Secrets and Styes
A Memoir

Gerard Smith

COPYRIGHT

Secrets and Styes by Gerard Smith

Published by Choice Publishing

Copyright © First Publication 2022 Gerard Smith

All rights reserved. No portion of this book may be reproduced in any form without permission from the author, except as permitted by Irish copyright law. For permissions contact:
Gerardfs338@gmail.com

Part Lyrics from 'How do you solve a problem like Maria' written by Rogers and Hammerstein. 'Beg Steal or Borrow' written by Tony Cole, Steve Wolfe, Graeme Hall. 'The first time ever I saw your face' written by Ewan MacColl. 'Evergreen' written by Barbra Streisand, Paul Williams. 'Sing a rainbow' written by Arthur Hamilton. 'Sealed with a kiss' written by Peter Udell and Gary Geld.

Cover by Homebird Design, Cavan.
Back Cover Image by Gerard Smith.

Editing: Norah Deay norah@norahdeay.com https://norahdeay.com

ISBN: 978-1-913275-55-6

Printed in Ireland

ACKNOWLEDGEMENTS

A special thanks to the doyenne of Irish Writers, Patricia Scanlan. Secrets and Styes is the result of her encouragement and support, for which I will be forever grateful.

And to the most avid of readers: Bernie Cawley Swift, her response to reading an early draft of Secrets And Styes spurred me on – THANK YOU.

DEDICATION

To my sister Maria, with all my love.

Prologue..7

Chapter 1: New beginnings.......................................13

Chapter 2: The Penman 19

Chapter 3: Uncle Tommy's Zephyr............................27

Chapter 4: An imaginary foe.....................................34

Chapter 5: The crow from the clear lagoon 41

Chapter 6: The truth about sausages.........................47

Chapter 7: Messages from above 53

Chapter 8: The Conspirators 60

Chapter 9: Saints and Sinners 67

Chapter 10: The Triumvirate......................................74

Chapter 11: The Guardians of The Congregation 79

Chapter 12: Noises that go bump in the day 85

Chapter 13: The knowing 92

Chapter 14: The Manifestation...................................98

Chapter 15: The cure 105

Chapter 16: The return...112

Chapter 17: The storm story.....................................118

Chapter 18: Into the night 125

Chapter 19: The hill..132

Chapter 20: The letter..139

Chapter 21: The stye of the storm 145

Chapter 22: The Tools 152

Chapter 23: The Procurement 158

Chapter 24: The Loading 165

Chapter 25: The Father 171

Chapter 26: The Three Wise women 177

Chapter 27: The chewing 184

Chapter 28: The healing..190

Chapter 29: The purge 197

Chapter 30: The Regression..203

Chapter 31: The talk 210

Chapter 32: Jesus...216

Chapter 33: Amble 223

Chapter 34: Ghosts 232

Chapter 35: Tall men 238

Chapter 36: All alone...244

Chapter 37: The Show 250

Chapter 38: Homecoming 256

Chapter 39: Found...263

Chapter 40: Coats..271

Chapter 41: Town Granny..279

Chapter 42: Potty Tastes 287

Chapter 43: Running..292

Chapter 44: School 296

Chapter 45: Green V Grey 302

Chapter 46: Manchester...305

Chapter 47: Full-Stop 308

Chapter 48: Revelation 313

Chapter 49 – Manchester: 1976....................................318

Chapter 50: A Star visit 322

Chapter 51: Bruce Lee 324

Chapter 52: Hairs and Veils 332

Chapter 53: The Telling 337

Chapter 54: Death 343

Chapter 55: 1977 Salford, Manchester, England 348

Chapter 56: No Show 354

Epilogue: Liverpool, September 1977 358

Prologue
1972: Salford, Manchester, England.

My ears pulsed to the beat of my heart. I unclenched my hands and wiped the sweat on my trousers, at once feeling fresh beads prickle my palms.

My breathing was fast and furious, propelled by nervous energy. I was about to commit a crime – a very grave crime.

......

My crime would be against Marjorie.

A fact that gave my violation its 'serious' status. You see, I liked Marjorie – quite a lot. Having to do this to her hurt me more than anything else in the world. But I had to; there was no other choice. So, aware doubt was beginning to pull me back, I put my hand on her front door and pushed.

The tinny tinkle of the bell alerted Marjorie of my entrance. My eyes focussed on the rainbow-coloured plastic strips hanging from the door frame. Marjorie's hands, clamped prayer-like, plunged through, and with a flick, the ribbons fluttered outwards, giving Marjorie the dramatic entrance that beguiled us kids.

But now, I wasn't beguiled by the sight of her; my smile was forced. There was nothing forced about Marjorie; her smile was always: ready, warm, welcoming,

"Hello Gerard, how are you this morning?" she asked, pulling strings tight at the back of her pinny.

"Alright," I said, hoping the one-word answer would hide the tremor in my voice. I stepped forward with my hands behind my back to conceal their shaking.

"What can I get for you?" she asked, patting her hair, set solid with lacquer.

I moved forward and hovered over the counter while an uncertain sound fell from me, "Erm?"

"Take your time," she said, stepping back to give me a good view of the brightly coloured sweet jars behind her.

Knowing I had no margin for error, I executed my diversion tactic immediately.

"Can I have a five-pence worth of strawberry bonbons, please?"

"Course you can, sweetheart," she said, turning her back on me.

Then – with a deft swiftness, my arm shot forward and plucked a penny Blackjack from its tray. I had it in my back pocket before Marjorie had even touched the bonbon jar.

I'd done it – I was now a bone-fide child-thief.

......

I skipped away from the crime scene, sucking on a bonbon. My crime had given me something I seriously needed – a sin.

As the child of immigrant Irish Catholics, I was on the cusp of a momentous occasion: my First Confession and Holy Communion. The learning and build-up to this rite-of-passage had caused me considerable anxiety, so it was a huge relief that I had a real-life sin to confess to Father Carey.

I swallowed my bonbon, and tightness gripped the pit of my stomach, stopping me in my tracks. The tautness gave way to a dull ache, which made me smile. For I knew what the pain was, it was the sin swaddling my soul, and my smile was for Father Carey – *he'd surely be proud of my brevity of sin.*

......

Although I had nerves, when confession day came, they were low-level compared to those I had while acquiring my sin.

I coveted the sin dearly because it meant I could enter the confessional box with the confidence that comes from telling the truth.

I'd heard playground whisperings that some kids were going to make their sins up. That was something I wouldn't do. I knew that lying in confession would have severe and lasting consequences – I wouldn't go there.

......

I rose early on the morning of my First Confession, washed, and dressed in grey shorts, socks and a crisp white shirt that had been left out for me.

Ready, I descended into the quiet of the living room, kneeled by the couch and began to rehearse.

Satisfied my confession was pitch-perfect, I rose and walked towards a solitary breakfast of Ready Brek and Vimto.

......

Our confessions were gender-segregated: boys in the morning, girls in the afternoon.

As always, even though it was a warm and sunny June day, the church was freezing cold. I sat mid-pew, shivering.

The sound of clattering teeth filled the holy space, momentarily stopping when the first boy rose from the pew and walked towards the confessional door with a confident stride.

He opened the hallowed door and stepped into the darkness, the door closing behind him with an ominous thud. We monitored his progress.

All ears were peeled on the door, straining to hear even the slightest hint of his sin. But we heard nothing; instead, we gave in to the cold and shivered nervously while awaiting our absolution.

When the door opened and he stepped out, I was struck by something that unnerved me – time.

The length of time he'd been in the box suggested a string of sins, and I wondered if my single sin would suffice. But I relaxed a little when I considered his plethora of sin was perhaps why the priests had singled him out to go first.

I relaxed further when subsequent confessions were swift. When my turn came, I was eager to get it over with.

Opening the confessional door, the light from the church gave me a glimpse of the tiny space, which eased me, for small spaces gave me comfort. Darkness surrounded me as soon as I closed the door, and I diligently dropped to my knees. Placing my palms together, my heart quickened, and I felt its beat in my every breath.

A sharp grating sound punctuated my thumping beats as a square shutter in front of me shot open, making me jolt.

It revealed Father Carey's big bald head in shadow. His featureless face looked like a dark moon in a black sky, and I stared in silence.

"Well, we don't have all day." The annoyance in his voice pushed me into my rehearsed routine.

"Bless me, father, for I have sinned. This is my first confession; these are my sins." I paused and tried to lubricate my mouth with a parched tongue. But I couldn't, so I delivered my sin with a dry, rasping voice, "I stole a Black-Jack from the corner shop. That is my sin, Father."

Relief coursed through me as I waited for my absolution and penance. But it never came. Instead, the moon face uttered a single word, "And...?"

I was thrown, wondering if I'd forgotten part of the routine, "And what, Father?" I whispered politely.

The moon grew larger as he leaned in, "You said sins, but you've only confessed one," his moon retreated, awaiting a response.

My head raced with my heart, and to my horror, my head took over, and made-up words spilled from me, "I swore at my mam, Father."

Such was my turmoil at doing the one thing I said I wouldn't, I couldn't take in what the priest was saying. All I knew was that when the shutter eclipsed the moon, my first confession was complete, and I was free to go.

But I was far from free. I felt the weight of a guilt-induced ball-and-chain shackle my feet, causing me to shuffle towards my penance. A penance that was worthless given I'd committed the ultimate sin of telling a lie in confession.

Kneeling at the penance pew with the other boys who basked in absolution, the burden of guilt pressed heavily on my shoulders. An inner voice scolded, *'You're so stupid Gerard, you don't even swear, you'd never, ever swear at your mam – what possessed you to say that?'*

It was a question I couldn't answer, and in the days that followed, I nervously awaited retribution.

......

The sun streaming through a gap in my bedroom curtains woke me; the beam of light pulled me from my bed, and I rose, feeling lighter, freer.

Walking to the bathroom, I felt my burden lift a little. The weighted balls of guilt around my feet lightened. The cold water I splashed on my face exhilarated me, and I liked my reflection in the mirror.

It had been a week since my seriously sinful act, and no fire or brimstone had been bestowed upon my family or myself. My week-long repentance and dislike of myself had been rewarded with forgiveness, or so I hoped.

I sighed and quietly spoke to myself, *"At last, maybe good times are beginning."*

Chapter 1: New beginnings

One week after my First Confession and Communion, I finally relaxed into being seven. Everything in my world was changing, becoming new. Our money had changed, something the adults were fretful about. But I loved this new money called decimal: golden, shiny new coins that glistened like a King's Ransom.

The house where we lived, a small Victorian Terrace in Salford, Manchester, was to be demolished. So: Mam, Dad, my brother, sister, and I were moving to a spanking new house, on a Council Estate called Paddock Field.

Of course, it was neither a paddock nor a field. Instead, it was a scattering of swiftly built breezeblock boxes, all finished off with a splattering of dazzling white pebbledash. But to me, the place looked positively palatial.

Mam and Dad brought us for the inaugural viewing of our new house on a grey summer's day. Dad opened the door, and we three kids ran in. The rapturous whoops and fevered excitement from my brother and sister instantly lit up the sterile, empty space.

Me, I stood silently open-mouthed in the oblong living room, overwhelmed by its modernity. Dad stooped to my level, "What do you think, Son?" I scanned the place, searching for the right words, "Dad, it's like a Space-Age-House." He chuckled and stood up, shaking his head, "You're right there, Son, sher I'd say it was built on another planet," he said, thumping a hollow, plaster-board wall.

"What do you mean?" I asked, thrilled by the thought that our new house may have been built on Mars.

Dad, a passionate Irish builder who was proud of his brick-laying prowess, explained, "There's no skill in their making; they're mostly made somewhere else, trucked in and assembled, they're not built." He looked at me, "You'd build a better house with your Lego."

I lowered my head to hide a sudden onset of shame. I hated Lego; my playing with it was a sham – to please Dad.

......

1972 was also the year that colour came into my life – via television.

I sprinted home from school, thrust by my thirst to watch Blue Peter drenched in colour. I dived through the door to see my brother, Dermot (five years older and fearless), lying on the floor, fiddling with a knob on the telly, "What are you doing?" I asked, slightly panicked.
"Calm it, I'm getting the colour right."
"But what if you break it? Please leave it alone," I pleaded.

Dermot was accustomed to my angst-ridden histrionics and carried on with his colour correcting while I wrung my hands and paced the room, worried he'd inadvertently botch my first coloured Blue Peter.

But he pulled back just as the opening peels of the nautical theme tune began.

I dropped to my knees, transfixed.

Then I saw them in glorious full colour: my beloved triumvirate of presenters and their pets. But something wasn't quite right. My face must have dropped because Dermot asked, "What's up? Is the colour too strong?"

My focus remained on the telly, "Look at Shep," I said, incredulous.
"I am. What's up with him?"
"He's black and white!"
"Yep, there aren't no multi-coloured dogs for colour telly, our kid."

My disappointment was profound, and I made a mental note to write to producer Biddy Baxter, questioning her decision to choose a black and white dog when everybody was getting colour tellies.
......

Now, at this time, I had two passions: Beauty Pageants and Horror Films. I would watch both with equal awe and fascination.

My sister Maria (seven years older) and I would watch Miss World together, curled up on the sofa with our pencils and makeshift scoreboards, while we steadfastly ignored Dermot's protestations and constant trilling, "Switch this rubbish over!"
I revelled in the televisual beauty, secure in the knowledge that if Dermot went anywhere near the switch-over-knob, he'd receive short shrift from our commanding big sister.

When the winner was announced, Maria and I would blub along with her as she made her victory walk amongst the glitterati in the Royal Albert Hall, while Dermot swivelled a disdainful head and left us to our snotty-nosed snivelling.

When it came to indulging my love of horror films, that was Mam's domain.

Mam worked evening shifts at The Salisbury, a vast Victorian pub on Salford Docks' edge (now Media City). Monday was her night off, which coincidently was the night that the BBC had their Appointment-With-Fear feature. This was a weekly horror film that usually came from the famous Hammer Horror stable.

Despite the fact I was only seven, Mam and Dad let me stay up and watch them, on Dad's conditional terms, "When you go home[1], don't be telling your cousins you do be watching these films, do you hear me?"

"Yes, Dad."

Mam opened her bottle of stout, positioned her ashtray on its stand, and we readied ourselves for 'The Curse of The Werewolf,' in Technicolor.

Mam took a sip of stout, then allayed Dad's concerns, "He never watches them anyway, Sean," she said dismissively.

And she was right because every time the music signalled a scary scene, I'd dive into Mam's lap and stick my fingers in my ears, waiting for her gentle shoulder tap, letting me know it was safe to emerge. When her tap came, I'd jump up and bellow, "What happened?"

Mam sipped her stout, "I'm not watching it for you; watch it with me or go to bed," she'd say, with a wry smile.

......

That first week in our new house was wondrous. But on the last day of school before the summer break, our big adventure beckoned.

Because Mam worked in the evenings, it was Dad who prepared

---

[1] Ireland was always referred to as home by Irish immigrants

and cooked our evening meal. He was in the kitchen cooking mince and spuds when I came in from school. He turned from the pan and wagged the wooden spoon at me, "You don't be fretting on the journey home now; Maria will look after you, do you hear me?"

"Yes, Dad."

'The journey home' was to Ireland. But Mam and Dad never referred to Ireland thus, it was always 'Home' – and us three kids spent our entire childhood summers there.

It was an epic journey, starting with a bus to the station, a train to Liverpool and then a taxi to the most exciting bit, the overnight Ferry to Dublin.

And what made the trip so daunting was that us three kids would make the boat journey alone. Due to economic necessity, Mam and Dad stayed in Manchester, only returning home for the last week of our stay.

Mam was meticulous with our clothes and appearance. On departure day, we were kitted out in brand new clothes.

"Now yous keep yourselves clean, and when you go into the town, I want the three of you looking immaculate, do you hear me?" she instructed.

"Yes, Mam," we trilled in unison.

……

In the second taxi to the boat, while Maria and Dermot took excited bets on whether it would be B & I's s the Leinster or Munster ferry, I'd feel the tears start to swell. I struggled so hard to fight them. It wasn't that I was upset leaving Manchester; I loved going to Ireland – I just so feared the sadness of Dad's goodbye.

He accompanied us onto the boat, and once he was sure our luggage was safely stowed, he'd pull Maria aside for a final pep talk.

"Could those not travelling to Ireland please disembark the ship immediately!"

When I heard those words from the tannoy, my floodgates opened, and Dad dropped down to me, his hands pressing on my shoulders.

With my head bowed, he gently shook me – there were no words nor a hug. When I lifted my head to look at him through tear-blurred eyes, I saw his jaw quivering, his lips tremoring, his eyes wet.

He, too, was fighting hard, and I felt bad. I wiped my eyes with my sleeve and nodded my head to reassure him I was okay. With that, Dad stood up stoic, turned – and walked off the boat.

He didn't look back or shout goodbye because he knew how much I feared the hurt that word caused.

And I knew how much goodbye hurt our dad.

Chapter 2: The Penman

With Dad out of sight, Dermot bolted for the gift shop, causing Maria to shriek, "Get back here now, or else I'm telling Mam!" He didn't look back, "How you plannin' on doing that, sis, you got special powers we don't know about?" Dermot disappeared into the brightly lit Aladdin's Cave.

Before departure we'd been explicitly briefed to stick together and go straight to the Pullman Lounge, wherein three reclining seats with blankets were waiting for us. Also, we mustn't talk to anyone other than the ship's staff.

Despite our youth, our inner-city upbringing made us streetwise. We were well aware of what we called perverts: how to spot a potential one and steer clear of their proclivities.

So, when Maria and I entered the gift shop to see Dermot chatting to a man, we were on guard.

As we approached, it became clear their exchange was heated. But I relaxed when I saw the man's B & I Badge and realised he was Staff.

The staff member wasn't happy, "I'll ask you again not to upset the displays. If you're looking for something specific, ask me," he said curtly.

Dermot was unfazed by his attitude, "I want one of those pens with the ship in it that sails when you turn the pen upside down," he said, continuing to destroy the shop man's carefully arranged merchandise in his search for the pen.

The assistant set off in the direction of said pens but was beaten to it, "You mean these?" said a man, holding the pen aloft.

Dermot beamed, "That's it."

The man placed the pen down, "I'll get that for the kid," he said, pushing other souvenirs forward.

This man was not a staff member, and I knew that an adult stranger giving or buying something for a kid was a sign of a potential perversion.

I stepped forward, thrusting my hand deep to retrieve my pocket savings. "Here, Dermot, I'll buy it," I said, holding my money-laden hand out toward my brother, taking care not to catch the man's eye as I looked him over.

Dermot dropped his voice, "Let him buy it, our kid."

I looked at Maria, also busy sussing the man. Lowering my head, I quietly asserted, "No, Dermot, we're not supposed to let strangers buy us stuff."

Dermot closed in on me, "Think of how many ice-cream-cones your money will get us in Hickey's on Saturday nights," he whispered conspiratorially.

Betty Hickey's was a sweet shop on the main street of Cavan Town, but to me, it was Willy Wonka's Chocolate Factory made real. A place I dreamt about. And right then, it dawned on me I was on my way to live that dream because my Granny had the Golden Ticket into Hickey's every Saturday night. I glanced at Maria, and when she nodded, I stuffed the money back in my pocket. Dermot grabbed his pen from the stranger man, and we sprinted from the gift shop, flinging a chorus of cursory thanks over our shoulders.

......

Now Dermot had his pen, Maria relaxed a little. Being the eldest, she was given the role of guardian, a responsibility she took seriously. But it was a position that came with considerable stress when we travelled with our wayward brother.

We settled into our Pullman seats. Well, I tried to – It was difficult to get comfortable. I was wearing shorts, and my scrawny legs stuck to the leatherette. My fidgeting legs made a farting sound every time I moved, eliciting much mirth from Dermot and resultant wrath from Maria. "Shhhhhhhhhh, stop laughing so loud, you're drawing attention to us," she admonished, looking around to ensure no nosey adults had tell-tale eyes on us.

The embarrassing noise issue was resolved when Maria re-upholstered my Pullman seat with one of her dresses retrieved from the luggage room. And once again, we settled – until the ship made the first departing shudder from its Liverpool dock, "WE'RE MOVING!" Dermot shouted, launching rocket-like from his seat.

Maria's arm shot across me, grabbed Dermot's shoulder, and pushed him down. He didn't tussle or answer back; instead, he sat down with a compliance that bothered me. This wasn't him. Although only seven, I knew my brother's mind, and right now, I knew it was whirring. His jaw jutted forward, "We're near the deck door!" he said, with an emphasis I couldn't place, which unnerved me.

"What does that mean?" I asked.

"If the ship sinks tonight, at least we'll be first in line for the lifeboats."

Maria instinctively grabbed my hand, "Take no notice of him. He's trying to wind you up."

I turned to him, "Dad told me they don't have icebergs in summer, so we can't do a Titanic," I said, confidently settling back into my seat.

Dermot continued staring at the door. "I'm not bothered about icebergs – it's bombs that's the worry – no one's checked for bombs," he said, rising from his Pullman again, drawing more unwanted attention to us.

"Sit down," Maria hissed.

Dermot stared ahead and insisted, "I have to go bomb searching on deck." He glanced at me, "Someone's got to do it, our kid." And with that, he was off, onto the deck. The place we had been expressly told never, ever to venture.

We three knew all about bombs. As the kids of Irish parents, we were accustomed to the playground taunts our parentage would engender every time there was an IRA bombing. But our parent's successful assimilation into the country had shown our English working-class community that most Irish people were not terrorists. When anti-Irish bullying did arise, our playground peers stepped in to quash it.

But the moment I saw Dermot fly out the door into the deck danger zone, it wasn't bombs that bothered me – it was the stranger man who bought him the pen that mired my mind.

......

Maria and I raced out the deck door after Dermot. Even though it was June, we were knocked back by a fierce sea wind. And, given the giant ship was shunting from a confined lock, its movements were staccato; one mighty jolt slammed us backside down onto the diesel smeared deck.

Maria's first instinct once we'd found our feet was to attend to our oil-slicked backsides. She spun me round, peering and swiping at my nether end.

"Bloody-Hell, oil on our new clothes, I'm gonna kill our Dermot when I get him," she said.

Her words smacked me with fear-inducing force, "Don't say that. What if that man gets him?" I said, spilling my worry.

She looked up and around, "What man?"

"The man who bought him the pen."

"Don't be daft," she said, dismissing but not easing my fears.

Despite my tendency toward tears, anxiety, and perceived sissyness from my peers, I wasn't a soft child. On the contrary, those combined traits had given me a strength that belied my years. Thus, it was with a warrior-like resolve that I followed my sister in pursuit of our brother.

The wind was against us, and we lunged forward to walk at a forty-five-degree angle to make progress. Our joint calls of "Dermot" were useless as his name was blown back in our faces; our voices muted by the blasting winds that were bolstered by the ship's departure.

After one futile circuit of the ship's deck, we were tiring. When we came by a side door, Maria pulled me towards it. Following a short door battle, we jumped back inside the ship with diesel-dirty clothes and wind-dishevelled hair.

A portly woman passed us by, "Would ya look at the heads of yiz, yer look like a pair of walking whin-bushes," she said, laughing at the sight of us.

Maria fumed as she tried to re-tame her hair, "Honest to God Gerard, I'm gonna batter him when I get my hands on him." But as rain lashed the ship's windows, her anger vanished, and she turned into a worrywart, "Oh God Gerard, I hope he's alright out there, I'm right worried?"

Maria's face was tight with concern. When I saw her hands begin a slow tremble, I took hold of one to halt her tremor.

"Let's go for a walk around the boat," I said, guiding her into the corridor. Maria was my anchor; it was time for me to be hers.

Also, I had an ulterior motive for this walk. While Maria worried about the elements harming Dermot, I worried about him coming to harm by human – from the potential pervert, Penman.

We walked the corridors and public spaces of the B & I Line's flagship, The Munster. And while Maria took every opportunity to peer outside, I inspected inside for Penman. All I wanted was a glance of him to reassure me that a Monster on the Munster hadn't kidnapped my big brother.

The café – he wasn't there.

In the toilets, I checked every cubicle – all empty.

I paused at the pub, "We can't go in there," said Maria, hoisting me back from the door.

I resisted, "Just a quick look," I said, opening the door and popping my head inside. It was hard to see through a thick fog of cigarette smoke, but I saw enough to know Penman wasn't in the pub.

I felt the first thumps of my heart in my ears as my anxiety began to rise.

The posh restaurant – no sign of a fine-dining Penman.

As my frantic search pulled us back to our beginning, the gift shop, I broke a sweat. Maria felt my clammy hand and stopped, "Gerard, don't fret, he'll turn up soon."

I couldn't hide from her knowing; my lips wobbled, "What if that man who bought the pen's got our Dermot?"

Her embrace smothered me in care; her words soothed me, "You know our Dermot, he'd kick the shins off anyone who tried to snatch him."

She was right; a ray of relief lifted me. But I knew Maria and I would not have the full release that comes with relief until we found our brother.

......

"We're safe to sail, our kid." Dermot was back in the Pullman Lounge, thoroughly soaked, rainwater puddling at his feet. "I've checked all decks and found no sign of bombing devices," he said, addressing me while avoiding Maria's eye.

Maria looked him over, "Dermot, you're wet through. Stay with our Gerard while I go and get you a towel and a change of clothes." She dashed off with nurturing haste.

The three of us slept soundly that night in our pre-booked Pullman seats.

......

As the boat docked in Dublin, Maria struggled to wake Dermot and me. When she eventually roused us, there wasn't time for toilet, face splash or teeth brush. Instead, we joined the other dishevelled passengers crowding the Munster's exit/entrance area, all patiently awaiting release.

When the door rose open, I saw him again – Penman. His gaze met mine. The sun rising on our summer adventure removed the sense of malevolency I'd previously felt for him.

He looked sleepy but smiley, hopeful and happy. He handed Maria a bunch of postcards with pictures of the Munster on them, "Enjoy your summer, kids," he said, with an Irish accent diluted with a Northern-English twang.

I'd miss-read Penman. He wasn't a Monster on the Munster; he was a kind man returning home – a Kindred Spirit.

Chapter 3: Uncle Tommy's Zephyr

Dermot couldn't control his excitement. He bounced, bumping, and bothering bleary-eyed, bed-headed passengers, all eager to step into Ireland.

Glancing around at the mass of people standing with cases of every shape and size, Dad's voice came to me, *"When I was a young fella travelling to England on the boat, we had to share it with cows, horses, hens, and sheep. It was Noah's Ark back then, Son."*

I relished the times when home-from-school-time coincided with Dad's home-from-work time. While Dad prepared food, I'd sit at our tiny kitchen table and ask him to tell me about his journey to England on Noah's Ark. I never tired of hearing it, nor did he of recounting it. And, the following day at playtime, while the lads played football, I'd have a rapt audience of girls all listening to me speak of Dad's adventures on the real-life Noah's Ark.

When we were swept along by the surge of human cargo disembarking the boat, I felt sad the Munster was no longer Dad's Ark.

......

We trundled down a wide gantry that wobbled under the weight of the luggage-laden passengers, then into a large arrivals hall where eagle-eyed Customs people scanned the crowds, pulling over anyone they considered shady. I stopped and stared at these chosen ones, trying to figure out what nefarious activity the customs men had seen in what looked to me like perfectly nice people.

For Maria, this was the high-stress point of our journey, the last hurdle, her Beecher's Brook. She had to get us onto Dublin's terra-firma without any adult authority discovering we'd travelled alone. And this feat was hindered two-fold – 1: Dermot's haste to get out, "Hey lad, slow down, you nearly took my bleeding leg off with that case of yours," shouted an angry English man. And 2: My nosey intrusion, "Do you know these people, or do you have something to declare, young fella?" asked a customs man. Maria grabbed my arm, "No, he hasn't; come on, Mam and Dad are almost outside," she lied, pulling me away while hyperventilating.

......

Once outside, the weight on Maria's shoulders dropped off, and she soared with relief as she roared, "UNCLE TOMMY, we made it, we're here," her hands free from responsibility, waving wildly with the release of it all.

Uncle Tommy was our dad's youngest brother, Granny's eighth child. Leaning against the bonnet of his shiny Black Ford Zephyr, smoking a cigarette, he looked like James Dean. And he possessed the same swaggering attitude as the Hollywood legend.

We raced to him as fast as our suitcases would allow. Dermot couldn't contain himself, "Fucking Hell, Uncle Tommy, when did you get this? It's fucking ace," he declared, his eyes wide with admiration for the car.

Uncle Tommy clipped his ear, "Watch your fecking language," he said, showing evident pride in Dermot's reaction to his motor.

There were no time-wasting pleasantries like, "How was your journey?" Instead, Tommy handed me a paper grocery bag, "You get sick in this, not in the car," he said, throwing our cases in the back – and with that, we were off.

......

Dermot sat in the front, constantly asking questions, "Can I do the gears?"

"You can't. It's a column gear change," said Tommy, tapping the stick by the steering wheel.

"Can I drive the tractor to the creamery?"

"No, I'll let you drive in the fields, not on the roads."

"Can I milk the cows?"

"You can, but if you get a belt from one, don't blame me."

"Can I help with slaughtering in the College Farmyard?"

"You'll have to ask the fellas on the farm?"

Their easy banter was a testament to shared interests and close bonds.

Maria and I sat quietly in the back, admiring the landscape. Our council estate was mostly grey, and we marvelled at the myriad hues of green that were rendered extra vivid by the clear blue sky of the early summer morning.

While Dermot chatted incessantly, I was aware of Uncle Tommy's glances at me in his rear-view mirror, "You're very quiet, Gerard, are you feeling sick?"

"Not yet," I replied, knowing nausea would present itself somewhere near Navan.

While Dermot was interested in earthly pursuits, my interests were considerably more celestial. So, when Tommy next checked in on my vomiting status, I leaned in, "Have you seen the ghost that haunts the college farmyard, Uncle Tommy?"

"I haven't. Your Uncle Paddy's seen him several times, says he's a tall fella in a long black coat."

"Aren't you frightened of seeing him?"

"Not at all."

"What would you do if you saw him?"

"I'd walk right up to him, say 'how-are-ya' – then walk on, right through the fecker."

I was enthralled and awed by Tommy's fearlessness, "Do you know who the tall-man is?" I asked.

"Indeed, I don't – there's a job for you. Do a bit of detective work, find out who he is; there's a lot of people who'd like to know."

I sat back feeling personally elevated. Dermot was good at so many things. I felt happy that Uncle Tommy had recognised something I might be good at. I was buoyed by his faith in me – and I decided to make discovering this ghost's identity my summer-time mission.

......

As expected, I spewed into the Dunne's Stores Grocery bag as we approached Navan. Tommy halted by a hedge, "Maria, make sure it all goes in the bag," he instructed.

Vomiting is extra hideous when three people home in on your every heave to ensure none of your stomach contents stray into the confines of Uncle Tommy's Zephyr.

......

With my sick bag discarded in a ditch, I settled into the rest of the journey with a post-vomit sense of calm. And with my stomach newly empty, all I could think of was Country Granny's culinary delights waiting to greet us on our arrival at what we called The House in The Hollow.

My mouth watered at the thought of a simple slice of her homemade current soda bread. Fresh from the range, still warm, served with butter and a generous dollop of damson jam, accompanied by a strong cup of sweet tea.

Afterwards, I would go straight up to the college farmyard to start my search for the tall ghostly man. But as I warmly planned my first day's adventures in Ireland, Uncle Tommy threw me a spanner, "We'll have to stop and drop into your Town Granny before we go out to our house."

Town Granny was Mam's Mother, a widow who lived alone in a terraced house in an area of Cavan town known locally as The Half-Acre.

Unlike Country Granny, Town Granny was a strict disciplinarian. Maria and I were slightly scared of her (Dermot was scared of no one).

While Dermot's reaction to this news was a nonchalant shoulder shrug, Maria and I were more affected. We glanced at each other, seeing the disappointment reflected in each other's faces. After a moment, Maria's face lit up, and she leaned in, "No, we can't, Uncle Tommy. Me and Gerard fell on the deck and stained our clothes. Town Granny will go mad and write to Mam saying we turned up looking like a pair-a-tramps."

Tommy remained focussed on the road, "Well, someone has to tell your mother. I couldn't believe it when I saw the state of the two of yiz this morning, looking as mangey as auld Johnnie Simons." He looked over at Dermot, "And this fella looking all flash and flah."

My dread deepened at the thought of Town Granny's derision at the sight of Maria and me. But it dropped away when I saw Tommy wink at Dermot. Maria playfully slapped his shoulder, "You're a right wind-up, Tommy." The Zephyr filled with laughter as it cruised through Virginia Town's main street.

......

We were now on our final stretch of the journey, and the atmosphere in Uncle Tommy's Zephyr was supercharged, not least because it was Saturday – Town Night.

An actual physical current of excitement travelled through me when I thought of us three getting dressed up and going into town with Granny for late-night shop opening. For us Manchester kids, Main Street Cavan was a veritable Aladdin's Cave on a Saturday night, a glistening pantomime full of colour and characters, treats and trinkets, laughter, lollies, and ice cream.

......

Uncle Tommy stopped at a petrol pump by the Majestic Cavan Cathedral.

"This lady needs a drink after that jaunt," he said, opening the door.
Dermot went to follow him; I grabbed his shoulder, "Lend me your pen." He threw it behind him and jumped out of the zephyr, grabbing the petrol pump and brandishing it like a gun, much to Tommy's annoyance.

Maria instinctively knew what I wanted to do, and she handed me one of Penman's postcards. I wrote – *Mam and Dad, we are here now.* I paused for a moment, wondering what else to write, then I remembered what Penman said to us and thought I should say the same to them – *Enjoy your summer. Love Gerard.*

Maria smiled, "That's lovely; we'll post it when we have more news," she said, squeezing my knee.

......

Uncle Tommy's refreshed Zephyr revved out of Cavan Town. I stared out the window, looking at all the familiar houses, unchanged from a year ago.

The houses soon gave way to fields and woodland. The Zephyr made a gentle upward ascent, and I saw a plume of smoke swirling and dancing up into the clear blue sky. I watched, mesmerised, for in that swirl of smoke was the promise of freshly baked bread, sweet apple, and sour rhubarb pies. But above all, it offered something every child needs to flourish – security.

My gaze followed the swirl of smoke downwards. It led to a sight that startled me – *in front of the house, slightly obscured in shadow, stood the looming figure of a tall-man.*

Chapter 4: An imaginary foe

Uncle Tommy's Zephyr freewheeled, making a slow rightward turn into the small, gravelled space at the side of the house.

I stared out the windows, trying to make sense of what I saw. But the bright sun dappling through the trees blinkered my eyes, making the tall-man flicker in and out of focus.

Tommy jerked the handbrake up, causing me to lurch forward and splutter, "Who's that man?"

"What man?" asked Uncle Tommy, opening the door and hauling himself out of the Zephyr. I didn't answer. Instead, I jumped out and raced round to the front of the house, stopping abruptly – there was no one there.

Dermot rushed past me and disappeared into the house, followed by an equally eager Maria, "Come on, Gerard, come in and see Granny," she said, hot on Dermot's heels.

Tommy's voice jolted me, "What are you looking at?" I looked back at him, looking over his Zephyr.

"There was a man at the door. I saw him when we wheeled past; he's gone now."

Tommy was emphatic, "All the men of the house are working at this hour, you might have seen the tall-man ghost, or you're raving from the journey," he said, walking past me and into the house.

34

I stood in the sun and noticed the silence. On my English council estate, noise was constant. Here, quietness surrounded me, and at that moment, it unsettled me – I dashed into The House in The Hollow, where Maria and Dermot's excited chatter shattered the spooking silence.

......

"Get that into you; there's nothing of ya. Do they not feed you over there?"

Granny welcomed me with slices of warm buttered current soda bread.

I tucked in while Maria answered for me, "He's a picky eater Granny."

Watching me eat her home-baked bread with gusto pleased Granny. She beamed and patted my shoulder, "Well, don't be picking the apples from the college orchard and bringing the vexed Bishop down to me, do you hear me?" she said.

I nodded my yes, while Uncle Tommy spoke, "It's Dermot who'll be vexing the bishop. Gerard'll be busy wandering, looking for the tall-man. There's no harm in that mammy."

I swallowed the bread and washed it down with a mouth full of sweet tea, "Who was that man at the door, Granny?" I asked. She looked at Tommy.

When he rolled his eyes, she looked at me, "There was no man at the door; the men are all out working," she said, wiping her hands on a cloth and stepping down into the scullery.

......

Maria and Dermot barely chewed their breakfast; such was their eagerness to get to the college farmyard. Dermot grabbed his wellies and ran out the door, while Maria paused, "You coming with us?"

"I'll see you there when I'm finished," I said, lifting my second slice of soda bread.

......

When Uncle Tommy left for work, I sat alone in the small room, the heart of the home. I listened to the various noises coming from the scullery – the sounds of Granny preparing dinner for her family created a nurturing symphony that soothed me.

Finishing my tea, I looked around, seeking difference. My young life had experienced a cacophony of change since I last sat in this room, yet everything here remained the same. The lack of change kindled warmth in the pit of my belly.

My attention turned to Jesus. He gazed down at me from his prime position above the table. I tilted my head to match the tilt of his and silently mouthed, "Help me find the tall-man, please." Then I winced at the open wounds on his outstretched hands and headed for the door.

......

Outside, the bright light momentarily blinded me. Once my eyes adjusted, I climbed the three small steps up to the road but noticing my city shoes, I turned back to get my wellies – that's when I saw something.

To my right, a shape moved. A grey silhouette sailed across the green grass, slowly disappearing behind the house.

I wasn't frightened. Rarely did I feel fear during the day; I felt protected by its light. I took off in the direction of this shadowy shape.

Turning around the gable of the house, I was hit by a blaze of colour. Wild roses, chrysanthemums, heather bells, geraniums, and poppies clustered together, creating a bouquet of epic proportions. But I had little time to admire its beauty, for a rustling sound broke the silence, and my eyes followed its source.

The natural bouquet was contained by a rickety fence, which formed the bannisters to narrow stone steps that led down to a stream – my favourite part of the house's environs.

The stream was home to minnow and tadpoles, the latter of which I would collect and delight in watching their metamorphosis. Walking towards the moss-covered, slippery stone steps, I knew there was something more than aquatic life down there.

I didn't feel a spectral presence. Instead, my earlier sighting of a tall-man, coupled with the rustling sound and shadowy silhouette, had given me a sense of something tangible – someone, or perhaps some thing, was down at the stream.

And yet, I still wasn't scared.

It was intrigue that compelled me to take the first step down to the stream, grabbing both sides of the bannister to steady myself. Bramble and other fauna grew wildly, converging to create a foliage tunnel that thrust the stream into a dim light.

The trickle of fast-flowing water was the only sound as I took another step downwards. About to take the third step, a series of hard splashes punctured the soft trickle, prompting me to hesitate.

Instinctively I squatted down, still holding tight to either side of the bannister. I focussed hard, and when my sight acclimatised to the dark ahead of me, I saw the figure of a tall-man again.

To be precise, I saw his wellington boots, which I followed upwards. He stood with his back to me, swirling his feet in the water. His considerable stature meant I couldn't see above his waist.

I leaned in, looking for any astral signs that might make him spectral. But I saw neither haze nor glow. No, he was human, and I called out, "Hello."

He swiftly turned and stooped; his face tilted up at mine – a black man stared at me.

He lowered his head into a beam of sunlight, which illuminated the bright blue of his eyes. I'd never seen a blue-eyed black man before. I stared back, charmed by the sight of him.

He stretched his hand towards me, "Ah, yous have arrived," said my great uncle Micky, granny's brother. He loomed up the stone steps and scooped me up in his coal-blackened hands, "Yee didn't give me time to wash the coal tar off me face," he said, hoisting me up like I was a mere baby.

I marvelled at the view from his great height. I felt exactly like Uncle Micky's nickname – Lofty.

......

"Lofty, what are you doing home?" asked my surprised Granny.

"I came home to greet the childer," he replied, slightly stooped as his height prevented him from standing fully erect in the house. Granny looked irked, "You'll see them at tea-time, get yourself back to work," she said, scurrying back down into the scullery to resume her own work.

Lofty's space in the house was on a battered chaise longue that ran the entire length of the front wall, nestled by the window. He sat down, "I'll clean me pipe, then be on my way," he said, swinging his long legs onto the cracked leather.

I watched him, fascinated. Not by his ritualistic pipe cleaning but by his conversation with someone who wasn't in the room. "Will you go and feck off now, be gone with ya." He made a dry spitting action, then continued to converse with an invisible yet antagonistic presence. "I did not, and well you know it, now don't be at me. You're always at me," he said, looking increasingly agitated.

"Who're you talking to, Uncle Micky?" I asked.

Immediately his agitation dropped away, and he looked at me, "Tis the finest of days. Would you get out into the sunshine and enjoy your holidays."

He drew on his pipe before resuming his verbal fight with an imaginary foe.

I matched his mood change, jumped from my chair, and pulled my wellies from my case.

Shoving them on, I excitedly told Uncle Micky of my mission, "I'm searching for the tall-man. Have you seen him?" I asked.

Micky re-lit his pipe, "I haven't, but I often see his friend." He inhaled, exhaled a great waft of smoke, leaned in, and said, "He has a big auld crow that looks out for him, if you ever see that bird perched on the corner of the byre, you'll know the tall-man's roaming."

......

I dashed from the house, eager to get to the college farmyard. The entrance to it lay across the road from the house. A rusting gate opened onto a manure saturated pathway, which led upwards to the farm complex. I couldn't open the gate, so I climbed over it, and as I did, the acrid sting of cow shit hit the back of my throat.

But I wasn't bothered by the invasive smell, for I was distracted by a call above me – *the screech of a circling crow's caw.*

Chapter 5: The crow from the clear lagoon

I climbed down from the gate onto the dung-sodden pathway. The crow circled above me, "Caw, caw, caw!" he cried. Looking up, I wondered was he warning me, "Hello, I called. "Rattle, ring. Rattle ring!" The change in his sound spoke to me. I waved, "Nice to meet you, crow."

"Clickety-click-click-click," I heard excitement in his response. He dove down and circled just a few feet above me. "Hello, Crow," I said. And with that, he swooped and settled on the gate.

Crow captivated me. I was used to seeing these black birds in horror films, where they hung around graveyards and gallows, signalling ominous happenings. But up close in real life, this crow wasn't scary, particularly when I recalled Dad's voice, "There's nothing to fear in a crow. It's only because they're black and ugly that they do be used in these films," he said."

"My friend, Mike Taylor, says the Devil disguises himself as a crow," I said, eager to hear Dad's take on Mike's playground pronouncement that petrified me.

"Not at all, son, there's no evil in a crow, only good. They do look after each other better than us people do. They even have funerals when one of them dies." He leaned into me, "When you're at home, and you see a crowd of them up on a gable, you'll hear them crying, mourning the death of a loved one. Crows are beautiful creatures; it's just their misfortune to be ugly looking things," he said, with knowing surety.

Crow's appearance and Dad's insight were revelatory to me. If Crow was tall-man's friend, then I countered that he wasn't an evil spirit, but more a lost and lonely soul, searching for someone or something. "How are you today, Crow?" He answered with a "Click" that stunned me – this bird was talking to me.

......

Crow jumped from the gate, but he didn't take off. Instead, he took to the floor by my feet and hopped off to my right – into the woods.

I followed him into the woodland, and felt myself become lighter as it became denser and darker. My feet traversed soft, spongy terrain instead of cold concrete slabs. I marvelled at the natural beauty of this environment compared to the manufactured artifice I was used to. Above all, I revelled in the solitude. There was no one here to hurl words at me – "Puff. "Pansy." "Sissy." No, it was just me, following a friendly crow towards the sound of flowing water – bliss.

......

My mind wandered, and amidst its wanderings, I lost Crow. He neither soared nor hopped below me. Not that I could see if he flew above, for the trees created a raggedy roof that offered only the occasional glimpse of sky.

So, I followed the rush of flowing water.

......

Eventually, I arrived at a clearing and a sight that made me gasp. A cascading crystal stream flowed over shiny rocks into an almost perfectly round pool, a lagoon framed by lush green ferns.

Peering into it, I marvelled at how clear the water was. A sense of pride washed over me when I thought about bringing Maria and Dermot to this diamond in the woods – I had found our own private oasis.

Sitting on a mossy stump, I drank in my surroundings. I felt quenched by the beautiful shapes, colours and forms that satiated my aesthetic senses.

"Caw, caw, caw," his call pulled me from my thoughts. Crow was perched on a branch on the other side of the pool, "Have you been here all this time?" I asked. "Click. Click," I took that for his 'Yes,' and smiled at the thought that he'd led me here.

Sitting on a stump with a crow for company, I felt safe and had the urge to chat, so I did. "In England, everyone thinks I'm odd 'cos I don't really like boy's things." Crow didn't ruffle a feather at my confession, so I continued, "Do you know Lofty, he's my great Uncle Micky?"

"Click, click," he answered.

I sat upright, "You do! Right, he talks to someone who isn't there. If they saw me talking to you in England, they'd probably put me in a Mental Hospital. But Lofty swears and argues all the time with someone who isn't there, and no one, not even Granny, bats an eye lid." I smiled, "You know summat Crow, it's easier being odd in Ireland."

But my reticence was never far away; I knew I wouldn't give full reign to my oddness, "I'm not gonna tell anyone about you, crow. I'll keep our friendship secret. You alright with that?"

"Click. Click."

His, 'Yes,' made me laugh aloud, "I can't believe I'm sitting here, learning to talk crow, with a crow."

When my mirth subsided, I turned serious, "Lofty told me about you, or at least I think you're the crow he's talking about." My heart fluttered; I took a breath and asked, "Are you tall-man's friend?"

My heart began to beat a little faster – "Click. Click."

I shot up, "Is he here, in the woods, with us?"

My heart turned up its tempo – "Click. Click."

"Show me where he is."

And now my heart raced – Crow remained silent, his eyes stilled, head tilted to the side as if listening to something.

I listened with him while watching for any movement or shadow amongst the trees that surrounded us.

My focus returned to crow. His head retreated into his body; wings hugged him tightly. It was as though he was fearful and priming himself for fight or flight.

Instinctively, my body language matched his, my shoulders drew in, I hunched a little as though I were protecting myself from some impending catastrophe.

And it came – a sonic THUD that forced me to the floor and crow to the sky. Crow soared, his squawking screams alerting his comrades of the shot that shattered our woodland idyll.

......

I was one of my school's fastest runners, but sprinting on an open sports field was a doddle. Running through woodland with its myriad obstacles wasn't. My right shoulder clipped a tree, and I shot backwards, landing with a crunch into beds of bracken and nettles.

My bare legs took the brunt of the nettles, but their sting was nothing compared to the thought of a bullet in my back – I jumped back up and continued my run.

The cobbles of the lane came into view, I increased my sprint. But an abject terror tore into me at the blasting thud of another shot, and I dove to dodge a bullet. My prostrate body skimmed the manure-soaked lane, drenching me in a cocktail of pee-diluted cow pooh.

There was no time for my city sensitivities; I launched back onto my feet to resume my flight

Reaching the end of the sodden lane, I began to shout for my protector, my real-life guardian angel, my sister – "MARIA. MARIA. MARIA!"

I stopped in the farmyard and looked around at the array of buildings that surrounded the concrete square. All was quiet, seemingly empty, yet I was full of fear – "MARIA – someone's trying to shoot me!" I shouted.

After what seemed an age, Maria appeared from a stone building. She stopped, stared at me, "You're covered in cow pooh," her face repulsed.

"I know, I had to dive in it to dodge a bullet," I explained.

She lowered her head, and to my horror, her shoulders began to shake, "Why are you crying, is someone trying to kill us?" I implored, tremors running through my small body.

Maria lifted her head – she was laughing.

Confusion stopped my quaking, "What's funny?" I asked.

She shook her head, "You watch too many of them horrible films, Gerard." She moved closer but was mindful not to touch me, "The farm man fired a few blanks to scare the crows, that's what you heard…"

…a third blast caused us both to yelp and squat defensively.

"There's no quiet way to stun a cow; the slaughterer didn't mean to frecken yiz." A young man stood by an open door. He looked me up and down, "You're soaked in shite; you've surely been christened by the country young fella," he said, turning back into the slaughterhouse.

I looked up onto the roof of the byre and was saddened to see no Crow.

Maria's hand tugged on mine, and still looking up at the byre, I allowed her to lead me blindly. When I looked forward, I froze – *a crimson river of fresh blood flowed from the slaughterhouse – and Maria was leading me into this horror.*

Chapter 6: The truth about sausages.

The smell of slaughter stung my nostrils – animal innards mixed with a triumvirate of bodily fluids: vomit, pooh and warm blood, all produced a metallic odour that permeated the air around us.

I tugged on Maria's hand, "I don't wanna watch 'em cut up a cow," I exclaimed, pulling her back. She looked at me, surprised, "You like horror, don't you?"

"I like watching it on the telly, with Mam." I looked down at myself, "And anyway, I need to wash this pooh off me," I said, disgusted by the smell of me.

Maria looked me over, "Let's get you down to Granny's," she said, pulling me towards the lane. I pulled back, "No, let me bring you to this place I've found; you'll love it," I said, excited by an imminent return to the clear lagoon.

……

Maria and I dawdled through the woods, picking wildflowers. Watching Maria delicately arrange her flowers into a circular bouquet, I asked, "Why did you want to watch the slaughtering? You hate stuff like that."

She stopped, plucked a poppy, added it to her arrangement, and pondered my question. Eventually, she looked at me, then back at her flowers, "Don't you think that farm lad's dead nice-looking?" she asked, a look on her face I couldn't read.

"I don't know," was my honest answer.

Maria stared wistfully, "He's got hair like Bruce Lee." That's when I understood the look on her face; it was her Bruce Lee look.

My sister liked looking at the Kung-Fu film star, Bruce Lee. And at that moment, she had the same look on her face that she had when she looked at his posters on her bedroom wall. I blurted, "I thought you only liked looking at Chinese men. Do you like looking at the farm lad as well, even though he's an Irish man?"

Maria laughed, "Yes, I think I do," her face flushed. She reached her hand towards mine, "Come on, take me to your lagoon and let's get you washed."

......

I was disappointed to learn that Maria already knew about my Lagoon.

"You were too young for us to bring you here during other summers; now you can swim, it's alright," she said, rinsing out my clothes. I breast-stroked the tiny pool; Maria came to the edge, "Can you do back stroke?"

I turned over, "Course I can," I said, proudly exhibiting my aquatic back moves. She looked down on me, my wet clothes piled in her arms, "You be careful; I'm going up to that field to lay your clothes out; they'll be dry in no time in this sun."

......

Floating on my back, looking up at the circle of blue sky through the trees, I became bothered.

Bothered by Maria liking to look at the farm lad, I drew my arms down into the water and kicked my legs until my feet hit the gravelly floor. Standing up gave me a new perspective – Maria looking at the farm lad didn't irk me; her involving me in her likey-lookings bothered me. I was addled, or was it annoyed? I settled on confused – why would Maria ask me if I thought the farm lad was nice looking? It was a question she'd never ask of my brother, Dermot.

......

My clothes had dried hard, like cardboard. But I welcomed the scratch of my shorts as I pulled them up since they gave temporary salve to the itch of my fast-presenting hives. Maria chuckled, "Look at your little legs; you look like you've got the measles." She foraged amongst flora and fauna, plucking a handful of leaves, "Come here," she said, patting her knee.

Sitting on Maria's lap, she gently rubbed the leaves over every one of my nettle stings, "Do you know what love is, Gerard?" Her question surprised me, yet recent events caused me to answer instinctively with another question,

"Is it when you like looking at someone's face and hair?"

"I think it's more than that."

"What else is it then?"

She shrugged, "I don't know myself, yet."

A thought popped into my head, and I said it, eager to help my sister understand what love is, "But you always say you love Bruce Lee's hair, so you can only love someone if you like their hair."

She finished treating my legs, "I suppose liking someone's hair's part of it." She threw down the leaves and gently eased me from her lap.

I felt my hair: thick, coarse, and dry. It lacked any Bruce Lee bounce or shine; it grew up and out in wiry coils. I hated my hair and deduced that if I loathed it, so would everyone else and thus – I would never have anyone like me the way Maria liked Bruce Lee.

......

Maria and I sat crossed legged, with a pile of plucked daisies in the space our legs created. I watched as she used her thumbnail to make an incision in the delicate stem, to gently thread another daisy through. Her chain was almost complete when we were alerted by an urgent rustling of foliage above us, followed by a thud as a wellington boot landed precariously close. We stood up to avoid a second flying boot – "Out of the way, I'm dive-bombing!"

A topless Dermot shot from the trees and launched himself upwards. Tucking his legs under his chin and clasping his arms tightly around them, he flew past us – a flying human ball.

His direct hit created a crashing tsunami that drenched Maria and me, almost knocking us off our feet. Maria responded with her usual – "Dermot, I'm gonna batter you!"

But I knew she wouldn't – because she never did.

......

Dermot was delighted to have taken an active part in his very first slaughter. Standing in the pool, he told us of the job the farm lad with the lovely hair had assigned him: "Right – I helped him pull out all the guts, and there are these slimy things like big, massive snakes called intestines. Right – and they're full of all the cow's shit. Right – so he told me to drag them over to the hosepipe and gives me a knife. Right – and I had to cut them open and clean all the shit out of them, so it was just the slimy skin left. Right – cos that's the skin what they use to put sausages in – right."

I laughed, "Stop winding us up; they don't do that. Sausages aren't cow guts."

Dermot hauled himself out of the pool, "Honest, our kid, it's not a wind-up," he said, drying himself with his t-shirt.

I looked to Maria for affirmation that Dermot was winding me up, but instead, I found myself studying her. I saw something in my sister I couldn't place. Despite her close proximity to me, I felt a shift; she seemed far away.

"Maria," I said, wanting to ask her the truth about sausages. She didn't answer. It wasn't that she was ignoring me; it was as though she hadn't heard me because she was concerned with something bigger than my sausage sensitivities. "Maria," I repeated, louder.

She jolted back to me and smiled, "Come on, we better get back to Granny's; it's dinner time."

Dermot pulled on his wet shirt, "Ace, I'm starving," his exit as rapid as his entrance.

I hung back, "I'll be down in a bit; I want to dry off in the sun."
Maria looked back, "Don't be long; you need to eat." She walked away – preoccupied.

The truth about sausages had killed what little appetite I had. And besides, something niggled me, a nagging sense that something was wrong with my sister.
……

To shake this nag, I felt compelled to return to the farmyard and divert myself with my summertime mission. I wanted to know why the farm man had to scare crows and whether it had something to do with the tall-man.

......

"Hello," I popped my tentative head around the open door of the slaughterhouse. The post-slaughter metallic smell hit me, as did the empty space; the life of the innocent beast hosed away, its slayers home to eat.

I welcomed the absence of workers; they weren't here to scare the crows with the gun.

Stepping back into the farm, I looked up, and towards the gable of the milking parlour, my heart skipped at the sight of him – "Hello Crow, nice to see you again."

I bobbed down; mindful people could still be around watching me talk to a bird. But when I was met with silence, I straightened up and whispered – *"Does this mean the tall-man's here?"*

Chapter 7: Messages from above

Crow was, as Lofty said, perched on the corner of the byre roof: watching, listening, constantly scanning his surrounds. Such was the intensity of his look-out that I had to repeat my question, "Crow, is the tall-man here?"

His head twitched, "Click. Click." The 'Yes,' sent a frisson of excitement through me.

Standing in the centre of the farm, I scanned the hayshed that spanned the back. Turning again, I looked over the terrace of stone-built buildings that acted as storage and office space. Confident the place was empty of workers, I spun full circle and faced the slaughterhouse. When I spoke, it wasn't to any living soul that may have lingered but to the deathly departed – *"Is there anyone here?"*

I waited for a response. When there came none, I upped my volume and asked once more – *"If there is anyone here, please make your presence known."*

A crash and rolling clatter from my left caused me to hunker down, head up, staring, like a cat, sussing a situation.

The clanging came from the byre. This was the building where my dad first saw the tall-man when he was a boy like me. So, I took a deep breath and walked in Dad's footsteps to its entrance.

To my disappointment, the metal doors were secured with a heavy padlock. I sloped around to the far side of the building, which was a jungle of ferns, bramble, and creeping ivy. But I spotted the indent of a window and deftly manoeuvred my way towards it, mindful to avoid any more stinging nettles.

At the window, I saw a wooden crate had been placed under it, *'someone else has used this as a way in,'* I thought to myself.

There was no glass nor even a window. Instead, an oblong-shaped opening presented a way in. It was about my eye height, but it didn't afford me enough of a view of the interior. I checked the state of the crate by giving it a shake. It didn't budge, and it seemed solid, rooted to its spot. Putting a tentative foot onto it, I pressed down; it still felt secure. I clutched the ledge and hauled my torso into the space, my feet dangling.

It stank of sour milk. Looking to my left, I saw the sound source; a milk urn had fallen from a wall. Its lid traversed some distance, hence the clattering sound. For me, this was no accident – it was a sign.

"Hello!" I shouted, my voice echoing back. To my right, I glimpsed a movement, the sudden jerk of someone hiding from view – "Hello, is anyone here?" Again, my echo was the only response. But yet, I did feel a presence.

Hauling myself in further, I was halted by a high-pitched scream of – "Gerard!" This caused Crow to take off with an equally pitched – "Squawk!" And before I had time to react, a roughly gnarled hand grabbed my leg.

I flailed and kicked, "GET OFF ME." But the grip tightened. When it began to pull, I kicked harder, using my other leg to repeatedly hit at the grabber.

The hand let go with a chortle and backhanded compliment, "For a scrawny fella, you're a strong fecker," said my Uncle Tommy. I pushed myself out and jumped off the ledge, landing as another scream of – "Gerard!" sliced through the silence. Uncle Tommy winced, "Jesus, Maria screeches like a banshee. Come on down and get some dinner before she bursts her lungs and our fecking eardrums." He lit a cigarette and walked towards the manure-soaked lane with me dawdling behind.

......

Granny put two potatoes on my plate of stew, "I only want one," I said.

Dermot glanced over the crust of his apple pie, "Eat them; you need them," he said, scoffing a hunk of pie.

The potatoes were un-peeled, their skins cracked, exposing the crumbly carbohydrate. I scraped and dug out the potato, allowing it to fall into the muddy, meat-strewn pool. Immediately I was comforted by the intense savoury taste and soft texture, "Mmmmmmm." My appreciative noise made Maria, Dermot, and Granny smile in unison.

The tastes and textures wakened a dormant hunger in me, and I woofed the lot with gusto.

......

On hearing the spark of an engine, Dermot's head bolted towards the door, "Tommy, wait for me," he shoved the last of his pie into his mouth and bounded for the door.

......

Granny took my empty plate, "We'll have you good and fattened up by the time your Mammy and Daddy are home; they'll not know you," she said, stepping proudly down into the scullery.

Maria finished her tea, "I'm gonna walk over to Aunty Margaret's." She left without looking back or asking if I'd like to go with her.

Feeling sleepy, I dismissed my sister's uncharacteristic departure and dived into one of the armchairs by the range. *'This Ghost hunting is a tiring business,'* was my last thought before I succumbed to a deep slumber.

......

A raised voice woke me with a start – "I'll tell you once more to feck off and stop annoying the head of me, do you hear me?"

Disorientated, I Jumped up, "Yep, I can hear you," I said, rubbing my eyes.

A coal blackened Lofty lay on his chaise longue, sucking his pipe between profanities. "Ah, but you're not talking to me, are you?"

He exhaled a string of smoke, "You were out for the count," he said, his demeanour without the earlier anger as he ignored my question.

"Where's Granny?" I asked, scratching my head to loosen my hair which had dried tight and sore.

Lofty's head tilted upwards along with a plume of exhaled smoke, "She's in the room above doing her messages," he said, swiftly returning to the fight with his imaginary foe.

......

I climbed the narrow staircase, turning right at the top. There was no door to Granny's bedroom, I entered. The light was dim, and when my eyes became accustomed, I saw Granny sitting on her bed, writing on a piece of paper.

Mindful I might be interrupting a private moment, I stepped back. "That was a quick visit," she said, putting her paper aside and looking over at me.

"Can I come in?"

She patted the bed, "Of course you can."

"Who're you writing to?" Immediately I regretted the nosey nature of my question.

"I'm not writing to anyone, Son."

"But you're writing."

She lifted the paper by her side, "I am. It's the messages for tonight."

"Messages for who?" I asked, intrigued.

"For me," she scribed another word on the paper.

"Why do you have to write messages to yourself?" I asked, bewildered.

"So, I don't forget anything," she put the pen down and handed me the paper.

I looked at the words written in an elegant handwritten script: *Sugar, Tea, Flour, Ham, Sweets, Biscuits, Barley Water...*

"This is your shopping list, Granny."

"She took the paper from me and began to write some more, "Them's my messages for tonight," she said, continuing her concentrated scribe.

Granny's hand was distracted from the list; her head lifted and tilted to the open doorway, "Is that you, Kitty?"

"Tis me, Mammy."

Granny knew everyone's sound.

......

Kitty was my Aunt Kathleen, Granny's youngest child. She two-stepped up the stairs and entered the room, "Welcome home, Gerard."

I waved, "Hiya."

She was laden with shopping bags which she placed on the second bed by the front window. Her excitement was infectious, "Wait till you see the dresses I got, Mammy, that new Dunne's Stores is great."

Soon the bed by the window was a riot of colour as Granny's bedroom became a fashion emporium. Mother and daughter discussed the dresses with enthusiasm. I looked on, in awe of the beauty on display, yet careful not to appear overly enthusiastic or step into their 'woman's world.'

I caught snippets of conversation between the fashion fawning that suggested an occasion was soon to take place. I listened, trying to thread the rapid-fire words together to glean what this event may be. But when Granny placed her hand on Aunt Kathleen's shoulder, lowered her voice and said in a whisper, "Do you think you'll see him?" I couldn't contain myself; I jumped from the bed, my intrusion loud and rude, "See who?"

When Granny looked down on me, she didn't look vexed. Instead, she smiled, "Kathleen's going to Rome to get married." She turned to Kathleen, "And God willing, herself and Tommy will get to see the man himself, the Pope."

On the dressing table, I noticed a card with this man on it. I took it and sat back on the bed, staring at him.

The Pope looked back at me with an intense stare; he held his hand aloft, a large, stoned ring on his finger. I opened the card to see a short biography. My eye caught a list – Pope Paul VI, Born: Giovanni, Battista, Enrico, Antonio, Montini, Maria.

The list stunned me because one of his names was Maria. My mind muddled – did this mean something?

Aunt Kathleen began folding her new dresses, "Where's Maria?"

Trying not to look too interested in the dresses, I answered, "She's gone over to Margaret's."

I placed the Pope back on the dresser. Granny's head tilted, her face pensive, "Did something happen to Maria up at the College?"

"No, why?" I asked, concern clouding me.

She straightened out her pinny, "She was very quiet at dinner time; she didn't seem herself at all."

Maria's quiet reflection and the shifting distance I'd felt at the lagoon returned to me, and I was hit with a sudden insight – I worried that the inclusion of 'Maria,' in the Pope's list of names was a message – *that my beloved big sister was in some sort of trouble.*

Chapter 8: The Conspirators

Sprinting from Granny's house, I stopped at the turnoff to the narrow-hilled lane that led up and down to my Aunt Margaret's house.

Resting my hands on my knees, I inhaled great lungsful of replenishing air.

I recovered to a soundtrack of bees buzzing as they hovered over the flora and fauna that framed the lane

The rustlings of wildlife fleeing from my footfall made me wary. I knew that, in time, I'd become accustomed to these noises, but at that moment, they instilled in me a low-level anxiety, which caused me to up my pace.

At the pinnacle, I looked down on the yellow cottage. It looked like a little buttercup floating in a sea of green.

Aunt Margaret was Granny's fifth child. She and her husband Jim lived in this cottage, less than a half-mile from The House in The Hollow – stone-made-twins.

......

A black bundle bounded towards me, barking uproariously, his tail wagging joyously. I scooped him up, "Hello Breifne," were the only words I could manage while trying to avoid his excited licks. I set him down, and knowing his boundaries, he sat respectfully, allowing me to enter the house without any more of his doggy greetings.

"How-a-ya, Gerard," said Aunt Margaret, wiping the laminate cloth that covered the table. I responded with an unenthusiastic, "Hiya," while scanning the tiny room. "Where's our Maria?" I asked.

"How would I know?" she answered curtly.

"She said she was coming to see you."

"Well, I don't see her here, do you?" She put down the wet cloth and looked me over with appraising eyes.

When I didn't respond, she enthused, "Well, tell us, any scandal from over the water?"

"Erm, no – I've gotta go. I need to find Maria and give her a message," I said, heading for the door.

"Wo-wo-wo – hold on ya-wee-pup-ya – what message, from who?" she asked, making a grab for me.

But, being as swift and nimble as a ferret, Aunt Margaret didn't catch me. I respectfully popped my head back through the door, "Sorry, it's a secret," I said, shunting back onto the lane before she had time to throw any more questions at me.

……

By the time I arrived back at Granny's, my t-shirt was wet with sweat. Granny was hanging washing on the line, her head be-decked with neat ridges of rollers, "Is Maria here?" I asked. "Didn't you say she's over in Margaret's?"

"She's not there," I said, trying to keep the lid on my fretting.

"She'll not be far, Son. The farmworkers will be back from dinner; she's probably up there," she said, nonchalantly pegging a vest to the line.

......

Climbing over the gate, I had a compulsion to return to the lagoon. Looking up at the clear blue sky, I asked, "Where is she, Crow?" But my friend wasn't around to answer or give me comfort and reassurance, so I ran through the woods, hoping to find Maria before she succumbed to some Papal foreseen Prophecy.

......

Maria's dress, strewn across a branch, stopped me dead in my tracks. Nervously, I took it down and forensically examined it for any violent signs: rips, dirt, blood.

Finding nothing, I sprinted for the lagoon, bringing the dress with me.

"Ta for bringing my dress – is someone chasing you?" asked Maria, wading in the water in her underwear.

My chest heaved with relief. 'No.' Moving closer, the sight of her caused my smile to waver, "You've been crying," I said.

"I haven't."

"You have, I can tell, what's up, tell me?"

"Nothing's up."

This was my big sister, my confidante and protector – now, our roles reversed.

"Please tell me, I can help you."

She shrugged dismissively, "Nothing's wrong, nothing you needn't bother about."

Her open-ended denial gave me verbal diarrhoea. "Something's up, cos you went all quiet when Dermot was talking about slaughtering – and Granny said you weren't a chatterbox at dinner time – and when Granny showed me her picture of the Pope it had your name on his list of names, and that means it's a message from the Pope that something's happened to you, something secret…something bad – tell me?"

I jumped into the lagoon when her bottom lip began to quiver. "What's happened?"

She wiped her eyes with the back of her wet hand, "Nothing – sometimes I wish Mam was around to talk to, that's all," she said, stifling her tears. She play-smacked my shoulder. "And don't be daft you, my name on the Pope's picture's not a message; your imagination's forever running away with you, Gerard."

"Why do you want me Mam, what's happened? Is it bad?" I repeated, trying not to despair.

"Nothing bad's happened."

"Then, if it's not bad, tell me," I pleaded.

She bobbed down to my level and looked me in the eye, "It's something private."

I stared back, "Promise me on Mam and Dad's life that it's not bad?"

"I promise."

"Will you tell me one day?" I asked, intrigued by my sister's private happening.

"When that day comes, you won't want to know," she said, wading to the edge of the lagoon.

......

After drying off, Maria and I returned to a packed house. Lofty lay on his chaise-longue, fighting his foe. Great Uncle Tommy sat in his chair by the range, ruminating. Uncle Michael (Granny's seventh child), on the chair next to him, waiting. Uncle Peter (Granny's sixth child) was in the scullery shaving. Great Uncle Frankie sat in his chair by the window, snoozing. Granny was in the scullery preparing tea. And on hearing our arrival, Aunt Kathleen bounded downstairs.

There was a Saturday evening air of excitement, which lent her greeting an extra helping of warmth. Aunt Kathleen homed in on Maria, "Your hair's gorgeous that length, and you've got tall. You look all grown up," she said.

Maria responded with uncharacteristic shyness, "Thanks," she said, gently catching Kathleen's sleeve and guiding her towards the stairs, where she whispered something in her ear.

I watched, looking for clues in their stealth-like interactions.

Aunt Kathleen looked towards the scullery and called out, "Mammy, can you come upstairs for a minute." It was said in a tone that all the males in the room seemed to understand, except me. Granny, seemingly knowing this code, skipped up the two steps. The three of them ascended the stairs in conspiratorial silence.

......

Outside, I stared at my legs; only for the red hives, they were almost indistinguishable from the white pebble-dashed wall I sat on. The sight of them made me smile, a smile entirely at odds with how I felt.

Something had changed in Maria. In a mere moment, my sister had altered, entered another realm that I wasn't part of or even allowed to question.

......

I waited on the wall, hoping Maria would come out and talk to me, tell me everything, spill her secrets like she always did.

When she didn't, I felt like I'd lost a part of her.

......

"Caw. Caw. Caw." Crow's call pulled me from my maudlin thoughts and gave me a hit of motivation – I may have lost something in my sister, but I was determined to find something with the tall-man.

Crossing the road, I stepped onto the first rung of the gate and looked up, "Will you be around tomorrow, Crow?"

The "Click. Click," of his 'yes' lifted me from my melancholy.

......

That evening I felt a little better. Partly because I wore my favourite clothes: a green t-shirt with a white horse and the word IRELAND printed on it, blue jeans with a good bit of flare, and brightly polished burgundy shoes with a platform height just on the right side of sensible for the fashionable seven-year-old.

Of course, the overall look was let down by the hair, but I wasn't going to let my cursed curls upset my *Saturday night in town.*

Chapter 9: Saints and Sinners

Maria, Dermot, Aunt Margaret, and I were seated snug in the back of Uncle Michael's car on our way to town.

Granny, up front, wore a green dress coat, matched with a green hat that nestled into her newly created silver curls, secured with a gold pin, a sparkling green stone at its end. She looked resplendent, regal.

......

Uncle Michael dropped us off on the main street before returning to collect the men of the house and deliver them to their respective pubs for Saturday-night-hoolies.

On the street, we met Dermot's best Irish friend, John O'Connell, accompanied by a young woman I didn't recognise.

The reunited friends threw their arms around each other's shoulders and launched into planning a summer of exploring, hunting, and fishing.
Despite a year since they'd seen each other, Dermot and John jumped right back into their friendship roles like they'd never been apart.

Granny acknowledged the woman, "How's things?" she asked, with a formality that wasn't like her.

"I'm grand Mrs Smith, and yourself?"

"Not a bother, sher we can't complain when we're having this weather."

"Is right, Mrs Smith, is right."

Dermot interrupted their phatic communion, "Can we go to the magazine shop, Granny?"

"Off yer go, but be back in Hickey's for half eight, or there'll be no cones for you," she said brightly.

The boys raced off, leaving a chorus of excited chatter in their wake.

The woman looked back at their sing-songy departure, "Isn't it great to see them so happy."

She looked to me, her stare making me uncomfortable, "Gerard prefers to be with the women?" she said, addressing no one in particular.

Granny didn't hesitate, "Gerard prefers to be with whoever he wants to be, isn't that right?" I nodded a 'Yes.'

The woman continued to watch me, "Wouldn't you die for a head of hair like that? It's always the boys that get the curls when it's us girls who want them."

I felt my face begin to flush, becoming self-conscious of the woman's appraisal of me in feminine terms.

Seeing my unease, Maria jumped in, "Why don't you go off to Connelly Brothers Gerard? We'll meet you back in Hickey's," she said, with a wink.

That wink meant the world, for it was loaded with Maria's good intentions for me.

......

A bell jingled to announce my entrance at Connelly Brothers gift and toyshop.

A Multitude of trinkets twinkled in the dim light, creating a moment's disorientation in me. But on focussing, my body tightened at the sight of a familiar man staring down on me from everywhere – it was Pope Paul VI.

His image loomed large in ornately gilded frames and small on delicate prayer books. On heaving shelves that surrounded me, he waved from dinner plates and teacups; he nestled next to porcelain statues of Holy Mary. He was on bottles of Holy Water, standing next to painted plaster statues of Saints. These revered icons were guarded by a poetic warning placed liberally along the shelves – *'Nice to handle, nice to hold, but if you break them, we say SOLD!'*

My unease at the sight of Pope Paul VI was tempered when I saw that he wasn't the star of this Holy Emporium. No, the star was Jesus.

He was top of the bill at Connelly Brothers, and the sight of him comforted me. To my eye, his image was more Poppette than Prophet. I saw David of Essex in his gentle face and luxurious locks rather than Jesus of Nazareth.

In contrast – the image of Pope Paul VI unnerved me. Because, given the change in Maria, the secrecy this engendered, and her name listed amongst his, I saw a conspiratorial malevolence in his dark eyes.

Driven by an urge to protect myself from potential evils, I picked up a small box containing Rosary beads. Noting they were within my budget, I took them to the counter. That's when I became aware of low-level mutterings.

An older lady was having a whispered conversation with a younger lady close to the counter. Wondering why she felt the need to whisper, I stopped. My ears pricked up when I discerned, they were discussing Pope Paul VI.

Knowing it was rude to eavesdrop, I took my beads to the counter in time to hear the old lady say, "He's spoken about the third secret, that's not right, it's not right." Her words slammed into me, shaking me with their relevance to my recent experience.

Yet frustration floored me as I couldn't ask the lady what she was talking about. I was taught not to talk to strangers, let alone question them.

....

The lady's words swam around my head, *'He's spoken about the third secret...'* Their conspiratorial conversation bothered me. Furthermore, I felt Maria was complicit in the conspiracy. I walked to Young's Newsagents with my head bowed, conjuring all manner of scary scenarios, while a strange feeling of cold isolation dragged at my heels.

......

Unlike Connelly Brothers, Young's Newsagents was bright, busy, and imbued with a cheerful atmosphere as people browsed and chatted. I looked around for Dermot and John – no sign of them. So, I walked over to the dark side – the Marvel and Horror comics.

I was an avid reader, with a reading age well above the average seven-year-old – a fact that elicited much pride from Mam and Dad.

My heart leapt when I saw copies of 'Creepy,' a horror comic from America. The cover illustration was of various creepy characters sitting at a candelabra be-decked dinner table in an old dark house. Standing at the head of the table, staring coldly at me, stood a tall man dressed in black.

I grabbed it and read the blurb: *'Tales of shock, suspense and secrets.'* It spoke to me – *'secrets,'* and a tall-man on the cover, all conspired to convince me this comic contained answers.

I turned to the inner back page, delighted to see it contained something else – an advert for Sea-Monkeys that could be purchased via postal order from America. I longed to own a family of these humanoid crustaceans that smiled at me from the back of my horror comics.

Swiftly, I turned the comic back to front to forget about Sea Monkeys for the time being. This summer, I had more pressing matters to think of. Taking Creepy to the cash desk, I was prepared to forfeit my ice-cream cone to seek any revelations contained within.

The comic induced a look of concern in the young cashier girl. She looked at me, "Will this not give you nightmares?" she asked, thrusting it into a paper bag with kind concern. I shrugged my shoulders because I didn't have the answer.

......

"Welcome home, Gerard. Will you be having a cone?" asked the lady assistant in Hickey's.

"Have I got enough?" I asked, presenting her with my change.
Her glance was swift, "You have indeed," she smiled and appeared

from behind her counter.

Being in Hickey's was a multi-sensory experience. The smells tickled and teased my taste buds: light sweetness gave way to chocolaty depths, which merged with spicy cinnamon and hits of citrus. These glorious sensations were bolstered by an aura of kindness that radiated from the assistant as she expertly handled a machine that sculpted a swirling flare of creamy whiteness onto a wafer flute.

She handed me the cream peaked torch, "Will you have sauce, Gerard?"

"Yes, please." And onto the icy swirl, she spun a spiral of crimson to contrast vividly with white.

The contrast wasn't only visual; the tart raspberry countered the smooth creaminess to create a momentary taste of heaven.

The assistant noted my bliss, "Go inside and enjoy it in comfort," she said, opening a curtain that led from the sugary retail space into Hickey's hallowed home.

......

The room was like an annexe to the rest of the house, and despite its smallness, the high ceilings and ornate cornicing hinted at the grandeur of the dwelling beyond.

It was a grandeur befitting the proprietor, Betty Hickey. She sat in a wing-backed armchair, in possession of a Hollywood star's towering personality and prowess.

To me, Betty was ageless, from another time and place. She wore a floral maxi dress, with matching scarf around her head, tied bandanna style. Her fingers were adorned with ornate rings, their multi-coloured stones glistening as she gesticulated. To top off her otherworldliness, there was her voice: deep, rich, and with a grand pitch that consolidated an overall presence that belonged on the big screen.

I sat on a small stool, relishing my ice cream while watching and listening to Betty Hickey, transfixed by her.

In my peripheral vision, I saw Granny being equally beguiled by Betty. Such was my sensory absorption that I didn't realise who sat to the right, behind me, "What do you be buying this kind of thing for?"

Her words tore me from the twin joys of ice cream and Betty. The woman from the street was flicking through my Creepy, a look of abject horror on her face.

Her question dripped with disdain, causing Granny and Betty to look our way. When sure she had their full attention, she held my Creepy Comic aloft and declared – *"A child shouldn't be looking at things like this; it's a sin."*

Chapter 10: The Triumvirate

Her judgement of my reading matter soaked me in a shower of shame, and I silently berated myself, *'Why can't I buy normal comics?' Why can't I like football magazines? Why can't I enjoy fishing books?"* I knew this woman had rumbled me; she saw my oddness, my difference, and was now exposing it to Granny and Betty Hickey.

Lowering my head, I waited for the other women to admonish me. Betty's voice came dark and delicious. "There's no sin in a comic; it's only cartoons, like Scooby Doo," she said, her words a salve to my shame.

While before I admired Betty Hickey's aesthetic, now I adored her person. Curiously, the woman didn't respond; instead, she handed me back my Creepy, her face crumpled in disdain for the comic and myself.

Granny's words followed, soft and light, "Isn't it great to see him reading. Gerard likes ghosty stories; many do, there's no harm in them," she said, relishing the final remnants of her cone.

This nonchalantly supportive attitude to my choice of reading material by the two senior women settled me. The younger woman's uncertainty of me still bothered, but less so.

So, when Dermot and John came bounding in, my enthusiasm almost matched theirs

......

Granny looked at the boys, bewildered, "Are yous not having a cone?"

Dermot answered without lifting his head from a fishing magazine, "We woofed them outside."

Betty guffawed, "Woofed them, like a dog."

He looked up, infected by Betty's mirth, "Yep, dead fast, cos they're dead nice," he said, through a smile.

"Is the ice cream in England not nice, Dermot?" asked Betty.

Dermot jumped off his chair, "Nah, it's horrible," he said before bursting into the song we council kids sang every time the ice-cream van arrived on the estate. "Bergen's ice cream, it tastes like Brylcream. The flakes are bad too, cos they taste like pooh. Don't eat it, you're right, cos it tastes like s…."

John jumped from his chair. "Settle, settle, Dermot!" he said, using his hands like a conductor controlling an orchestra; his gentle admonishment and gesticulations designed to spare the woman any offence.

John was the polar opposite of my brother. Where Dermot was impetuous, feisty, and wilful, John was calm, considered, and collected.

Dermot's reaction was swift, his singing stopped, and he returned to his magazine. A quiet descended, in which I noticed the woman assess Dermot. It was clear his song sullied him somewhat in her eyes – yet she seemed sure of my brother; she knew where to place him in her world.

Granny broke the moment's silence, "Do English cones taste like Shite, Dermot?" she asked, chuckling. Betty joined her in low-level laughter while I stifled my mirth.

The merriment was interrupted by Maria, who appeared from behind the curtain, "What's the joke? Tell us." She said, placing her shopping bag on the table.

As if to diffuse any more talk that would upset the woman, Betty asked, divertingly, "What've you been buying?"

Maria's face lit up as she delved into the bag, "I got this gorgeous dress, for best," she said, pulling out a billowing confection of white.

Betty homed in and held the dress up, looking it over with her fashion-forward eyes, "It's Broderie Anglaise, isn't it just exquisite? You could get married in this, Maria."

I couldn't resist and jumped up to get a closer view, "She's going to marry Bruce Lee," I said, scrutinising the dress to ensure it was befitting of my sister's big day.

I wallowed in its delicate beauty; before being thunderstruck by a revelation – perhaps this was the secret, Maria was getting married, and she hadn't told me. I railed, "You can't get married in this; it's not long. Wedding dresses are supposed to be long nowadays."

Maria tussled my hair, "Don't be mad, I'm not getting married; and besides, do you think I'd choose a dress without your expert eye,' she said.

"Does Gerard like picking out frocks?" I spun around to see the woman gazing at me with the same expression, a look of uncertainty about where she should place me in her world. Realising my reaction to the dress was probably too passionate, I sat down and flicked through my Creepy.

To my surprise and delight, nobody answered her. Not out of rudeness, more out of distraction, as the three women were ensconced in girly talk, the two boys immersed in boy talk, and me in my Creepy.

The woman left the room, taking her uncertainty of me with her. She didn't say goodbye.

......

"When are you gonna wear your new dress?" I asked Maria as we walked to post my card.

"At the end of summer, when Mam and Dad come over, and I've got a bit of colour," she said, taking my hand.

This is when I felt happiest, hand in hand with my big sister. I felt safe and free to say anything, "That woman doesn't like me."

She tugged on my hand, "Don't be daft; everyone loves you," she said, pulling me into a shop.

Maria looked at the postcard, "Do you have Dermot's boat pen?"

"No."

The shopkeeper pulled a pen out of his jacket pocket, "There you go."

She began writing but stopped abruptly, looking at the shopkeeper with concern, "Do you sell single envelopes?"

His hand shuffled under the counter, "We do surely," he said, handing her one.

Maria continued to write, her face tight with concentration. Once finished, she put the card into the envelope, causing me to assert, "NO – you don't need to, I put the address on it already. Postcards don't need to go in envelopes."

"This one does," she said, licking the edges and ensuring it was sealed.

Why would Maria want her message to be unseen by others?

I remained silent, for I knew the nature of secrets. They were whispered, hidden, sealed away – until lost in time.

But I would find this one. I suspected it was hiding somewhere between the triumvirate of *Pope Paul VI, Maria, and the tall-man.*

Chapter 11: The Guardians of The Congregation

"Gerard, wake up, we're late," Maria's shout was accompanied by a vigorous shake of my shoulders.

I'd slept so deeply I found it difficult to lift my body. I managed to reach an arm towards Maria, "Late for what?" I asked. She grabbed my hand, hoisting me up.

"Mass," she said, hurriedly brushing her hair.

The smell of cooking bacon wafted into the room, its savoury hit waking me up. Great Uncle Frankie was Sunday morning chef, concocting a culinary feast we'd enjoy after Mass while he left for the later ceremony.

……

A crowding congregation marched with silent solemnity up the steep hill that led to the jewel in Cavan Town's Crown – The Cathedral.

The granite and limestone of St Patrick and St Felim's Cathedral glistened in another blue-sky day.

Holding Maria's hand, we strolled, my head bowed in thought, thinking about Patrick and Felim. The week before we left Manchester, I recalled asking Dad, "Do Patrick and Felim live in the Cathedral?" He'd spluttered a laugh and pondered, "I suppose they still do, in spirit; that's how it got its name."

Passing through the doors, I stopped, halting Maria with me, "Were Patrick and Felim brothers?" I asked.

Maria dabbed two fingers in the holy water font. "Don't be silly; they're Saints," she whispered, tapping her sacredly wet fingers onto my forehead.

……

She pulled me into a pew as the Priest, dressed head to toe in white and gold robes arrived on the altar. Three boys in plain white, their hands clasped in prayer, followed him. I watched the Priestly preparations with a warm glow – because I thought that when I was grown up, it would be nice to live in a Cathedral like this with my best school friend – just like Patrick and Felim.

But the warmth soon evaporated when Maria's mumbling caught my eye. Her head down, I saw her mouth moving in silent prayer. This struck me as odd, never had I seen my sister embrace prayer so fervently.

I stared at her moving mouth, trying to discern her words, but I couldn't fathom any. She reminded me of a fish out of water, yearning to be thrown back to recover the life before – the sight of her made me sad.

Maria noticed my stare, looked at me and mouthed, "What?"

I whispered, "What're you praying for?"

Her lips tickled my ear, "We're at Mass; that's what you do."

"Tell me what you're praying for, and I'll pray for it too," I said, hopeful I might get some clues in her response.

But a sharp trio of shushing sounds, from a woman in front, a man behind, and a woman to our left put paid to that glimmer of hope. We immediately lowered our heads for the rest of the religious ceremony.

......

With Mass over, there was a marked contrast in the atmosphere outside Patrick and Felim's Cathedral.

The respectful silence accompanying the congregation's entrance was replaced with a relaxed sizzle as they burst into chattering. It felt like a collective tension had been released as people opened up – and talked.

I became acutely aware of the words that surrounded me. More significantly, I figured that if people were relaxed, secrets might be spilt. And so, I mingled – and listened.

......

I soon deduced that the main topic of conversation was the weather. "Isn't this weather great," asked a woman, dressed in a pink trouser-suit, of a man who appeared distressed by his own Sunday suit and boot.

"It might be great for you, but it's killing me," he replied. I stared up at him, open-mouthed, waiting for the weather to make its final blow and finish him off right there, on the concourse of Patrick and Felim's Cathedral.

But it never happened. Instead, they both looked annoyed at my intrusion, "Who do you belong to?" asked the woman, perspiration prickling her forehead. I closed my mouth and scarpered into the crowd.

My time was limited, for soon, Frankie's feast would beckon – so I moved stealth-like through the thronging crowd, my ears like a satellite, ready to home in on any trigger words.

Disappointingly all I picked up was innocuous talk of weather, work, and football. But I spied someone of interest – the old lady from Connelly Brothers shop, she who spoke of secrets.

She wasn't alone. Another lady and a man were in her company; their heads close in talk. They stood apart from the rest of the crowd, the slight distance distinguishing them from the congregation.

I sauntered over with my best nonchalant impression. As I neared, I saw them talking ten to the dozen, their mouths moving in rapid-fire. I quickened my pace, eager to pick up some of their streaming words – *"Hail Mary Mother of God...*

...they were reciting the Rosary.

I stopped in my tracks and watched as they fingered their Rosary Beads while praying in trance-like fervour. Now, I knew that this was the mother of all prayers, one that packed a powerful protective punch. So, I figured these people were acting as The Guardians of The Congregation – they knew something the rest of us didn't.

"Gerard!" Maria's call pulled me away from The Guardians, and I ran to her, my head spinning with questions.

......
Squeezed into Uncle Michael's car, these questions looped around my head.

What were the Guardian's protecting us from? What secret did Maria seal in that envelope? What had caused the change in my sister? The questions caused me conflict, for I was aware they were derailing me from my Summertime purpose – searching for the tall-man.

Maria's voice pulled me from myself, "You're very quiet, Gerard."

"I'm thinking."

"What about?"

"Things."

"What things?" she asked, nudging my elbow with hers.

Uncle Michael's car pulled into the side of the house, causing Dermot to shout at the top of his voice, "SAUSAGES, WE'RE COMING TO GET YOU."

Maria laughed and jumped from the car, disinterested in any answer I may have given her.

......

Great Uncle Frankie had created a mighty, meaty breakfast. Bacon smothered the range, surrounded by mounds of fat sausages, all framed by slices of fried brown bread – it was culinary art in its purest form.

Dermot grabbed a fork and violently stabbed a sausage, which retaliated by spurting a torrent of juicy fat in his face. The hot fat didn't faze my brother; he wiped his face and went straight for the kill, biting off and devouring half the beast with barely a chew.

I sat at the table sandwiched between uncles Michael and Peter. I savoured the salty bacon and crunchy bread from Frankie's breakfast buffet. I was about to relish my second rasher when Uncle Tommy piped up, "You've no sausage, Gerard."

Alarmingly, my eye caught sight of Uncle Tommy stabbing a sausage and thrusting it towards my plate.

"Here, have this one," he said, releasing it from his fork with a knife. I didn't have time to say, 'No,' as I watched the offensive missile launch itself at my plate, scoring a direct hit on my remaining rasher.

"NOOOOO!" I hollered, causing my relations to halt their eating and look at me, mouths agape.

"What has you screeching?" asked Granny.

I stared at the sausage, settling on my beloved bacon, and opened my heart, "I can't eat bacon when it's been touched by sausage!"

"Why not?" asked Granny, concerned.

I loosened my tongue and told the truth, "Because before they're filled with sausage, they're full of shit!"

My relations swivelled their heads and continued with smiling chews while Uncle Tommy exclaimed, "A bit of cow shite did no one any harm." He retrieved his porky missile from my plate and bit into it with relish.

......

My relations' smiling dismissal of my sausage sensitivity made me feel silly and apart. I left the table and took myself away, leaving their breakfast banter in my wake.

Alone on the tree-tunnelled lane to the farm, I heard the caw of a crow; the sound made me feel together.

"Hello, Crow," I said. "Caw, caw, caw," his response gladdened me, which in turn made me see that my social interactions with humans were awkward, while my engagement with crow was comfortable.

On this lane, watching Crow circle, I felt warm contentment that stayed with me as I ambled up into *St Pat's College Farmyard*.

Chapter 12: Noises that go bump in the day

Walking along, I spoke openly with Crow, "Dad says ghosts are people who die suddenly, and they don't realise they're dead. He saw the tall-man when he was my age, said he looked sad like he was looking for something he'd lost and couldn't find." I stopped and looked up, "Crow, did the tall-man die all of a sudden?"

"Caw."

His yes motivated me. It gave me a springboard into his identity – I could ask about people who'd died suddenly on the farm or at the college and deduce from there.

Upping my pace to match Crow, I ran with him into the farmyard, stopping in the middle to watch him circle, scrutinising his territory. My heart sank when he flew off without a caw goodbye.

When he didn't settle on the corner of the byre, his observational post, I knew the tall-man wasn't here; instead, humans probably were. Yet the place was deathly quiet, especially given a whole herd of cattle had been milked a short while before.

Welcoming the quiet, I thought with clarity. I wondered what the tall-man may have lost in the farming space in which I stood. Was it a personal item?

When Mam lost her engagement ring, she couldn't rest. I recalled the look of sorrow mingled with panic as she ran out the door to retrace her steps. I also remembered the joy as she came racing back, proudly brandishing the ring on her finger. "It was on the sink behind the bar; I'd taken it off to wash my hands," she exclaimed, glowing with relief.

Looking around, I took in the enormity of the space, the number of buildings and out-houses, offices, and hay sheds. Eventually, I settled on the byre. If I was to find any lost personal items, I had to start somewhere. I turned towards the milking parlour to start my search.

......

This time, I climbed through the side window un-encumbered by any grabbing uncles. It was warm and smelt of cow pooh and sour milk, a combination that didn't bother me, now that I'd become accustomed to country flavours.

My search began by walking along the concrete milking booths. I soon realised it was hard to find what you don't know you're looking for. But I continued, looking for a glint or a glimmer of light amongst the concrete that might lead me to a tall-man clue.

But my search stopped when I heard a sound.

A shuffling.

Instinctively I called out, "Is that you, Uncle Tommy?" mindful my joker uncle might try to startle me again.

"Tommy!" I repeated, my voice raised.

The shuffling continued.

Looking towards its source, my eyes settled on the main metal doors.

"Hello, who's there?"

When there came no reply, I became spooked.

Now, despite my extreme youth, I was a horror film aficionado, so I was acutely aware of how sounds could be used as tropes to trick and scare. I knew a shuffle and a rustle could become the jolting jump of a rat or the flapping bolt of a bat.

Thus, I listened with an experienced ear.

The shuffle came again – its sound dragging and heavy, not that of a rat or a bat.

I walked toward the door with slow, sure steps, constantly glancing to my left to make sure my way in was my way out should I need to flee.

In front of the doors, I noted a narrow gap through which I could peek. Leaning in, I froze – another eye peered back at me.

The shock of a bump and rattle threw me backwards.

Searing pain shot through me as my backside smacked on the hard concrete floor. But there was no time for tears or fears as the door rattled again, this time accompanied by an angry male voice – "Come here to me you. When I get me hands on you, I'll throttle ya, you little fucker ya!"

It wasn't Uncle Tommy's voice, nor was it any voice I recognised. No, it was the sound of a man who wanted to avenge my trespass – I heard the murder in his mind.

Fear finally found me.

I scrambled to my feet, the fright making me fumble and tumble back on my bottom again.

But a massive thump of the doors put a rocket up my backside – I launched myself at my way in and quite literally flew out, landing in a bed of bramble and nettles.

The nettles stung, and the brambles scratched, but self-preservation dulled the pain. I closed my eyes, lay still, and played dead.

Playing dead was fruitless. After a few minutes of motionless silence, I opened a tentative eye. All I saw was bramble, so I opened my second eye and lifted my head, careful to cause no identifying rustle.

A flash of red caught my attention – I lifted my head further.

Horror engulfed me when the realisation of what I saw hit me – the unmistakable sight of Maria's red wellington boots coming up the lane towards the milking parlour.

Instinctively I made to jump up and save my sister from the same fate as mine, but the sound of her voice halted me, "leave him alone, you, don't hurt him!"

An icy pick spiked my heart, while a dull thump hurt my head.

For the tone in which my beloved sister delivered her plea to save me hurt; because it was said without conviction, instead her tone was cheery and light-hearted.

I waited for his response, but none came. Instead, Maria's high-pitched scream cut through the farm. I jumped up in time to see her fleeing – with the man in hot pursuit.

A weapon, I needed a weapon. Seeing nothing with which to hit the man, I raced into the farm. My delay had served me poorly, they had fled, and I had no idea in which direction my fleeing sister and her harm-intending pursuer had gone.

My ears pulsed to the sound of my heartbeat, hindering my ability to listen for Maria and her pursuer. But her scream cut through my beats, and my head spun to its source – the avenue leading up and into St Patrick's College, a local boarding school.

The college was a magisterial building, imbued with a Dickensian sense of story and authority. The place scared me, but I had to go there to save my sister – I sped off towards the scholarly space.

I'd barely made it to the avenue when I was stopped in my tracks by another scream – it came from Maria, but this was a different sound.

Although the sound was piercing, a lilt at the end seemed to lead to laughter.

Listening intently, I deduced that Maria's scream had somehow transmuted into hysterical peals of laughter.

To my mind, this was impossible; the sound of fear could not become the sound of joy. I stared at my feet, puzzled.

My sister had changed, and now, I had a good idea what had caused her difference. But I couldn't, wouldn't say it – not yet.

……

Maria's laughter was accompanied by rushing footfall through gravel and foliage, and almost as quickly as it started, it stopped. The quiet caused me to look up, "Gerard, what you doing here?" asked

Maria.

She looked dishevelled, her face flushed red from exertion.

"I'm looking for the tall-man," I answered. Her appearance startled me, for the lids of her eyes were painted in a blue shadow, emphasising the pale blue of her eyes, and her eyelashes appeared thicker, blacker.

She looked at me strangely, as if she were nervous, "Go on then, go looking for him in the woods," she said, pointing behind me.

I looked back towards the woods, and when I looked back to my sister, I jolted to see the farmhand sidle up behind her. My hand shot instinctively forward in a protective gesture, "Don't hurt us!" I shouted.

Maria stared at me, her brow furrowed, "Don't be daft, Gerard, he's not going to hurt us," she said, looking at the farmhand with an apologetic expression.

I didn't hold back, "I was in the byre; he said he was going to throttle me when he got his hands on me. He was banging on the door and everything." My rant was swiftly halted by Maria's pronouncement – "Stop it, Gerard!"

I stared at them, standing side-by-side yet apart.

My sister looked embarrassed by me, while the farmhand seemed amused.

"Why are you laughing?" I asked him, confused.

He walked towards me; I took a step back, halting him, "You're like a wee freckened dog."

That's when I noticed his hair; it glistened and shone in the sunshine.

Maria joined him, her smile matching his, "He was talking to a stray cow Gerard, not you."

I began to heat up, flushing with foolishness. I lowered my head to hide my reddening face, "Sorry, I thought you were talking to me," I managed to mumble.

Doing a swift about-turn, I sauntered towards the woods. Maria called after me, "Gerard, are you alright?"

"Yeah," I replied, forcing nonchalance through clenched teeth.

......

The sight of his hair stayed with me as I wandered towards the woods. He had Bruce Lee hair, just like the posters on Maria's bedroom wall in Manchester.

I called him the boy with Bruce Lee hair and entered the woods – *alone again, naturally.*

Chapter 13: The knowing

"Dock leaf, dock leaf, in and out, take the sting of the nettle out," I repeatedly recited while I salved my stinging legs with God's good leaves.

As I did so, a calm came over me, more so when a fluttering Crow landed on the post by the lagoon.

"Hello Crow," I said, starting a fresh dock leaf on another hive, "Caw," he replied.

I looked at him, "I wish you could talk to tell me about this secret stuff that's going on."

When he didn't respond, I continued talking, "My sister's changed, you know, something's happened to her." I continued salving my legs, ruminating on whether to say what I was thinking – aloud.

"Caw, caw, caw," said Crow, prompting me to look at him and say the unsayable – "I think she's possessed."

I put the dock leaves down and stood up to explain more, "Spirits of dead people can go inside alive people, you know, I've read about it in my comics and stuff." I felt suddenly purged for articulating what I'd been frightened to do so.

"There's no other reason for her change, Crow; she's been possessed by a spirit." I threw the dock leaves down and stood up, my mind whirring, "I have to go back," I said, compelled by a need to observe Maria. Crow took off and glided in the direction of the farm, with me in hot pursuit.

......

Crow settled on the corner of the byre, quietly watching. When he took off again, he soared along the avenue that led to St Patrick's College. Despite my unease with the place, I didn't hesitate in my pursuit.

The sound of other kids accompanied my run – bursts of Sunday morning merriment emanated from the orchards that surrounded me, as boys, borders from the school, indulged in illicit adventure.

My sprint continued until the boys' noise dimmed in the distance, giving way to other sounds. I ran towards a cacophony of chaos. Angry voices transmuted into swelling cheers of elation, which suddenly dropped to drones of disappointment.

These sounds ebbed and flowed like an ocean storm carrying me along in their wake until I burst through the clearing on a great choral crescendo.

I stopped abruptly; this chorus was not for my arrival. No, a goal had been scored. Players and spectators cheered in celebration of the heroic, game-winning scorer.

Deflated, I placed my hands on my knees and dropped my head to recover from my sprint. Crow had led me to a football match, not my sister.

......

This world I'd run into was alien to me. I didn't understand the language, the culture, or the physicality of this game that was so revered, yet I secretly reviled.

The cheering chorus continued, and I lifted my head to watch the celebrations. My focus was on the players as they milled about the pitch; I saw that they weren't men but boys on the cusp of maturity. Their parents mostly made up the spectators, who swarmed the pitch; proud fathers back-slapped triumphant sons while loving mothers soothed their dearly defeated.

But a splash of red pulled me from the celebrations – Maria's red wellies.

Instinctively, I crouched like a wily fox staking out its prey. My sister was on a grassy embankment that led down onto the football pitch. My heart lurched when I saw she was sitting next to him – the boy with Bruce Lee hair.

The sight of them together instilled in me a strange feeling for which I had no name. All I knew was that I had never felt like this before; it was an unpleasant emotion. I wanted it to go away, but the more I looked at them, the deeper this feeling became. Soon, I had to look away before I was swallowed whole by this strange pang that pulled me to my knees.

Sitting on my heels, I stared at green grass, trying to make sense of this monstrous feeling. It was a type of sadness, laced with anger, and accompanied by a looping question, "Why was Maria with him when she used to be with me?"

......

Soon, I realised that sitting on my hunkers watching my sister interact with this boy, a stranger to me, was odd behaviour. So, I rose and walked towards them, trying to affect a casual confidence suggesting I'd chanced upon them rather than sought them out.

The boy with Bruce Lee hair noticed my arrival, pointing towards me. Maria jumped up, "Gerard, what you doing here? I thought you were ghost-hunting?" she asked. I thought I heard annoyance in her question but couldn't be sure, so I said, "I heard all the cheering and wondered what it was for." I was pleased with the authenticity of my reply.

The boy with Bruce Lee hair looked towards the players departing the pitch, "You missed a great game; some of those boys are future superstars. They made the whole county proud when they lifted the cup for Cavan," he said, bristling with pride.

His pride puzzled me, "Why did they lift a cup?"

He smiled, "It wasn't any auld cup wee-fella, t'was the Hogan Cup, the winners' trophy for the All-Ireland Gaelic Football Championships."

I lowered my head to disguise another reddening face.
Maria's voice lifted me, "Have you had any sightings?" she asked.

"Not yet."

Looking at her, I was struck by her height. She seemed taller; she stood the same height as the boy with Bruce Lee hair.

He leant towards me, "I've seen him," he said in a hushed voice.

My head shot up, "Have you, what does he look like?"

He leaned back, "Ah now, I only seen him in the dark, but I can tell you, he's a fierce tall fella."

One of his words hit me like a bolt – "fierce."

Fierce was not a word I'd associated with the tall-man. On the contrary, my image of him, moulded by Dad, was one of a kind soul, searching for something lost, a spirit far removed from anything fierce.

My mind began to piece together threads: the change in Maria, her new height, the secrets, the Rosary reciting Guardians of the congregation – the tall-man.

My new understanding of the tall-man's fierce malevolency led me to a horrific possibility and a light-bulb-moment – perhaps my beloved sister was possessed by him!

My heart sank as my head soared with scenarios.

A scene from the Cathedral returned to me, the Rosary praying led by the lady who whispered secrets in Connelly Brother's shop.

My hand flew to my pocket where I felt the outline of the Rosary beads I'd purchased in the presence of this lady.

Fate was leading me towards the truth.

I needed proof of possession – I pulled the beads from my pocket and thrust the plastic cross towards Maria, "Do you like my new Rosary beads?" I asked calmly.

She instantly recoiled, screaming, a piercing, ear-splitting screech. The extremity of her reaction to the sacred cross was all the proof I needed – an evil spirit, the fierce tall-man, possessed my sister.

Maria continued to scream and flail wildly, even when I put the beads back in my pocket.

Turning away, I heard the boy with Bruce Lee hair, "It's only a wasp. Stop trying to swipe it; you'll make it more vexed," he said, his words laced with laughter.

But I saw no wasp; I saw the truth.

......

Two emotions I understood all too clearly engulfed me: fear and loneliness.

I feared for Maria, and in losing her to a demon, I felt lonely without her kinship. But more so, the burden of knowing pressed heavily on my slight shoulders. This was my secret, and I had to keep it sealed tight to save my sister.

This responsibility made me feel even more alone, isolated by *the knowing*.

Chapter 14: The Manifestation

Lying awake in the darkness, I listened to the soundly sleeping breaths of my uncles: Mickey and Peter, with whom I shared the room, and my brother, Dermot, with whom I shared the bed.

I wished I could sleep like them. But how could I, when my sister lay in the adjacent room, an evil spirit lying dormant inside her while she slept. My mind tormented me as it played images of how the fierce tall-man would manifest himself in Maria.

......

The birds began their dawn chorus before I finally succumbed to sleep.

......

I flailed violently in the bed as Dermot shook me, "Get up, our kid, we've gotta go to Town Granny's for our dinner," he shouted, shaking me some more.

Bleary-eyed from too little sleep, I sat up and did the thing I instinctively did every morning, patted my hair down. Sleepily trying to tame my whin-bush, the revelations of the previous day slammed back to me, "Where's our Maria?" I shouted, hurtling into the other room.

Staring at the two neatly made beds, I repeated my question with rising urgency, "Our Maria, where is she?"

My raised mood bemused Dermot, "Have you two been on the red lemonade or summat?"

I moved closer, "What do you mean?"
"You've woke up all jittery and jumpy, like our Maria." He leaned in, focussing on my face, looking for something. Seeing nothing untoward, he pulled back, "But our Maria's got reason to be, you haven't."

A chill hit me, "What do you mean?"

He exited the room, me shadowing him, "What's up with her?" I asked again,
bracing myself for his answer, "Summat's growing in her eye; she's right flipping out about it," he said, unconcerned.

……

I took the stairs two by two, following the sound of Maria's distressed voice into the kitchen.

She arched backwards over the sink while Granny leant over her, cradling her head. I homed in as Granny gently opened Maria's eye with her thumb and forefinger while ignoring her incessant chants of, "What is it, what is it?" and protestations, "Leave it alone, stop touching it!"

Granny pondered before pronouncing, "You have a stye." She released Maria and patted her hair reassuringly, "You probably got it from that cheap make-up you're using."

Maria rushed to the small mirror on the wall and thrust her face into it, "It looks horrible; how can I get rid of it?" she asked, rubbing her eye vigorously.

Granny grabbed her hand, "Stop. You'll make it worse. Leave it be."

Maria looked at her, "I can't go out looking like this, can I?"

Granny took a pot from the cupboard, "You've to go to your Town Granny's today. Don't be worrying, it probably feels worse than it looks – you look grand," she said, piling potatoes from a paper sack into her pot.

Maria continued to stare at her eye, her face gnarled with revulsion and worry.

Me, I stood and glared with her. The white of her eye was vivid red, and in the corner of her inflamed eye-rim, a little mound lurked. Although no bigger than a facial spot, I worried it harboured a growth, a malignant manifestation of the fierce tall-man's wicked intention.

Dermot broke my dark thoughts with his cheerful exuberance, "Seriously, Maria, you can hardly notice it," he said, patting her shoulder.

Granny, happy with her portion of potatoes, climbed the two steps up to the range, readying herself to prepare the main meal of the day.

"Dermot's right, Maria," she stopped, halted by a thought, "do you know something, Milly Doyle lives up beside your Town Granny. I think she has the cure of the stye."

Maria turned from the mirror, "She can cure styes?" she asked, buoyed. Granny continued to the range, "I'm sure I heard tell she can."

On hearing this, Maria's face visibly softened, and she took my hand, "Come on, Gerard, let's go."

......

Our Monday dinner dates to Town Granny were mandatory.

We three didn't enjoy these sojourns; rather, we endured them, always eager to get back to the freedom of the fields. But for me, this trip was different because I was on a mission to meet the magnificent Milly, who I hoped would hold the key to exorcising the spirit of the fierce tall-man from Maria.

......

Dermot was, as always, turbocharged and took off on the three-mile walk before us. Maria and I were delayed while she pinned her hair to fall over and cover her offending eye.

She power walked while I dawdled behind her. She stopped and looked back, "Gerard, will you hurry up? I don't want us bumping into anyone when I've got this ugly eye!"

I ran to her and took her hand, "Do you mean the boy with Bruce Lee hair?" Her head shot in my direction, "Is that what you call him?" she asked, with a smile.

It gladdened me to see her smile, and I was pleased with myself for being the bringer of this positive amid her possession, "Yes," I said proudly.

Her smile lingered, "I like that Gerard, I'll give him that nickname if I ever see him again," she said, quickening her pace and bringing me with her.

"What do you mean, will you not see him ever again?" I asked, curious.

"I'm not seeing him looking like this, that's for sure," she said, feeling her hair to ensure it covered her eye.

......

In town, I noted most of the shops were closed. This meant the narrow main street was without the bustle of the previous Saturday evening. The lack of human presence shrouded the place in sleepy silence.

Maria and I had the town to ourselves, and I didn't like it. The lack of people lent the place an eerie atmosphere that worsened my sense of foreboding.

As we walked, it soon became clear to me that we were not alone. A figure in the near distance caught my eye, my head instinctively shunting forward to get a better sense of what, from a distance, looked like a kid of my age, dressed in black.

Nearing the figure gave me greater clarity; it wasn't a kid. It was a lady in a shawl, sitting on a concrete post by the corner of the market square. Immediately I tensed, and Maria sensed my unease, "What's up with you?" she asked, stopping. I pointed, "That woman, what's she doing?" Maria looked, "She's doing nowt, just sitting down minding her own business," she said, pulling me forward.

My heart paced – I felt this lady had been placed here for a purpose; she was part of this dark narrative I was taking part in.

Closing in on the lady, I saw she was old, her face framed by the black woollen shawl, was withered, gnarled with age. I pulled back on Maria's hand, stopping her. She reacted with an irritated pull-back, "Gerard, it's an old lady. Stop being such a scaredy-cat."

In truth, it was Maria I was scared for. I was on the outside, and I didn't want her to cross the lady's path, so I swiftly changed sides and grasped her left hand, "I'm not scared, come on," I lied, pulling her into a slow jog.

Our change in pace caught the attention of the lady, her gaze fixed on us.

I feared she might be part of this darkness that Maria was caught in, so my caution was justified.

Her eyes homed in on mine, and as mine fixed on hers, I'm sure I saw knowing in her gaze – something in her eyes gave me reassurance. I relaxed.

Then, she reached out as I was next to her, offering her up-turned palm to me. I brushed my hand against hers before briefly departing – sure there was goodness in her touch.

......

As we reached the bottom of the hill up into the Half-Acre, where Town Granny lived, I felt a renewed sense of positivity.

The sun burst from behind a cloud, boosting my mood further. I tightened my grip on Maria's hand, guiding her towards the cure.

At the top of the hill, we were met by two women and a man who pushed a pram. One of the women smiled, nodded, and said, "How-are-yis?" Maria returned a smile and lowered her head in silent response.

When they passed, I saw the pram was empty. When I looked up, the man's appearance startled me, I stopped. My halt caused Maria to jolt me onwards, "Come on, Gerard, I hate people seeing me like this," she admonished. I carried on, looking back at the man with the pram, "Maria, did you see him?"

"I saw you gawping at him. It's rude to stare." Her answer frustrated me,

"But did you see his face?"

"No, I didn't."

"He was wearing make-up, blue-eye shadow – *like the one you've been wearing.*"

Chapter 15: The cure

Maria looked back, but the three people were already out of sight. She gave me a quizzical look, "Was he really wearing eye shadow?"

Happy she was now engaged with me, I replied. "Yes, and he had red stuff rubbed on his cheeks. Why does he wear make-up like that?"

She shrugged, "He probably just likes women's things, some men do." Her answer flummoxed me. I wanted more explanation, a rationale for why a man would make up like a woman, why the two women with him, nor my sister seemed bothered by it, and more importantly, why it bothered me?

But there was no time for more questions, as we saw Town Granny climbing the stone steps of her small backyard. She was looking out for us, and by her stance, it was clear we were somewhat late. We upped our pace and ran to her.

A short, compact woman dressed in a white cotton blouse, buttoned tightly at the neck, a blue pinstriped pinny tied tightly around her ample middle.

She stood at her gate, straight and stern, "Dermot's finished his dinner; he's off down the town; what kept yous?" she asked.

Maria didn't hesitate, "Sorry Granny, it's my fault; I woke up with this thing in my eye and was worried about it," she said, pulling back her hair.

Granny took a cursory look, "You have a stye; Milly has the cure." She lifted the latch on the gate, "Come and get your dinner first before it dries up altogether."

......

Town Granny lived in a small house, part of a terrace built to house the returning soldiers who'd fought in the First World War.

Her husband, our granddad, was long dead. We knew nothing of him because he was never spoken of. Town Granddad was an enigma to us; he played no part in our life's narrative.

......

Maria and I followed Granny down the steep concrete steps, through the back door, into a narrow kitchen, then straight into the small living room.

The sulphurous smell of over-cooked cabbage hit me, instantly ridding me of what little appetite I had.

......

Of course, Pope Paul IV and Jesus were there, each having their very own walls to hang from. They were joined in reverence by America's finest Catholics, JFK and RFK, who hung in proud profile from a third wall.

A table and four chairs formed the centrepiece of the small room. A recess to the right contained a coal-burning range, which pumped out a hazy heat, creating a stiflingly uncomfortable temperature on what was already a warm summers day.

I pulled at the collar of my t-shirt, "Can I open a window, Granny?" I asked, wanting respite from the smell and heat.

"No, the room will fill with flies." She pulled out two chairs, "Come on now, sit yourselves down."

Soon, a new dilemma was put in front of me: Town Granny's dinner.

I winced at the plate, on which lay a shrivelled chop with its culinary companions: three dried potatoes and a mound of odorous old cabbage. Beads of sweat pricked my forehead as I wondered, *'How will I get through this?'* Granny proceeded to add insult to her injury by brandishing a jug, peeling back a thick brown skin and depositing a glutinous gloop of gravy from it.

When it splatted on the plate, I couldn't hide my repulsion, "NO! I don't like gravy, granny – I only like it when it's part of a stew," I implored, instantly regretting my outburst.

She ignored my plea and plonked another plop on my plate, "Don't be acting the maggot; there's starving childer would be glad of that feed," she said, sailing her gravy boat over to Maria.

While she saw to Maria, I scraped gravy from my chop and began plotting my way out of this dinner. Maria's good eye met mine as granny glooped her plate. In her glance, I knew she saw what I was thinking.

But she followed her glance with a swift smirk, and that simple gesture reminded me my sister was not herself. Maria always supported me with my foodie fussiness – that sly smirk came from the fierce tall-man, I knew it.

Maria began to eat her food with a casual relish. I looked at mine and knew I had to get this grub gone before my sister's cure could begin.

Granny's eagle eye was trained on me, determined to watch me consume every morsel of her meal. I began cutting into the chop while silently praying for divine intervention.

And to my relief, it came – a rap at the door diverted Granny. I wasted no time cutting and scraping half the chop into my lap. Granny moved to the door. Before turning the knob, she scrutinised my plate. On seeing the diminished chop, she smiled, "Good lad, eat that up now, you need it, there's not a pick on you," she said, opening the door and disappearing into her small hallway.

Maria usually picked at her food, but I noticed her eating with an intense relish, further evidence of the fierce tall-man's possession of her.

Still, I used her distraction to my advantage and managed to get both parts of the chop into my pockets. Two potatoes sank nicely into the mug of milk, but the cabbage was a problem.

There really was only one solution, and that was my tried and tested: side-of-the-plate-illusion.

I deftly mashed the remaining spud and moved it to the side of my plate, stuffed the cabbage into it and created a narrow moat that ran halfway around the rim, giving the illusion of a mostly empty plate.

Happy with my work, I relaxed in the knowledge the mostly clean plate should appease Town Granny.

On hearing her talking animatedly at the doorstep, I seized the moment – grabbed my milky-spuddy mug, raced to the toilet by the kitchen and flushed it away. I returned to the table just as Maria finished her plate.

She lifted her head, looked at my plate, "You've done alright there, Gerard."

I nodded at her plate, "So have you. You told me you don't like Town Granny's dinners; how come you've woofed it all?"

She stared at her plate, "I don't usually, but I was dead hungry – I don't know what's got into me."

My body bristled at Maria's admission that something had got into her. But when the door opened, an electric current shot through me, lifting me to my feet, forcing me to exclaim – "It's you!"

Granny, perturbed by my rude greeting of her guest, shot back, "It's who?"

The woman: short, round, and rotund, answered for her, "It's me, Milly. Who did you think I was, Raquel Welch?" she asked, a guttural laugh made her ample bosoms wobble, which in turn rattled the row of holy medals pinned to her pinny at the right breast.

Slumping to the chair, I was angry with myself for my impetuosity. I stumbled over my words, "Erm – no one – erm – hello Milly."

In truth, I was stunned to see she was one of the three Guardians of the Congregation who prayed the Rosary outside of St Patrick and St Felim's Cathedral.

Her appearance lifted me; I felt the forces for good were on our side. But I had to keep quiet; Town Granny already saw me as odd, so I suppressed my relief at seeing Milly and affected nonchalance.

Granny gave me a raised eye, but a glance at my plate cheered her, "You ate a good dinner; will you take a mineral?" she asked, taking my plate and empty mug.

I didn't know what a 'mineral' was, so I answered, "No thanks," rather than risk any more culinary chaos.

Milly smiled at me, "Isn't he bonny for a boy."

I hated being called bonny, and not wanting her focus on me, I diverted her accordingly, "Maria's got a stye in her eye, can you cure it, please?"

"And he has manners, too; you're a pet," she said, placing her hand on Maria's shoulder.

Maria slowly rose, standing with her back to Milly, who turned her around at the shoulders until she faced her. "Push back your hair," she instructed. Maria complied while Milly rose on her toes to look at the eye. I watched as she studied the stye with her studious eye.

Eventually, she returned to the flat of her feet, "Tis a familiar sight alright, my Saints will put this right." She grabbed Maria's head and thrust it into her bosom with force. Maria yelped, then mumbled something illegible as Milly's breasts muffled her.

I moved in closer, fascinated by Milly's ritual, and determined to decipher what Maria mumbled.

But all I heard was gibberish, as though Maria was speaking in a different language.

I moved away, frightened of this foreign tongue emanating from my beloved sister – *I watched Milly do God's good work.*

Chapter 16: The return

Maria's face flushed as we started our return journey to The House in The Hollow.

"That was horrible," she said, rearranging her hair across the offending eye.

"Did you feel anything leave you?"

"No, course not."

"Do you think it'll take the badness out that's causing the stye?" I asked, hopeful.

We arrived at the pinnacle of the Half-Acre, the decline forcing us to pick up pace, "Who knows, suppose it can't make it any worse." She turned to me and stooped down, "Does it look any better?"

I tippy-toed up, readying to look – but a physical force winded me, throwing me to the ground. I tried to get up, but with every exertion, I was dragged back down. It was as though I were in a dream wherein I couldn't run away from the unseen beast. In my confusion, I became aware of Maria, flailing, kicking, screeching. It was my right side I had no control of. A continual tugging dragged me along until a loud tearing sound released me.

Disorientated, I managed to find my feet with Maria's help. I looked down; my trousers were torn, my right leg exposed. Maria's voice gave me clarity, "What did you have in your pocket?" I followed her gaze; a dog hungrily guzzled the chop, along with my trouser pocket. I thrust my hand into my intact pocket and threw the contents towards the dog. "Town Granny's chop," I said, running swiftly down the hill onto the relative safety of the main street.

......

Maria and I stopped outside a small local post office. I immediately checked my left pocket, relieved to feel my Rosary Beads were still safe. When I looked at Maria, she was almost doubled up, clutching her stomach, laughing – the sight of her pleased me. *'Maybe Milly's cure had rid her of the tall-man,'* I hoped.

When her mirth subsided, she straightened up, "Oh Gerard, what're you like; that dog could've had your whole leg," she took my hand and pulled me forward, my trouser leg flapping like a torn sail in the wind.

......

A kind of serenity enveloped me as I walked hand in hand with Maria along the main street.

The honk of a car caused us to look in the direction of a sleek black vehicle cruising to a halt beside us. The front passenger seat flew open, a smiley looking man leaned forward, "Tis the young Smiths home from England, isn't it?" he asked. Maria bobbed down to his level, her hand over her eye, "Yep, that's us." The man smiled, "I'm Pippy, a friend of your Granny's; jump in, I'll give yous a lift back out to Drumalee."

......

Sitting in the back seat of Pippy's car, I felt his warmth and kindness. His presence soothed me as he gently chuckled on hearing my choppy dog story, "That'll teach you to eat yer dinner," he said as we pulled up outside the house. "Tell your Granny I'll pick her up at the usual time for Bingo," he said by way of goodbye.

......

Maria rushed into the house, while I stopped to look at what was parked on the road to the left of the house – a pram. Looking it over, I knew it was the same one I'd seen on the half-acre, pushed by the man in makeup and his two female companions. Except, while then it had been empty, now it was full of junk.

Wondering if it had been dumped there, I entered the house to let Granny know – and in the dim light, I saw him again. On the middle chair by the stairs, flanked by his female friends, the man in makeup was sitting in silence, sipping water from a mug – while I stood, gawping.

Granny was in the scullery, while footfall above told me Maria was upstairs – I was alone with these people.

"Hello," I said.

"Well," they said in unison, nodding their heads.

Their response threw me, but I smiled without question.

The man took a sip, "You're the wee fella we met coming down the hill."

"Yes, I am."

He pointed to my trousers. "Did you have a fight with Lizzie's dog, or is that the latest fashion over in England?" he asked, causing the two ladies to lower their heads and giggle nervously.

I laughed with them, my stare still fixed on his face. I so wanted to ask him why he wore makeup. With that question on the tip of my tongue, I was grateful another fell out, "Where've you been?" I asked.

He was the spokesperson, "Over at the tip, rummaging," he said. He put the mug on the floor and rose, the two women rising with him. He looked into the scullery, "Thanks, Mrs Smith, we'll be going," he said, walking to the door, followed by his ladies in waiting.

Granny shouted after them, "Mind yourselves."

Immediately, I jumped on Lofty's chaise longue and watched as he manpowered the pram onto the road, the ladies walking behind in single file. The sight of them recalled another-worldly version of the Three Wise Men, bearing gifts to be delivered to an unknown deity. They enthralled me; their otherness elevated me. Their difference made me feel there was a place for me in the world.

......

When they were out of sight, I joined Granny in the scullery where she washed lettuce leaves under the tap.

"Did you see that man? He was wearing make-up," I said, sure she'd give me an explanation.

But instead, she shrugged, "What harm is he doing?"

"But men don't wear makeup," I shot back.

She shook out the lettuce, "That fella does. For one so young, you do think too much, Son," she said, putting the lettuce into a colander and going out into the back garden – leaving me reeling with questions and confusion.

......

I returned to Lofty's chaise longue, lay down and tried to fathom why his appearance bothered me so. I knew he wouldn't be allowed to walk through my Manchester council estate with makeup on, without inviting scorn and possible violence from some. I wondered if the rules were different in Ireland.

But my ruminations on Makeup Man were interrupted by Maria bounding down the stairs. "You know what, Gerard, I think it looks a bit better; Milly's cure might be working," she said, pulling her hair back and thrusting her face in mine. "What do you think?"

I sat up, peering into her offending eye. I saw no change, yet lied to salve my sister, "Yep, it does look a bit better."

Cheered by my response, she beamed, "I don't think that eye shadow caused it. I think it's probably got something to do with what happened at the lagoon," her voice lifting.

I jumped off the chaise longue, "See, I knew something happened at the lagoon; what was it, tell me, please?"

My reaction induced an eye-roll in Maria and marked change in mood, "God Gerard, you can be such an annoying kid, you know!" She bounded up the stairs two by two.

Shocked by her reaction, I grabbed the Creepy comic and took myself off to the lagoon.

......

Sitting on a mossy stump, I opened Creepy. But I couldn't concentrate; the horror therein wouldn't divert me from the hurt I felt at Maria's outburst. She had never, ever raised her voice to me, let alone call me an 'annoying kid.'

Setting the Creepy down, I stood up, hoping Maria would come to find me, say sorry, and rationalise her change for me.

But she didn't.

Sitting back down, I stared at Creepy's cover. The central tall-man stared back at me, "What do you want with my sister?" I asked aloud. When there was no response, I looked skyward and shouted, "Crow, where are you? I need someone to talk to!"

But there came no, "Caw," the only sound the trickle of water, serenaded by the gentle rustle of trees as a wind began to gather.

The pages of my Creepy began to flutter and flap, finally resting open on the inner back page, which carried the advertisement for Sea Monkeys. The sight of them gladdened me, and I homed in to look closer. "I will have a Sea-Monkey family one day, and I'll look after you like the best daddy in the world," I said, closing the magazine and sticking it up my t-shirt to protect it from the droplets of rain that were beginning to fall.

With the sky darkening, I ran swiftly through the woodland to shelter *from the rapidly brewing storm.*

Chapter 17: The storm story

Within seconds the heavens opened, throwing down great mug-sized rain portions accompanied by a howling wind that pulled the trees to-and-fro, threatening to drag them up by their roots and toss them skyward like plucked feathers.

I dived into a ditch with a thatch of thick bramble that created a rainproof roof. I recalled this place from the previous summer when I used it as a den to hide from the world. I sat back and relaxed in its naturally woven womb-like space.

In small spaces I felt safe, secure in a tightness that would induce claustrophobia in others, yet in me created a curious sense of well-being. In our Manchester Council House, we had an old pram with a large hood that folded over; Mam would use it to take the weekly wash to the laundry. When it wasn't in laundry use, I'd often climb into it, pull over the hood and escape from the world into my comics.

And in this bramble womb, which gave shelter from the storm, I felt the same sense of contentment as I pulled Creepy from my t-shirt.

......

But I couldn't focus on the Creepy Tales because my own story was more compelling.

The fact that Maria had admitted to a 'happening,' at the lagoon that morning made me fear that she was complicit in her possession, that she had willingly given her body to be used by another soul to fulfil a physical purpose that they could not carry out while in spirit.

The raging storm gave me greater clarity – a clap of thunder and a flash of light made me re-think my opinion of her possessor, the tall-man. Perhaps he wasn't fierce, like the boy with Bruce Lee hair said. My first appraisal, coloured by Dad, was probably closer to the truth of him being a kind soul. This theory was bolstered because I knew my sister wouldn't willingly allow an evil entity to use her body for some nefarious activity.

Yet her calling me an "…annoying kid," wasn't her. All her barbed words were reserved for Dermot, not me. The vision of her eating hungrily at Town Granny's table returned to me; she ate more like man than girl. She herself said, "I don't know what's got into me."

I wondered about talking to Dermot about her. But that thought was quickly quashed when I clearly envisioned his reply. "You're mad, our kid; stop being so stupid and think like normal lads," would probably be the tone of his response. And I wouldn't blame him for it, for I knew I wasn't like, 'normal lads.'

At that moment, sheltering from the storm in a naturally woven womb, I yearned to meet another lad like me, who'd understand my concerns and worries. But sadly, I realised I was him, the only 'odd-little-lad' in the world. I retreated further back into the ditch, rested my head on my knees and closed my eyes.

……

"Gerard, Gerard, Gerard!" I woke, startled – where was I – who was calling me? I was cold, uncomfortable, my legs cramped up when I tried to move them.

"You look like a curled-up rabbit stuck in a hole," hands pulling at my ankle, a light blinding me.

I shouted back, "Get off me!"

"Get out, our kid; I've been looking all over for you. It's a good job Maria remembered this hiding place, cos you could've been here all night," said Dermot. The annoyance in his voice matched that of Maria's as she'd marched up the stairs, away from me.

The time and space dawned on me, and as the newly crowned annoying kid, I unfurled myself, emerging from my bramble womb into the calm after the storm.

My hair was Velcro for Flora, and at that moment, every species of Irish Fauna was stuck to it. I stood up, my right leg exposed, covered in hives and scratches, my Creepy half hanging from my t-shirt, "I fell asleep," I explained, pulling a twig from my hair.

Dermot looked at me and shook his head, "You look like the Son of Catweasle," he said, laughing and running off in the direction of the farmyard. Almost out of sight, he turned and shouted out to me, "Go back to the house, our Maria's been dead worried about you."

Dermot and I had opposing tastes in TV Programmes, but we both enjoyed the show, Catweasle. The protagonist was an ugly, scrawny old man with a great big bush of hair. Of course, I looked like his son. So, I added 'ugly' to my 'annoying' status and wandered back to The House in The Hollow, leaving my shred of confidence to wilt in the bramble womb.

......

The sun went down as I reached the house, and its light welcomed me into the home. It was a comfort to see all present and correct in their usual places: Frankie, Granny, Big Tommy, Michael, Peter and Lofty on his chaise longue, fighting with his imaginary foe, engulfed in plumes of pipe smoke. Great Uncle Frankie guffawed, "Look at the cut of you; have you been through the wars?" he asked.

They looked at me with non-judgemental smiles while I checked myself over.

Satisfied I was alright, I answered Frankie, "I haven't cut myself, and I've not been in a war; I fell asleep in a ditch." I peered into the scullery, "Where's Maria?"

Granny pointed upwards, "She's hiding upstairs."

"Who's she hiding from?" I asked, intrigued.

"Callers,"

"What callers?"

"Ones calling for a ceili," said Granny.

Before I could ask what this thing was, Uncle Michael piped up, "I think she's smitten with that young fella from the college. She's afraid he'll call and see her with the stye," he said, chuckling.

"What does smitten mean?" I asked.

Michael flicked his head back, "Go up and ask her if she's smitten; she'll tell you what it is."

I took the stairs slowly, wary of this thing called 'smitten,' which my sister might have.

......

Maria was sitting on the bed by the window, her head engrossed in her book, Black Beauty.

As soon as she saw me, she put the book down, "There you are, I've been worried sick." She threw her arms out, "Come here." In her arms, she held me tight, "I'm so sorry for snapping at you," she said, rocking me gently from side to side.

"How can I stop being annoying? Will you show me?"

I felt her shoulders shake and pulled back, "Are you laughing at me?" She was laughing, but she seemed to be crying as well. "What's up with you?" I asked, confused.

She wiped her eyes and patted the bed, "Sit down." I waited for a revelation from her.

But none came. Instead, Maria gently foraged for woodland fauna in my hair. When she spoke, her voice was soft and wistful, "You're not annoying, you're lovely. I said that because I'm angry with this stye, that's why," she said, pulling a berry of some sort from my hair.

I wasted no time, "Are you smitten?" I asked.

She gently nudged me with her elbow, "I bet Michael told you to ask me that, didn't he?"

"Yes." When she didn't answer, I asked, "What does smitten mean?"

She shook her head, "It's a teasing word that people use, that's all."

And before I could probe further, she pulled me back into my story, "Tell me about the tall-man. Have you got any clues who he might be?"

I told my unfolding narrative with fervour; "He's not fierce like the boy with Bruce Lee hair said. I think he's a kind man like Dad said. He's lost something before he died, and he won't go to heaven until he's found it; do you believe in ghosts?" I asked.

She didn't hesitate, "Of course I do; there's one in Town Granny's house." I felt the back of my neck prickle as she continued to forage in my hair, "How do you know, have you seen it?"

"No, I've felt it."

"Did it touch you?"

"It was last year. I was in bed in the back room and couldn't sleep; the sheets tightened around my feet like when someone was sitting on the bed. I couldn't move, started praying. Whatever it was stood up and sat further up the bed until I could feel it sitting at my shoulders." She paused for a moment before concluding, "Ghosts only roam at night, Gerard – that's why I don't think you'll find the tall-man during the day."

A thought hit me, and I fired it out, "I bet that ghost was trying to possess you?"

Her head swivelled with certainty, "No, he was looking for something else in that room, not me." I noticed her skin, flawless white in the dying light, "Only Demons like the Devil possess people; you should know that with all those stories you read, Gerard."

A feeling came over me, an unease at what Maria was saying. I needed to be downstairs in the security of light and family as my body bristled, processing what Maria was trying to tell me – *she was actually possessed by the Devil himself.*

Chapter 18: Into the night

I couldn't sleep. Partly because I'd slept so deeply in the ditch, but more so because my mind was drenched in doom.

I envied Dermot, who slept deeply beside me, unencumbered by the horrors that haunted my head.

I sat up.

The sound of deep sleep breathing surrounded me; the luxury of their slumber tormented me.

I swung my feet onto the floor.

Something Maria said returned to me, "Ghosts only roam at night, Gerard..."
I gently eased off the bed.

"...that's why I don't think you'll find the tall-man in the day," she'd said.

I put one foot forward, mindful to avoid any creaks.

Stealth-like, I moved into Granny's room and stopped, allowing my eyes to become accustomed to the darkness.

Granny, Aunt Kathleen, and Maria slept – oblivious to my presence.
I made it to the middle of the room when Maria moved. I halted, my hand on my mouth silenced my breathing.

She unfurled from her foetal position, stretched onto her back, outstretched her arms, and emitted a gentle sigh.

She didn't wake.

Nor did Aunt Kathleen, despite Maria's right arm falling on her shoulder.

My sister lay prostrate, arms outstretched, swathed in a slither of moonlight. My gaze moved up her body, her long hair tousled, framing her face – she looked like the picture of Jesus that hung in every Irish home.

I took the serenity of her image to be a good sign and emboldened by it, tip-toed around the room, making it out onto the small landing, safely.

I needed three things: my rosary beads, wellies, and Dermot's torch.

The rosary beads hung protectively around my neck. The remaining items were in the small hallway. I had a hurdle to reach them – the stairs.

They were a minefield where a misplaced foot would send an explosive creak ricocheting through the silent house, waking my family and exposing my night-time search. I had to tread carefully.

A brainwave hit me, or to be precise, I saw the bannister. I cocked my right leg over it, and gripping tightly, I edged myself down. My backside hit the bottom knob without a thud – I'd arrived downstairs, silently.

Tip-toeing to the door, I opened it a fraction into the tiny hall space. With precision quiet, I put on my wellies, picked up the torch and opened the front door that thankfully was never locked.

I stepped out into the darkness. Except it wasn't dark, it was blindingly black.

As a council house city kid, I'd never really experienced true night-time darkness. The inky black of a rural Irish night was unsettling. Even the summer moon gave little respite to the relenting dark.

Not wanting to switch on the torch until I was midway up the lane, I set off blindly, using my instinct to make it to the gate. Tucking the torch into the waistband of my pyjamas, I climbed over.

The squelch of my jump from the bottom rung made me flinch, its sound shattering the silence. I remained stooped, my eyes fixed on the house like a wary cat. Satisfied there was no waking light, I turned and began my journey into the night.

......

Midway up the lane, I switched on Dermot's torch. The beam of light flooded the pathway, bathing the space in an artifice that made it feel and look unreal, like a forest film or theatre set. I looked from left to right, a strange feeling of familiar warmth enveloping me – I felt like I was standing in a Hammer Horror film. With that thought, the warmth evaporated, replaced with a cold chill when I realised I didn't have Mam to protect me from any impending scary bits.

I braced myself and continued onwards until I reached the perimeter of the farmyard. Again, I noticed how the artificial light gave the familiar buildings a theatrical artifice that unnerved me. Was this new look a deception to trick me into a false sense of security?

The question raised my guard. I swung swiftly round for fear of what might creep behind me. The torch shed light on an empty lane – and I spun back around for fear of what might creep in front of me. I saw nothing untoward.

Venturing a little further into the farmyard, I stopped, looked, listened. The only sound was the steady beat of my heart, accompanied by the undulating heave of my chest.

I saw something – a movement that confused me rather than scared me – it was my breath pluming upwards into the black sky. It wasn't cold, yet this visual suggested a physical chill amidst the warm stillness of a summer night.

I shuddered – moved forward – halted when a shape shifted to my left. I primed myself, ready for defensive fight or flight. A shadow floated over the walls of the outbuildings to the left of the farm. I swung to the right to see what physical form cast this shadow – the torchlight revealed no one, nobody – nothing.

I spun back in time to see the shadow leave the end building and meld amongst the trees that formed the avenue up to St Pat's College. Its shape changed, became uniform, spherical, indiscernible. It traversed the trees, disappeared, then reappeared from around the gable of the byre, resting on that building's far wall.

The byre. The Crow – I shot the torch to his observational post, "Crow, are you there, is he here?" I asked, my whispered voice amplified in the silent night. The beam of light showed no avian sentinel, nor came a "Caw," reply.

But I was not alone. For, at last, I felt it, the presence that is intangible yet present. But I knew it wasn't him, the tall-man. This was someone guiding me towards – something.

My eye caught a movement again. The shape slowly floated along the wall of the byre. I watched with a wondering eye, not quite fearful, more questioning. Once again, it left the wall, mingled amongst the trees, before resting on the front of the slaughterhouse – it had come full circle.

I rubbed my eyes and re-focussed. The shadowy shape kind of ebbed, flowed, and pulsed for a minute or so before shifting along the slaughterhouse wall until it reached the door – then it was gone, no more, vanished.

I looked around, turned full circle in the farmyard space. All was as it was before: empty, silent, unreal, perhaps surreal. Disappointed I had neither clue nor answer, I pointed the torch at the slaughterhouse door – it was open.

......

I didn't go in. Instead, I sat cross-legged on the concrete floor and shone the light through the door, swivelling the beam around, hoping the harsh light would illuminate the shadow, reinvigorate the shape to show itself again. It didn't.

From where I sat, the slaughterhouse seemed empty. But I didn't believe it was. Something was in there – waiting.

Waiting for what? I didn't know. To find that out, I had to go in. I inhaled deeply and stood up.

Taking a step forward, my mind wandered back to that first day of our holiday – Maria leading me into this killing room as blood from a newly slain beast seeped from it.

Maria taking me into a place that was an anathema to her had struck me as strange – wrong. Now, I wondered if this place was the genesis of her change, the beginning period of her possession.

The open doorway of the slaughterhouse framed me; its height emphasised my lack of stature. *Was I big enough for this?*

Yes, I was – I walked in.

The smell hit me, a warm odour – not unpleasant, somewhat reminiscent of the batteries that ran my train set, reassuring. I pointed the torch upwards, picking out the heavy meat hook. Thankful no carcass hung from it, I circled the space; it was cleansed, clinical, ready to welcome a new beast to the slaughter.

There was no sign of the shape and shadow that had led me in. Yet I felt there was something here, waiting to be found, "Hello," I said.

No response.

I drove Dermot's torch all around the concrete room, letting it linger on tiny specks. Only when I identified the specks as spots of brown blood that had avoided the power hose did I move on.

But then, my searching beam noticed something, a thing foreign to this place, an importation. In the far-right hand corner, I saw it, out of its place. I moved closer and bathed it in light, "I didn't know it was lost, yet I'd found it," I said.

Moving closer, I crouched down and stared for a few minutes before picking it up. For some reason – I kissed it.

It was Dermot's pen, the one with the ship in it; bought by the Penman, whom I'd thought was a Monster on the Munster – but he'd turned out to be a kind man.

I wondered if this was a sign that Penman was now in spirit.

Chapter 19: The hill

Food. I rolled over, stretched, then furled back into a foetal position.

In that strange state between waking and sleep, I was conscious of food. The smell of it woke me, and I stretched again. My stretch revealed an empty bed that made me catapult upright. The room was open, with my uncles' beds neatly made and no Dermot to be seen or heard.

It dawned on me that it was dinnertime, and swinging myself off the bed, a sharp pain shot through my thigh, making me wince – Penman's pen caught up in my pyjamas, stabbed me.

Thankfully its stab was only superficial. I swiped the blood from my graze and placed the pen on Granny's dressing table. Something held me there, gazing at the pen with its encapsulated miniature boat. I felt it was symbolic. Of what, I didn't know. But I was happy it was found, safe and sound.

......

"There you are; I thought you'd gone missing again. Where were you?" asked Granny as she kneaded dough in a bowl.

"I was in bed."

"What, you're only getting up now?" she said, forming the currant-speckled dough into a ball.

"Yes."

"I thought you were up and out early this morning, with Maria and Dermot."

She threw the dough onto a tin tray, forming it into a round pattie took a knife and scored it, creating a cross that would define four equal parts when baked.

She used the knife as a pointer to the range, "Your dinner's there for you, but it should be breakfast you're having. Maria and Dermot have been and gone; I was waiting for you to come in from the fields." She put the knife down, wiped her hands with a tea towel, "What has you sleeping so late?" she asked with concern.

I shrugged, "Don't know," I said, not wanting to divulge my nocturnal ramblings.

Granny put the dinner of stew and potatoes down in front of me. "Are you sickening for something, pinning for England, maybe?" she asked, picking up her bowl and throwing in a handful of flour.

"No," I said, taking a morsel of meat on my fork.

"Well, it's not right, you should be out enjoying this good weather, not lying idle in bed." She added a pinch of soda, salt, and a glug of buttermilk to her bowl, her right hand moving rhythmically to amalgamate the ingredients.

I ate my food in silence, mesmerised by Granny's instinctual making of the soda bread that would sustain and supplement our diet in the coming days.

The combination of eating food while watching Granny make it induced in me sustenance that energised me. Finishing my plate, I asked, "Did Maria still have that stye this morning?"

"She did. It looked no better, she's still fretting about it," she said, making my dread return.

I sat up, "Do you know where Maria and Dermot have gone?" I asked, wanting to go to Maria and assess the stye myself.

"They've gone out to the creamery with Tommy," she said, nestling her plain soda bread next to its fruity brethren in the heart of her range.

"Is it walking distance?" I asked, sliding off my chair. Granny took my plate, "Indeed it isn't. It's away out the Dublin Road." She was about to descend into the scullery when she noticed the sight of me and stopped. "You're still in your pyjamas." She pointed upwards, "Get up them stairs and dress yourself before anyone calls and sees the cut of you at this hour of the day."

......

Walking through Granny's room en-route to my clothes, a postcard of the Munster peeking out from underneath Maria's pillow caught my eye.

I paused, looking from postcard to Penman's pen. Maria had written on my postcard to Mam and Dad and put it into an envelope – Top Secret. Was this another secret? Who was she writing to? My hand stretched out to it but swiftly withdrew. I couldn't betray Maria's trust, even though she was possessed. I ran into the next room and quickly dressed to divert myself from peeping at the postcard.

......

The sun appeared from behind a cloud, welcoming me outside.

With one foot on the step, I waivered – *go back and look at that postcard.*

No.

I stepped up onto the road – *it might reveal loads of secrets, go back.*

Turning back, I stared up at the bedroom window – *this is your only chance for a look at what's written on that card, go back.*

A compulsion pushed me down the step; conflict pulled me back up. I stayed there, on the cusp of uncertainty, until I heard, "Caw. Caw. Caw." Crow's call compelled me to run from the house and follow him back up to St Pat's college farmyard, ensuring my prying eyes were far away from the postcard's reveal.

......

"Ahh, wee fella, how-are-ya?" asked the boy with Bruce lee hair, hosing off his wellington boots.

"I'm alright," I said through recovering breaths.

He looked at me with a friendly smile that somehow flattered me. I felt he liked me, "What has yous running? You're running after me, and that sister of yours is running away from me," he asked.

I quickly corrected him, "I wasn't running after you, didn't even know you'd be here."

He turned off the hose, "Well, your sister was. I said, 'Hello,' to her this morning, and she ran from me like I was the Devil himself. What happened to her?" he asked, hanging the hose on a hook.

"She's got a stye in her eye, and she's smitten, so that's probably why she ran away," I explained, happy I had an answer that wasn't the whole truth but wasn't a lie, either.

He laughed, "Is she smitten with me?"

"I don't know what smitten is."

"Then how do you know she is?"

"Uncle Michael said she is; that's how I know."

He took off thick rubber gloves, placed them on the windowsill and ran his hands through his hair. I watched with envy as silken strands slipped through his fingers with ease, falling back together to create a gloriously glossy face frame.

"What's smitten?" I asked.

He paused, pondered, looked at me and said, "I wouldn't know how to explain it. Ask Maria, she'll tell you, she's a great girl with words, so she is," he said, turning to enter the slaughterhouse.

I jumped forward, halting him, "I did ask her; she said it's like teasing."

He nodded, "That'll do, that explains it, now you have smitten," he said, slinking back inside, his hair shining like black silk in the grim slaughterhouse light.

……

I stood in the square and thought – some boys in my class in my

Manchester school tease me for my curly hair and looking like a girl. Now I knew, they were smitten with me.

So, I deduced that smitten was a bad thing, and my mood sank – my sister was possessed and smitten, things were going from bad to worse for Maria and me.

......

Back at the gate, I stood transfixed by The House in The Hollow. It was so near yet seemed so far. The compulsion to run came over me again. Needing out of the hollow and into height, I ran for the hills surrounding Aunt Margaret's house.

......

I sneaked past Margaret's house and climbed over the gate that led into rolling fields, beginning a steady climb upwards. All was peacefully quiet, and I felt the dooming content in my head reduce as I climbed higher. At the pinnacle of the hill, I stopped and looked down upon the rolling countryside, lush green fields occasionally dotted by a homestead that looked lonely and remote – like me.

......

Looking up at a clear blue sky, I began to sing my version of a song that now had a relevance I had not previously known –
"When I'm with her, I'm confused.
Out of focus and bemused.
And I never know exactly where I am.
Unpredictable as weather.
She's as flighty as a feather.
She's a darling! She's a demon. She's a smitten!"
How do you solve a problem like Maria?"

Maria and me – this was our song, the one that kicked off the splendour of our Saturday nights. How I loved those times together in her small bedroom in our Manchester council house, surrounded by images of Bruce Lee with his inky black hair glistening in the cosy lamp-light of Maria's space. We'd sing along to the Sound of Music at the top of our voices while eating spoonful's of Butterscotch Angel Delight and slurping Carnation Cream straight from the tin between tracks.

Now alone, singing aloud atop a hill in Cavan, I longed for that sister back, the Maria that solved all my problems and everybody else's. At that moment, the words of the song became prophetic. I stopped singing and said out loud, – *how do I solve this problem with Maria?*

Chapter 20: The letter

A flutter to my left was a momentary distraction from myself. It was Aunt Margaret hanging clothes on her washing line. Although I was within sight, I sat down, as I didn't want her to know I'd passed her house without calling in.

I wanted to leave the hill, get back to Granny's to see Maria, yet I'd have to pass Margaret's, and she'd ask, "Any news?" And of course, the news I had couldn't be divulged, nor was it the kind she'd want to hear or believe.

I began to slide myself down the hill. Once out of Aunt Margaret's range, I stood up and began to walk, hoping the fields would lead me back to The House in The Hollow.

It wasn't long before I reached an obstacle. A wall of trees nestled in a valley created an impasse, or so I thought. About to turn back and ready to brace myself for Margaret's questioning, I heard crow's call, "Caw. Caw. Caw."

His song suggested a place behind this green curtain, and I paced up and down until I found a narrow gap through which I could squeeze. Wanting to protect my face from any scratching brambles, I edged in backwards until I felt the release from the foliage and space behind me. Standing straight, I turned and saw that I was in an orchard.

The only other orchard I knew of was the one that belonged to St Pat's College, a forbidden place that could only be visited by trespass. This place seemed to belong to no one. I felt it was mine – my own secret orchard.

"Hello Crow, where are you?" I asked. His lack of response told me he'd flown away, but I was happy he'd led me here.

The complete stillness and tranquillity instantly eased me. Looking around, I saw the trees stood and flourished in their own space; the branches of older trees were free to reach out unencumbered by their younger siblings, who were not yet bearing fruit. They each had their own appearance, which gave them distinct personalities. I felt I was with a family who welcomed me, a stranger, into their home.

Walking to the family's elder, I reached up and plucked one of its low hanging fruit. I marvelled at the beauty of the apple, its colour a pale green smudged by swathes of pink, its shape, perfectly round. It seemed almost sinful to bite this natural gift.

But bite it, I did – the juice, sweet and warm, seeped down my chin. Sitting down, I feasted on its flavour, savouring every bite as it salved my thirst and satisfied my yearning for sweetness – the perfect dessert.

As I sucked the last remnants of juice from the core, I knew why the St Pat's boys risked reprimand to feast on this forbidden fruit. Standing up, I reached for another but swiftly retracted my arm when I saw this was not my secret space – I was not alone in the orchard.

Tensing, I feared I was to be punished for feasting on what was not mine.

......

He stared at me through large, sad eyes – a donkey. I stared back, "Have you been here all this time?" I didn't expect an answer; it was me thinking aloud. Besides, I liked talking to animals; it was a source of comfort.

Donkey stood still, the only movement being his slow doe-eyed blink. We both stared for some time, staking each other out. Eventually, I made the first move and put one step forward. Donkey didn't flinch. But something behind him did, and I immediately took that step back.

My punishment was coming.

A man emerged from the foliage and stood alongside the donkey. I instantly became defensive, "I'm sorry, is this your orchard? I didn't mean to come. I just found it when I was trying to get back to my Granny's," I babbled.

He put a soot-blackened hand on the donkey's back. "There's no harm in us being here, the Smith's don't bother," he tilted his head backwards, "not like the bishop beyond at the college," he said, his voice slow and soothing. He smiled – one single tooth in the bottom of his mouth stood like a lone iceberg in a sea of black; it made me laugh, and I at once felt at ease with this man.

"What has you laughing?" he asked.

I checked myself and respectfully stopped giggling, "Nothing."

"I'm Gerard Smith," I said by way of introduction.

His gummy grin lit up his age-ravaged face, almost black with dirt, "You'd be a nephew of Jim and Margaret, home from England?"

"Yep, that's me."

His smile widened, "Then this is your orchard." He reached up, plucked a piece of fruit, and handed it to me, "Have another of your Granny Smith's apples."

His appearance struck me as I ate the apple. It was a hot day, yet he wore a heavy suit, complete with shirt and tie, fastened tight at the neck. Time had blackened his clothes, and when I looked at the shirt collar, I could only faintly see where the collar ended, and his neck began. The aged fabric had fused to his skin. I deduced that constant wear had glued the clothes to his body. My eyes travelled to his feet. He wore wellington boots, the bottoms of which were wrapped in newspaper, bound tightly with brown string that wound all the way up the boot to his knee, binding the boots to his lower legs.

His hand fumbled in his pocket, "Can you read?" he asked, pulling me from my private appraisal of his apparel.

"Yes, I'm a good reader for my age."

He moved towards me, the donkey shadowing his every move. When he stopped in front of me, his odour hit me – a stinging smoky smell that tickled my nose. He pulled from his pocket a blue piece of paper and handed it to me,

"Read this out for me, will ya."

I took the paper, "Can't you read?" I asked.

He nodded, "I can, but it's nice to hear someone else say the words," he said, with his solo toothed grin.

I opened the single piece of paper and looked at the handwriting in blue ink. It was joined up lettering, and I had to concentrate carefully to decipher it.

Eventually, I saw the words and read aloud – *'My Dear Johnnie. We had a terrible thunderstorm here, and Mrs Warren died of the fright. We were at her funeral yesterday. I hope you are keeping well. I am great.*

> *Do write soon.*
> *Yours Evelyn.'*

I looked to him; his head tilted sideways, his grin stretched wide, yet it was sadness that I saw on his face. Handing him back the letter, I asked, "Who's Evelyn?"

He gently folded the paper and placed it back in his pocket, "That's my sister."

With a jolt, my sister's predicament returned to me, "Why is Evelyn writing to you? Where's she gone?" I asked, trying to suppress my self-interest.

When Johnnie didn't immediately answer me, I imagined a place where Demon-Damned-Sisters were sent to die of fright simply by listening to the weather and other natural phenomena.

Stepping forward, I asked, "Johnnie, did something happen to Evelyn?"

When he looked at me, I saw his old eyes were wet, "I wouldn't know; she left home long ago."

"Why did she leave?" I asked.

With wistful eyes, he said, "Daddy passed to heaven, and not long after, Mammy joined him up above." He wiped an eye with the back of his palm, dampening the deep ravines that crisscrossed his aged face, "A lock-a-years later, Evelyn took a notion and off she left the homeplace." He swivelled his head, "She took the heart of the home with her, so she did." His grin returned, "But I have her letters; they're a comfort to us, aren't they?" he said, patting the donkey's back.

His patting hand drew my attention to something I hadn't noticed, "There's grass growing on his back," I said, chuckling.

Johnnie giggled with me, "He has his own meadow, so he has," his hand brushing the grass.

I had an urge to bring the conversation back to his sister, "What's that thing you said Evelyn took, a notion?" I asked.

He thought a moment, "I wouldn't know." He paused before continuing, "Notions happen in people's heads; who knows what they are?"

Intrigued, I asked, "Are notions good or bad?"

He smiled, "They could be either, I suppose." I wanted to ask him if 'notions' were the same as 'possessions,' but I couldn't, partly because I was afraid of his answer, but more because I wasn't ready to talk about Maria with another human being.

No, I would keep my knowing between Crow and me – for now.

……

I liked my new friend, Johnnie. I felt Evelyn's 'notion,' and Maria's 'possession,' gave us a connection, and I promised to visit him again. But I'd left him in haste, as his letter had given me a thought. Maybe Maria was planning on leaving like Evelyn and was writing that postcard to me – *I sprinted to The House in The Hollow, desperate to read the postcard.*

Chapter 21: The stye of the storm

I sprinted through the door and leapt up the stairs without saying hello. On the small landing, I stopped, primed myself to enter the bedroom and pry.

But I was too late, "Granny, is that you?" asked Maria quietly.

"It's me," I said. Her smile welcomed me into the room, "Orr, where've you been?"

"Out," I said, glancing past her to the pillow. She followed my gaze, "What you looking at?"

"Nowt," I said, disappointed to see the postcard was no longer protruding from the pillow.

Without thinking, I asked, "Why did you run away from the boy with the Bruce Lee hair?"

She physically jumped at my question and stood up, "Who said I did?"

"He did."

"Who did?"

"The boy with the Bruce Lee hair did."

She took my hand, sat on the bed, and drew me into her, "Tell me what he said?" she asked, a myriad of emotions flooding her face.

"He said he said, 'Hello,' to you, and you ran away from him like he was the Devil himself."

I studied her face trying to understand the emotional response to what I'd told her.

She looked hurt, "Really, were those his exact words?" I felt bad for causing her upset and wondered if I should lie to protect her. But I couldn't, so I simply nodded 'Yes,' and lowered my eyes.

"Where were you talking to him?" she asked, her face tight and troubled.

"Outside the slaughterhouse, he'd finished killing a cow," I explained.

She tilted her head up, "Look at my eye; does it look any better to you? Be honest," she asked, brushing back her hair.

Leaning in, I zoomed into the corner of her right eye, my focus on the stye. A white pimple sat in the middle of red, inflamed skin. Like an eye within an eye, it stared back at me with malevolent intent, and fearful it might spurt its possessive poison at me, I jerked and jumped back hastily.

Maria gasped in horror at my reaction. "Oh my God, Gerard, does it look that bad?" she exclaimed, jumping from the bed, thrusting her face into the dressing table mirror.

Realising the extremity of my reaction, I came back with, "No, no, it's the same as it was, it hasn't changed, honest!" And that was the truth; it looked no worse nor better than the previous day. But I couldn't go beyond the truth and tell her of my knowing, not when she was so distressed by the stye.

Her pained expression upset me, "Gerard, you jumped the way you do when you're watching horror films. Don't lie to me. Do I look that horrific?" she pleaded.

A strange sensation pricked at my chest; it was my heart aching, and to prevent it from breaking, I leaned in and hugged her. My sister could never look horrific to me; even in the grip of possession, she still looked the epitome of pretty.

She hugged me back as I backtracked, "Honest, it doesn't look bad; I jumped cos I thought I saw a spider behind you," I lied.

When she began to shake, I pulled back; she was laughing gently, "Gerard, you're not even scared of spiders." She pulled me back, "You're just trying to protect me; you can do that properly by telling me the truth." She pushed back and looked me in the eye, "Honestly, does it look dead horrible?"

Looking at it from a safe distance, I was able to judge it objectively. "No, not horrible, it looks really sore," I said, happy with my honesty.

She glanced at her reflection, "Sore doesn't look pretty Gerard, that's the truth of the matter," she said, fixing her hair over her eye.

Perking up, Maria spun around, "Gerard, will you do me a favour?" she asked.

"Course I will," my reply matching her renewed enthusiasm. But she immediately deflated, her shoulders slumped, "Nah, don't worry, he'd be gone home by now, and I don't even know where he lives."

"Who?" I asked.

She smiled and pulled a leaf from my head, "The boy with Bruce Lee hair." Her mood elevated again; she held my shoulders. I could almost hear her mind singing, "Will you go back to the farm in the morning and tell him I wasn't running away from him. Tell him I had to rush to the chemist cos I'm poorly, but when I'm better, I'll go to the pictures with him."

A rush of excitement hit me, "Can I come to the pictures with you?"

"No, Gerard," she said emphatically.

"Why not?"

"Because it's a grown-up film, kids aren't allowed in."

Indignant, I replied, "But you're not a grown-up!"

She returned to her reflection in the mirror, "I am now," she said, in a slow voice that chilled me.

I knew she was still a girl because we're not a grown-up until we're eighteen. This was her possessor talking because I knew he was definitely an adult.

I remained quiet while Maria toyed with her hair, experimenting with different ways to disguise the nasty stye in her eye. When she seemed happy with one configuration, she turned to me, "You and me can go to the pictures when a kid's film comes on."

"Alright," I said, forcing a smile through my disappointment. Maria, satisfied with my answer, picked up Penman's pen, turning it up and down. She watched almost trance like as the ship sailed to-and-fro.

I broke her staring stupor, "The man who bought Dermot that pen's got lost somewhere."

Putting the pen down, she asked, "What do you mean?"

I didn't know what I meant, the words tumbled out, surprising myself, "Dermot lost the pen in the slaughterhouse; I found it there."

Maria smiled, "That's good, it means the man's found where he's going, good lad Gerard." She picked up the pen again and took a notebook from the drawer. My interest piqued, I took a step back to give her space, and more importantly, watch what she was doing.

Maria opened the notebook and began to write.

Coldness enveloped me, and I wrapped my arms around myself for warmth against a foreboding chill. Taking a slow step to the left, I studied her face.

All I saw was an intense concentration, and unable to contain myself, I asked, "Who're you writing to?"

"Mam," she answered, her hand continuing to scribe.

I moved forward, "Why?"

"Because I want to."

There was no info in her answer, which concerned me. I stepped closer, "Maria," I said, hoping she'd stop and look at me.

"What?" Her focus remained on scribing.

I braced myself, took a deep breath and asked, "Are you taking a notion?"

She snapped the pen down, "What are you talking about?" she asked, amusement in her voice. I didn't want to mention my new friend, Johnnie.

I had a strong sense that our meeting and the information he'd shared with me was private; so, I asked, "Are you leaving us?"

Her answer was sure, "No, I'm not; I'm writing a letter to Mam, that's all." A gentle chuckle accompanied her return to writing.

"Why are you laughing? Are notions funny?" I asked, bewildered by her merriment.

She held out her arms, "Come here." I walked into her embrace, warm and comforting, "I'm laughing at you. You're so cute with all your questions."

She unfurled her arms from around me, put her hands on my shoulders and pushed me gently back, "You're far too young to worry like you do." She gently shook me, "like Dad says, you need to stop fretting so much."

Maria pulled me into her again, and as she did, we heard the sudden pelt of rain against the window, "Blimey, there's a storm brewing," she said. I pulled back, jumped on the bed, and stared out the window. Great sheets of rain ricocheted off the window. Although there were no accompanying peels of thunder, Evelyn's letter and her account of the storm laden death therein returned to me. I warned Maria, "You have to be careful, cos you can die of storm fright, you know!" But my warning elicited more mirth in Maria, "Stop fretting, Gerard." She sat on the bed, "And if that was true, you and Mam'd be dead ages ago with all those frightening films you watch."

As the rain and wind raged outside, Maria stood up, "It's so safe and cosy in here; the perfect evening to read some of your spooky stories together, Gerard." She looked around the room, "Where's your Creepy comic?"

My mouth dropped; this was not my sister – *Maria hated creepy stories.*

Chapter 22: The Tools

My Creepy lay crumpled on the bed I shared with Dermot. I picked it up and flicked through its pages. The horror felt wrong, or more accurately, it didn't feel right to be consuming it with Maria. I knew her sudden interest in Horror was not her. It was he who was to blame for her change, her possessor.

I decided to confront her, "Maria, you hate horror; why do you want to read it now?" I asked, brandishing my Creepy.

When she went to take it, I pulled away. Maria looked at me warily, "You've been acting really strange lately, what's up with you?"

"Nowt's up with me." My answer laced with obvious irony.

She leaned in, "Are you sure?"

"Yes, why are you asking me?"

I was aware of her eyes studying me keenly, "You've been getting all nervous and jumpy." She raised her good eye, "You know you can always talk to me about anything."

A thought hit me, and I stepped back to process its possibility – was this Maria's possessor talking through her? To confuse and unnerve me, making her problem mine?

My School Priest's Pre-Communion words came back to me with chilling resonance, "The Devil is a devious beast, he sets out to trick us into doing his evil work for him. Only through your devotion to God can you be saved from him." All that day, I repeated the sound of a word he said that I didn't understand and asked Dad when he came home from work, "What does devious mean?"

Taking off his work boots, he pondered before explaining, "It means telling lies to get your own way. Don't you ever be devious, Gerard; it's not a nice way to be in life," he said patting my hair.

I wouldn't fall for this devious demon's tricks.

Clutching my Creepy, I stared at its inside back cover, wanting to divert the demon and lighten my mood. I thrust the comic towards her, "Can we talk about this wonderful world?" I asked, pointing to the advertisement for Sea-Monkeys.

Maria stared at the advertisement for a moment before reading aloud, "Enter the wonderful world of amazing live Sea-Monkeys." She chuckled and continued to read, "Own a bowl full of happiness – instant pets." I watched her as she read the rest of the ad, silently mouthing the words.

I was happy to see her look so engaged. "They look so cute. I wonder if they really look like that?" she asked while looking at the illustrations of the adorable little humanoid creatures that seduced me so much.

Excited by her enthusiasm for the pets I yearned for, I jumped on the bed beside her, "If I had them, we'd find out what they look like. Can I send away for them?" I asked, hopefully.

She scoured the advertisement, "I'll ask Mam in the letter I'm writing, you'll have to send away from them when we're back in

England." She closed Creepy and handed it back to me.

Maria assessed the storm outside. I joined her at the window as the storm retreated, taking with it Maria's sudden interest in horror. "You're right; I don't want to read a scary story; I want to write this letter to Mam." She turned her back on me in an obviously dismissive manner.

She wrote with intense concentration, her hand racing across and down the page as words poured from her at a rapid pace. I stepped forward, "Don't forget to ask Mam about the Sea-Monkeys?"

She stopped writing and turned slowly, "Gerard, can you leave me alone, please?"

Speechless, I simply nodded and turned into the bedroom. I lay on the bed I shared with Dermot and clamped my eyes shut to delete my surroundings, wishing I could do the same with the contents of my mind.

......

"Gerard, get up and dressed." Through sleep-blurry eyes, I saw Granny looking down on me, "You'll not be sleeping into dinner time today," she said.

I turned over, pleading, "Just five minutes more, please?"

She was insistent, "No, get up, you have to eat and get out into that lovely morning."

I was about to protest further when she said something that catapulted me up, "Come down and comfort Maria; she's awful upset at that stye. It's worse it's getting."

......

Bounding down the stairs, I heard Dermot, "I won't lie, it looks like you've been in the ring with Muhammad Ali." His words made me wince.

On hearing my footfall, Maria turned to me – shamefully, I flinched at the sight of her.

Her eye now raged red and so swollen it was closed. Her good eye saw my flinch, "I know Gerard; your face says it all." She pulled back her hair, "Come and have a closer look; Dermot says it'll get worse before it gets better. What do you think?"

I floundered and took a step back, "Yes, yes, he's right; that's what Dad always says about bad stuff," I said, taking another step back. "I don't need to get closer; I can see from here that it looks really sore," I said, trying to conceal my fear of her eye.

Granny came down the stairs behind me. "Heed Dermot, these things get worse before they get better. If it's no better tomorrow, we'll go into Dr McKenna's," she said reassuringly. This cheered Maria a little, and as she turned to eat her soda bread, I bolted back upstairs.

I dressed in a torrent of turmoil, unconcerned that my t-shirt was on backwards, I needed to be out of the house – to think.

......

Dermot and Maria were chomping and chatting at the table as I ambled towards the door, hoping to sidle out unnoticed. But of course, as I opened the door, Maria halted me, "Aye you, where'd you think you're sneaking off to?" she asked. I opened my mouth, but no words came out; instead, I ogled her eye. It seemed to pulsate, goading me with possessive knowing.

Finally, thanks to Johnnie, I found some words, "I fancy a Granny Smith's Apple for breakfast, I'm gonna go and get one from the orchard near Margaret's."

Maria looked back at me, "Stop staring at my eye like that; you're making me feel dead self-conscious about it."

"Sorry," I said, sheepishly opening the door.

She relaxed a little, "Remember to do that favour for me, the one we talked about last night, won't you?"

I smiled because I now had a good get-out clause, "I'll get my apple, then go up to the college farm to give him your message."

Granny chuckled, coming up from the scullery with her mixing bowl, "Have you Gerard doing your courting for you now?" she asked, putting down her bowl and handing me a piece of buttered, currant soda bread. I took it and was gone before Maria had time to answer Granny.

......

I ate Granny's bread while I walked. The bursts of sweet currant were imploded by salty butter, both of which melded into the doughy texture. My enjoyment of this simple fare was such that I stopped and sat on a wooden post to savour the last comforting remnants. The culinary comfort gave my mind clarity, and I put my thoughts in chronological order. 1. My knowing meant I knew a doctor couldn't rid Maria of her stye. 2. Yet Milly hadn't delivered The Cure with her Holy Medals. 3. So, I had to look to a Higher Order to exorcise the demon from my sister.

Finishing my bread, I walked the short distance to a natural spring water well. This oasis was located in the corner of a field and accessed via a tiny wooden gate. It was a perfect natural stone-clad barrel, which carried a constant supply of the clearest, freshest-tasting water. I knelt down on its mossy mat and, using my hands as a ladle, scooped and drank the cool claret, feeling an inner cleanse as it coursed through my body and calmed the pit of my stomach.

I felt replenished. A positive energy to purge my sister of her possessor coursed through my veins. With the help of all that is good and holy, I could do it myself. But I needed tools to help with my mission. I had to obtain two things: a gun and ammunition. And I knew where to get both.

Closing the little gate behind me, I looked up at the cumulus clouds sailing gently in a bright blue sky; they reminded me of the ship in Penman's pen. I inhaled deeply, then said aloud, "Dear God in Heaven, please help me in my good mission."

When I made it to the road, I began a power walk that soon turned into a sprint. I had to meet with the boy with Bruce Lee hair – *urgently.*

Chapter 23: The Procurement

As I ran, I became aware of a 'clippity-clopping' sound behind me. Stopping to look back, I saw Johnnie approaching on a small cart being pulled by his donkey.

He halted by my side, "Where you off to in such a hurry?" he asked.

"The College Farm," I said.

Johnnie shuffled himself a little to the left, "Jump on, I'll drop you at the lane." His smoky smell wafted over me like soothing incense while we clip-clopped onwards.

A question instinctively fell from me, "Johnnie, is a notion the same as a possession?"

Immediately I regretted asking him, and before I could retract it, Johnnie had answered. "Not at all, a notion is all in the head, and a possession is something you own." He gently tapped the donkey with his stick to shift him up a gear.

I wasn't sure whether Johnnie had understood my question, so I swiftly followed it with a safer one, "Any more letters you want me to read?" I asked breezily. He tapped the donkey again, the increased speed making me grab hold of the side of the cart.

Johnnie answered wistfully, "No. My next letter from Evelyn will come at the end of the summer. If you're still here, you can read it out to me, you're a great wee reader."

His answer gladdened me, "Thanks Johnnie, I liked reading your last one," I said, feeling lifted by his compliment.

I smiled and hoped Evelyn's letter arrived before I left, hoping it might give more insight into what sisterly notions were.

……

Johnnie pulled the rein on Donkey, who dutifully stopped at the lane up to the farm. "Thanks, Johnnie; I'll see you in the orchard again soon," I said, jumping from the cart.

Johnnie shouted after me, "Come up to the house some time and meet my mouse; he's a loveable wee fella." Waving after him, I shouted back, "I will."

……

Midway up the lane, a cloud sailed over the sun, which sucked the colour from my surroundings. I stopped for a moment and noted how the light changes ambience and creates mood. With the vibrant colours dulled, my mood dropped to one appropriate for my mission ahead – dark.

……

On reaching the farm, I looked skywards. The cloud cover gathered, crowding out the sun to create a square canvas of grey around me. My roving eye travelled up to Crow's viewing post; he wasn't there. I didn't expect him to be, for I now knew where the tall-man was, and I had to get the tools to rid him from my sister. I had to steel myself, focus.

……

I focussed on the slaughterhouse, braced myself and walked towards it. The wooden door was closed, I knocked. When there came no response, I lifted the latch and gently pushed it enough to decipher it wasn't locked.

Leaving the door slightly ajar while my heart raced, I looked behind me. Seeing no one around, I sidled into the slaughterhouse.

All was neat and tidy, everything in its place, which told me there would be no slaughter on this day. There was a concrete butcher's block in a recess, and on seeing what lay upon it, my body prickled with horror. Tentatively I walked towards the array of tools for violent animal destruction, a mix of repulsion and compulsion pulling at me, making me feel physically torn.

Stopping at arms-length, I flinched at the myriad blades, serrated saws, hatchets, and other implements designed to hack, break, tear, and slice animals for our consumption. But it was the device designed to initiate the process of ridding life from the beast that held my focus – the gun.

The violence inherent in this inanimate object hit me with a force that made my legs wobble. I reached out to steady myself on the concrete block. But rather than step away, I took deep breaths, steadied myself and stepped forward, reaching out toward the gun.

"What are you after?" The question shook me, I spun round. The boy with Bruce Lee hair looked at me quizzically.

I was quick to answer, "You. I've got a message to give you, from Maria."

He held his hand out, "Give it to me, so," he said.

"So what?" I said.

He smiled, "So I can read it."

"Ah no, it's not a letter message," I explained.

"Then tell me, so."

"So what?" I asked again, confused.

He thrust a hand through his glossy locks, "So I know what the message is."

I heard a hint of irritation in his voice. Feeling foolish, my face started to heat, and I spilt out Maria's message with speed to hide my reddening face, "She said she wasn't running away from you, she had to run to the chemist because she's poorly and when she's better she'll go to the pictures with you," I said, swiftly lowering my head.

"What is she sick with?" he asked.

"She didn't get sick," I answered, my head still lowered.

"Then what's wrong with her?"

I wanted to open my floodgates and tell him all about my knowing, to have his broad shoulders share some of my burden. But I held back, "She's got a stye on her eye."

There was a pause before he answered, "Those things can be brutal, alright. Tell Maria to come and see me when she's feeling better in herself." On hearing this, my head shot up, my whole being flushed with a furious desire to purge my sister of this brutality.

The boy with Bruce Lee hair's demeanour changed, became

serious, "Now listen to me," he said, crouching to my level, "I saw you reaching out for the bolt pistol there." He threw a glance towards the block, "You should never handle that; it's very, very, dangerous." He put his hand on my shoulders and leaned in, "Do you hear me?"

I nodded my yes, then asked, "Is it loaded?"

He gently shook me, "It's always loaded, and I want you to promise me you'll not go near it; promise me you'll not be messing with guns?"

His eyes widened with concern. I nodded, "I promise."

But behind my back, my fingers were crossed, which meant my promise wasn't morally binding.

Happy with my answer, the boy with Bruce Lee hair stood up and smiled down at me, "Now, will you do me a wee favour?"

"Yes, what is it?" I asked, wanting to oblige.

He ruffled my hair, "Will you ever dress yourself properly? Your t-shirt's on back to front," he said, chuckling. I nodded and felt my face redden again with embarrassment for my lazy error.

......

Back in Connelly Brother's Holy Emporium, I slowly walked by the Saints who shimmered in the dim light. I paused at a large picture of Jesus and crossed myself before continuing to search for a weapon.

It didn't take me long to find what I was looking for.
......

Ensuring it had what I needed, I took the gun, gave it to the man, held out my hand and said, "Take this, is it enough?" He took my coins, gave them a count and said, "Take that back; you have more than enough. He handed me back two coins. I took them, gave thanks, and swiftly departed.

......

With the pistol in my pocket, I ran to load it, hoping and praying I could get access to the ammunition. As I walked, I caught sight of the old lady in the shawl sitting at the corner on the concrete post, her hand outstretched to no one. I felt she had the knowing because the sight of her motivated me, and I powered onwards, determined to complete my mission.

......

Although I knew what I was about to do was wrong, I was doing it for the right reasons. So, it was devoid of any burdensome guilt that I began a slow ascent to the open doors of the magnificent Cathedral of St Patrick and St Felim's.

I stood alone in the place of worship, feeling tiny in its vast space, like an insignificant speck of humanity. Yet what I was going to do was of great significance, as I was fully aware that it would bring me to God's attention, again – for I was about to commit the sin of stealing from his church.

A flickering light caught my eye; my heart soared when I saw a possible way out of this sin. Slowly, I walked up the aisle towards the light.

Pausing at the altar, I gazed at the full-length image of Jesus, his arms outstretched, his modesty protected by a swathe of green sheet. Three men flanked him to his left and two to his right. I recognised the near right-hand man as St Patrick and thus deduced that the man behind him was Felim. These two men intrigued me. I felt connected to them, especially as Felim was brown like my best friend in Manchester. I was drawn to them but pulled myself away and back into my mission.

......

My penny dropped with an echoing clang into the metal box. Taking my penny candle, I placed its wick onto the flame of another, igniting it. I placed the candle on a holder and watched, mesmerised as the flame pirouetted like a tiny dancer giving me a private performance. After a silent prayer, I popped my final penny into the box to pay for what I previously intended to steal —Holy Water – *the ammunition I needed to purge my sister of her possessor.*

Chapter 24: The Loading

Felim and St Patrick stopped me as I walked past. In them, I saw togetherness, a unity that induced fluttering warmth in me. Forcing myself away from the image of the Cathedral dwellers, I turned and walked down the aisle to re-focus on my mission.

Happy I was alone in the beautifully ornate entrance area, I rushed outside and scanned left and right. There was no one around, satisfied my coast was clear, I took the pistol from my pocket.

My breathing was heavy, and my hand shook as I dipped the barrel of the pistol into the Holy Water font. Taking deep, calming breaths, I pulled slowly on the plunger. The sucking sound of the pistol filling with saintly imbued liquid filled me with a spiritual serenity. Satisfied I was fully loaded, I wiped the pistol on my t-shirt and placed it in my pocket.

......

I strolled down the sweeping drive of the Cathedral, my head down, deep in thought about my mission—how to create a scenario wherein I could shoot Maria in the stye. But I stopped – it was Felim and St Patrick that grabbed me again.

The image of them together popped into my head, physically halting me. Their togetherness confused me, for, in it, I saw the same connection that seemed to be pulling Maria and the boy with Bruce Lee hair together. I turned to go back and look again to see if their image would give name to the emotional feelings they were both instilling in me. But a voice called out to me, *"Gerard, turn away and stop this wrong-thinking – immediately!"* I spun around, *"The Devil is devious, don't have him divert you with these thoughts,"* he shouted. I raised my head to the sky and sucked in the air to stop myself from drowning in a clammy shame. *"Get back to your mission, now!"* This voice was my own, yet it was so loud and clear that it seemed to come from someone else in another time and place.

The sun behind me elongated my shadow, making me tall, like a man. I stood, transfixed by the shadowy image of myself stretched in stature, grown into adulthood. My inner voice returned, *"That's your future, Gerard, run away from it!"* The words hit me with force, and I bolted down the driveway of the Cathedral like a rabbit out of a trap.

On the pavement, I slowed and wandered onwards, perturbed by the maturity in this authoritative inner voice that had been released by St Patrick and Felim.

……

A familiar figure ahead gave me a welcome distraction, and I walked towards her.

"Well, hello, young Smith," said Milly. The warmth in her voice pulled the shutter down on mine, instantly easing me.

"Hiya," I said.

She smiled, "What has you up visiting the Cathedral?"

I stalled, wanting to tell her of this strange new voice that spoke of my future. But I wouldn't, shouldn't, couldn't. So, I answered with a partial truth, "I was praying for Maria's stye to go away because it's got worse."

Milly's smile dropped, "Didn't I give her the cure – give it time, the Saints will do God's good work," she said, her hand instinctively resting on the line of Saintly Medals at her breast.

Her eyes flickered over me, resting at my head, "Is them Rosary Beads you have round your neck?" she asked.

"Yes, I got them at Connelly Brothers."

My response gladdened her, "Aren't you a great wee lad? It's special you are." She placed her hand on my head, muttering a prayer.

Her prayer lifted me from the doom of my inner voice as I felt being blessed by one of the Guardians of the Congregation would help me with my mission. Also, I'd never been told I was 'special' before, so it was with a spring in my step that I bid Milly, "Goodbye,' and skipped off on my mission to shoot Maria in the stye.

......

The day was warm, and I absorbed its pleasantry while I walked, buoyed by Milly's appraisal of me. Strategies for 'Mission Stye' tumbled through my head. On reaching the summit of the hill leading down to Granny's house, I decided the best option was to simply pretend I was playing with my new toy – and – "KERPOW" – shoot Maria in the stye.

To achieve success, I needed to ensure two things: one, to get Maria alone. That wouldn't be a problem. The second thing was more so; I would have to concoct some kind of contrivance to convince Maria of my newfound interest in this boy thing, the gun.

167

And with a literal bolt, I found it – in the boy with Bruce Lee hair. He used a 'bolt pistol for his work, and I was using a 'water pistol for mine. Positivity surged through me, as I knew the Saints were aligned and giving me answers to guide me with Mission Stye.

My motivation was bolstered further when I realised that Maria would want to spend more time with me now that I was interested in guns and learning to use them, just like the boy with Bruce Lee hair.

......

The revelation that the Saints knew of my knowing greatly relieved my burden. I felt a physical weight lift from my shoulders. This newfound lightness turned my amble into a steady walk down the hill to the House in The Hollow.

A white van approached the house, stopping at the door. I watched my uncles Michael and Peter appear from it and into the house. Their arrival from the chicken farm told me it was lunchtime.

Knowing Granny's table would be busy, I decided to wait a little before going in for my helping of rhubarb and custard, hoping Granny would let me skip straight to my favourite part of the dining experience.

But the experience of my inner voice flickered back to me, and I looked up into the expanse of blue, looking for crow, wanting his distraction. I saw no sign of him nor any other avian life. I sat in warm silence, fighting the strange feelings from the cathedral that were beginning to creep back into my head. "NO!" I said aloud, jumping up and striding toward the house.

......

Smoke from Granny's range rose from the chimney like swirling plumes from Lofty's pipe. I jumped down the short steps and into the darkness of the tiny hallway, a space I always paused in as it made me feel safe.

"Are you coming in, or will you eat your dinner in the hall?" asked Lofty, opening the door and stooping to accommodate his stature in the small space. "No," I said. He tousled my hair, "Go on in; there's a space at the table for you." He inhaled his pipe and exhaled a plume before leaving to complete his working day.

Dermot launched himself onto Lofty's chaise-lounge. "Yessssssss, Evel Knieval misses the ramp," he shouted, feigning a death-defying roll onto the floor, coming to a halt at my feet.

"Where's our Maria?" I asked, scanning the room. Nobody answered.

Instead, I saw Dermot looking up at me, "Our kid, look at yourself," he said, judgement in his tone, disgust on his face.

"What?" I asked, seeing Michael, Peter and Granny looking at me with crumpled faces. "What's up, what've I done, what you all looking at?" I asked, trying to control my creeping dread.

Dermot pointed to my nether region, "You've pissed yourself!"

His exclamation filled me with horror; I looked at my trousers, drenched from my crotch down, "Nooooo!" I shot towards the bathroom, the words, 'Please God,' on a silent loop in my head.

In the bathroom, my hand shook as I grappled with retrieving the pistol from my sopping pocket. My inner voice angrily criticised me, *"Idiot, you've all the Saints on your side, and you let this happen; you should've learned from the chop and dog incident,"* while my outer voice quietly countered it with a pleading whisper, "Please God let there be some left, please!"

I tried to look into the barrel of the gun, but my hand shook, and I couldn't see it properly. I placed it on the toilet cistern and stared closely.

Nothing, not even a drop of Saintly Salvation remained.

My Holy Ammo soaked my nether regions and would get nowhere near Maria's stye – *Mission Aborted.*

Chapter 25: The Father

A gentle tap at the door, "Who is it?" I asked, trying and failing to dry my trouser leg.

"It's me, Maria; who're you talking to?" Searching for an excuse, she tapped the door again before I had time to find one, "I've got some clean trousers; Dermot said you wet yourself."

I opened the door a fraction and stuck my hand out.

"Will you come out and talk to me when you've cleaned yourself up? I've missed you."

"Alright, see you in a minute," I said, hurriedly changing into the dry trousers.

......

Maria was sitting at the dressing table brushing her hair. I sat on the bed, trying to get furtive glances at the stye. It looked no better, but I took small comfort that it looked no worse. "I thought you'd grown out of wetting yourself after you did it at school when Mam went into to talk to your teacher. Why couldn't you hold it in this time? Were you nervous of something?" she asked.

Her question transported me back to a shameful experience in the school gymnasium. Standing in the queue for the vault-horse in my vest and underpants with my peers. The boys before me all rushed toward the vault with a competitive push, clearing the beast with effortless athleticism. My anxiety grew with every cheer and applause for another boy's perfect performance. When my turn came, I had neither focus nor physical push; instead, I stood, rooted to the spot. There came a gentle nudge from the boy behind me, "Hurry up, I want my turn." But instead of pushing myself forward – I pissed myself.

The boy behind me jumped the queue to avoid my nerve-induced torrent, which bounced off the gym floor and pooled outwards, "Eurgh, Miss, Gerard Smith's weeing!" he exclaimed. I stood in my pissy pool, the growing sniggers of my classmates worsening my embarrassment.

That incident had prompted the teacher to call in my mother to ensure all was okay at home. So, with an enthusiastic push, I rushed to put everyone right on this none peeing incident.

......

I grabbed the pistol and rushed back into the bedroom, holding it aloft proudly. "I didn't wet myself; I bought this water pistol, and it went off in my pocket when I was walking home. I didn't notice it leaking," I said, happy I wouldn't have to experience the judgement the gym incident engendered.

Maria smiled wide, "Aww, that's so funny," she said, taking the gun from me. She looked at it, her fingers caressing its contours, "Why did you buy this? You don't like guns?"

Her question stunned me, for, in it, I felt that Maria knew of my knowing. But then, 'No,' I realised the truth here was my sister simply knew me, so I smiled, "I do now."

Maria put the gun down and looked at me quizzically, "Why, where's this interest in guns come from?" she asked, tapping the bed for me to sit.

"Because the boy with Bruce Lee hair uses a gun," I said.

"He uses a gun for his job, not to play with," she said.

I jumped in, "I'm using it for my job, as well." When she asked, "What job?" My tummy lurched. I was dangerously close to spilling my truth. But like a God-send, an answer sprang from me, "To water the flowers in Granny's Garden."

Salvation – it worked. Maria beamed, "Orr, that's so sweet." She turned back to the mirror, "Your way of using a gun is nicer than how they use it on the farm," she said, peering into the mirror to stare at her stye. Her reflection stared back at me, "Did you buy that gun because you like the boy with Bruce Lee hair, Gerard?" Her question pulled me back to our time at the clear lagoon when she'd asked me if I thought he was, "…dead nice-looking?"

Back then, it bothered me, and this new enquiry irked me more so, simply because she'd never ask Dermot these questions. And the tone of her delivery induced in me a low-level-anger. Her tone was not quite, 'accusatorial,' more, 'searching' – as though she were looking for something from me.

My inner voice raged, "*I bought it to save you from possession and shoot you in the stye, to get rid of it!*" But I managed to suppress it, my outer voice emerging, measured, "I told you why I have it, don't you believe me?"

My answer changed her tone, "Course I do," she said, squeezing my knee. She turned back to the mirror; I watched her playing with her hair. My sister seemed to be appraising herself, "I just want to talk about him, that's all, Gerard."

She stood up, thrust her arms wide, threw her head back, and twirled like Maria from The Sound of Music on the top of her mountain, "I like him; I think he's gorgeous," she sang. I jumped up, eager to join her in one of our treasured sing-alongs.

But Maria guided me back onto the bed, placed her hands on my knees and asked, "Did you give him my message this morning?"

I didn't instantly answer as her curt cutting off of our sing-song, along with the word she used to describe the boy with Bruce Lee hair, was hurting me. I remembered Dermot had told me that I looked like the son of Catweasle, and this, combined with my wiry hair, ensured I wasn't gorgeous. Therefore, it was clear my possessed sister no longer liked me.

She gently shook me, "Well, did you?"

"Yes."

"What did he say?"

I relayed his words with a cold detachment, "Those things can be brutal. Tell Maria to come up and see me when she's feeling better about herself." My delivery was low, quashed by the hurting.

Her abject joy was poles apart from my aching sadness, "That's dead nice, he's so understanding; not like the rough Manchester lads." She closed her eyes and clasped her hands in prayer, "Stye, stye, go away and never come back another day," she chanted – a dark version of our sunny Saturday's Sound of Music, Maria

Her chant merged into excited chat, but I couldn't take her words in. I sat on the bed, sinking in hurt, which was being attacked by something like hatred. I wondered whom this hate was for, and in so doing, my stretched shadow on the cathedral concourse returned to me – I hated myself.

......

Whenever these feelings came over me, I wanted to be around Dad. His gentle manner and ever-watchful eye elevated my sinking in horrible feelings. With him not around, I preferred to be alone to deal with my dark feels. So, with Maria basking in Bruce Lee glory and pulsing with possession, I took myself off to the clear lagoon to wander my way out of myself.

......

At the gate, I stopped, evaluating the road into town. I wondered if I should walk back to the Cathedral and re-load. But 'No,' I decided to climb the gate to escape from secrets and styes for a while.

......

The fact I could tell Granny, Uncles Michael and Peter, and Dermot the truth of my wet trousers gave me some comfort. The thought of their smiling faces and gentle chuckling over my mishap lifted me a little.

Sat on my mossy stump, I had a desire to talk to someone. I looked for any signs of Crow; he wasn't around. With my head in my hands, I released a loud sigh, and with it came a moment of great revelation as my inner voice spoke with a positive vibe. *"You must speak to God the Father and seek his guidance to lessen your burden and exorcise your sister."*

I raised my head, took a deep breath and began, "Dear God the Father, I'm asking for you to bring me help for my sister who is possessed by the Devil. I will promise to be a good boy all my life so I can get to heaven one day." I paused for thought, then continued,

"Please, God the Father, can you give me a sign that you'll bring me help in my mission? I'm only seven and can't do it on my own." I finished my plea by kneeling and saying one Our Father and three Hail Mary's.

......

Feeling better, I wandered to the farmyard. I wanted to see the boy with Bruce Lee hair, to discover what made him gorgeous.

Cleaning his wellington boots with a hose-pipe, he seemed pleased to see me, "How-a-ya Gerard," he said, turning off the hose. I liked that he called me by my name. "How is Maria today?" he asked.

"Her stye's still there, but it hasn't got worse," I explained.

"That's a good sign." He placed the hose on a hook on the wall, "Will you give her a message from me?" he asked.

"Yes," I said, happy to be useful.

"Tell her before she goes back to England, I'll take her to see The God Father."

Chapter 26: The Three Wise women

I felt myself lighten; his message lifted some of my burden. I watched him walk up the avenue and waited until he disappeared from sight before I looked skywards, "Thank you, God, the Father, for sending me that message, I'll make sure Maria gets it," I said before taking off at speed down the manure covered lane.

......

With dinner over, Granny was in the scullery, washing dishes and prepping for the evening meal. She didn't notice as I flew up the stairs in a flurry of excitement to deliver a message from above.

Maria was on the bed by the window reading Black Beauty, chewing on the end of Penman's pen, which bothered me. I wanted to tell her to stop biting the pen, but when she saw me, she took it out of her mouth, slammed the book shut and sat upright, "Gerard, what's up?" she asked, alarmed by my panting physicality which she took for distress. Such was my breathing, I couldn't get the words out, I raised my hand, taking deep, recovering breaths. Maria leapt off the bed and made to hug me, but I backed off, knowing her hug would impede my recovery. "Gerard, what's happened? You're scaring me."

I managed to drop two words between breaths, "I've got...."

Maria crouched to my eye level, "You've got what?"

Two more fell from me, "A message...."

A tentative smile played on her face; she grabbed my shoulders, "From the boy with Bruce Lee hair?" she asked, feverishly.

"Yes."

Maria shook my shoulders; the extremity of her joyful expression made her stye bulge, and I threw my head back to avoid any demonic spurts.

Feeling sufficiently recovered to deliver the message in full, I pulled free from her grip. "Before you go back to England, he's going to take you to God The Father." Maria reacted with a triumphant spin before chuckling in my direction. "What you laughing at me for? That's what he said."

I felt irked by her merriment. "You muddled up the words," she said, still chuckling.

Indignant, I shot back, "No, I never, that's what he said."

She jumped back on the bed, "It's The Godfather, Gerard; a film that's out at the end of the summer. You should know that! You love films."

"Is it a horror film?" I asked.

She didn't hesitate, "No, it's about an American family," she said, with a knowing authority.

I was scathing in my appraisal, "That sounds boring."

Maria answered with a strangely dismissive voice, "It's a grown-up film; you wouldn't like it."

"Does it have singing in it?" I asked.

"It might do, but it's not a musical."

The depth of Maria's change was deepening. I struggled to fathom it. "But you love The Sound of Music and Mary Poppins, and they've got singing – don't you like musicals anymore?"

"Course I do, but I want to see a more grown-up film when it comes out, that's all."

I still held onto hope the boy with Bruce Lee hair taking Maria to see this film may have to do with exorcising the demon. So, I asked, "Is God in the film?"

"I really don't know, Gerard." She picked up Black Beauty, a gesture clearly designed to dismiss me. Opening the book, she peeped over its rim at me, "Why don't you go out and look for the tall-man."

Maria wanted me gone!

Stunned, I stood rooted to the spot as vivid images flashed before me – of Maria and me in her Manchester bedroom singing along to the sound of music. This reminiscence reel continued with footage of our Saturday mornings, scrutinising wedding magazines to pick out her dress for her marriage to Bruce Lee; my approval mattered to Maria. The visuals changed to more recent scenes, the three of us alone on the Munster; I physically felt her protective hold and pull as we searched for Dermot while I fretted about his possible abduction by Penman.

And now, she was letting go, pushing me away at a time when I needed her most.

Disconsolance dragged me down; the sting of tears pricked my eyes. Maria, aware I was still in the room, put her book down, "Go on then."

I managed a weak "Alright" before my bottom lip gave in to quiver.

She didn't say, "Goodbye," or, "be careful," or, "be back in time for tea." All the things she'd say before this thing got into her, this entity I was losing my beloved sister to.

......

Outside I sprinted up the road, stopping at a little clearing past John O'Connell's house. When sure I was alone and out of sight, I dropped to the floor and sobbed, my tears flooding the fauna around me. I didn't hold back; I couldn't. I lay prone, burying my face in the grass to soften the sound of sobbing.

Maria's rejection of me caused an almost physical hurt, but it was my loss that stung most. The loss of the only person with whom I could be myself, the loss of the one who indulged my non-boyish likes and loves. But above all, it was the loss of someone whose company I loved, adored, and cherished.

My body heaved and shook as it was battered with emotions, many of which I didn't understand; until I was blasted with one I recognised all too clearly – anger.

The anger halted my tears, the sobs subsided; rage took over, and I pummelled the earth with my fists. The physical pain I felt in my hands helped suppress a hurt that lurked deep inside. But I wasn't angry with Maria, her possessor, or the boy with Bruce Lee hair. It was myself my anger was for. Something about me wasn't right, and it was this intangible thing I raged at.

I longed to be like my brother. He fitted into the world without a care or cumber. Images of him indulging in some fantastic adventure with his best friend John popped into my head. I was shackled by myself, and I longed for Dermot's freedom. He was without burden. Nothing bad ever happened to him.

......

A compulsion pushed me back to the Cathedral. I needed to see St Patrick and Felim, to see if the sight of them would make sense of the strange self-anger that puzzled me. Standing up, I tidied myself, swiping leaves and bracken off my clothes, drying wet eyes with the back of my hand, composing myself. I set off back into town.

......

The walk eased me a little. My mind moved towards thoughts of Sea-Monkeys as I realised Mam and Dad would soon receive Maria's letter, wherein she asked if I could get them. Nurturing these little creatures gave me a purpose, the thought of having them helped to settle me a little.

......

The late afternoon sun was hot. I became aware of the dampness on my t-shirt, and I stopped to wipe the beads of sweat trickling down my face. Looking ahead, I saw what looked like a mirage in the hazy heat of the distance. Waiting, I watched as this vision travelled out of the haze and into my reality, where I was able to identify them as what I had come to call the Three Wise women – the two women and their pram-pushing makeup-clad-man-friend.

That I included the man within a female context without question struck me. It wasn't a hard, stinging strike, more of a telling tap. His wearing makeup enlightened me. While I had no desire to wear makeup, nor be anything other than the boy who didn't enjoy boy's pursuits, it was his difference, his expression of himself as herself, that gave me comfort. My inner voice spoke, *"If he can find his place in this world, then so can you, Gerard."*

......

In moments, they were upon me. The man stopped, parking his empty pram by my feet. His fellow wise women flanked him. The way they stood, their configuration reminded me of the fresco of Jesus and the saints in the cathedral. I stared at Makeup-Man with an intrusive intensity. I noticed his discomfort at my intrusion and instinctively said, "You look nice," by way of explanation and apology.

Astonished, he looked either side at his companions before breaking into a broad smile, "Did yis hear that?" he asked, elbowing each of them. The women looked at each other and laughed uproariously. They were laughing at me for telling a man he looked nice, and I felt my face redden. One of the women interrupted her merriment, "Don't be giving him notions, now," she said. The man play-tapped the woman's shoulder and addressed me, "Don't mind her, she's only jealous." His smile widened, "Thank you," he said, taking rein of the pram and manoeuvring around me.

A few feet ahead, Makeup-Man called out, "What's your name?" I turned to him, "Gerard." He held his hand aloft, "Mind yourself, Gerard," he said before taking off again with his wise companions.

Watching them walk towards their rummage, I knew he had the knowing and was telling me to mind myself during my mission. But it was what his companion said that diverted me, "Don't be giving him notions."

Old Johnny's words about his sister returned to me when I met him in the orchard, "...Evelyn took a notion, and off she left," he'd said mournfully.

I worried that I'd unintentionally given Makeup-Man a notion, and he was going to leave his two wise women friends bereft like Evelyn had Johnny.

I abandoned my return to the Cathedral and ran towards the Three Wise Women – *wanting to make amends with Makeup-Man.*

Chapter 27: The chewing

They'd travelled quite a distance ahead of me, and feeling myself tire, I shouted out, "Excuse me!" They stopped, turned, waiting for me. I reduced my run to a power walk and was soon upon them.

Seeing them looking at me, waiting for me to give a reason for stopping them, I began to gabble. "Erm – I didn't mean – I mean – what I said – I meant – I'm sorry…."

Makeup-Man, seeing my struggle, helped me out, "There's no need to say sorry for being a nice wee fella."

His words gave me focus, "No, I know; what I mean is, I didn't mean to give you a notion that might take you away from your friends," I said, happy to get it off my chest.

The woman who said it piped up, "Don't worry about that; we'll handle any notions he has." Both women linked their arms through his, "We take care of each other, so we do, we have to."

"Are you sisters?" I asked.

"We are," said the woman, nodding to the other. She slapped Makeup-Man with the back of her hand, playfully, "And he's as good as," she said, causing all three to take to the road again, propelled by peels of joyous laughter.

Wanting to wish them well, I shouted out, "I hope you find something nice today."

Makeup-Man shouted back, "You never know; one man's rubbish is another man's treasure."

Treasure. I liked that word. Watching them walk away, I treasured the sight of them, for their unity filled me with hope that one day in my future I'd find friends like Makeup-Man's. Friends who'd treasure my intangible difference the way the two wise women treasured his visible difference.

......

Before I returned to the Cathedral, I realised I needed a sit-down. Hoisting myself onto a short wall, I felt a tingle in my tummy. It was similar to the one I'd felt when Dad took me on a rollercoaster in Belle Vue Amusement Park in Manchester. That day had been the happiest of my life, and somehow, I felt this day was comparable to it. The fear and despair I'd experienced only moments before in the room with Maria were akin to how I felt as the coaster approached the pinnacle of the hill. And the rush of excitement and exhilaration The Three wise Women instilled in me was akin to the thrill I felt as the coaster raced down the drop.

But on that day, I'd had Dad by my side to share those highs and lows. Without his companionship, I knew this day would never hit that level of happiness. It was with a modicum of hope that I set off to re-load my pistol at the Cathedral.

While I walked, I ruminated on a self-revelation – I realised that to feel happy, I'd have to feel sad. Just like that day on the roller coaster with Dad, I knew I'd have to hit the lows before I could feel the highs. It was a grown-up insight, the maturity of which unnerved me because if I felt like this as a kid, would it intensify as an adult? My inner voice spoke with authority – *'Don't grow up, Gerard, it's a trap!'*

......

With the loaded pistol safely in hand this time, I decided to visit the newsagents for a browse to see if the new edition of Creepy was in.

The faint paint-like smell of ink-pressed paper welcomed me when I entered Young's Newsagents, warming me with its promise of escape from my own story into other narratives. Browsing the comic section, I saw there was no new edition of Creepy. Disappointed, I made to leave.

But the girl at the counter called out to me, "Excuse me!" It was the same girl who'd sold me my Creepy. I was concerned she was going to tell me I could no longer purchase the comic. I approached with apprehension.

Her sunny smile eased me, "You're the wee boy home from England."

"Yes."

"Do you have an older sister with long brown hair?"

"I do, Maria.'

She reached under the counter, "She left this. Can you make sure she gets it back?"

My jaw wobbled and dropped at the sight of it – Penman's pen.

Such was my astonishment that I took it without saying thank you and left the shop.

......

This simple pen had become symbolic to me. Holding it in my hand

and looking at it, I believed it represented abandonment. Dermot had left it in the slaughterhouse; now Maria had left it at the newsagents.

Yet it always found its way back to me. I wondered why. Not having the answer, I focussed on the pen, noticing Maria had chewed the top off it. This upset me because I knew the destructive force of Maria's possessor had done the damage. I wondered how she had got to the shop and what for? It would have to be for something significant, given she was in hiding with the stye.

But the pen provided me with good reason to return and ask Maria these questions. With the pen in my left hand and the pistol in my right, I set off –back to my mission.

......

My return journey was interrupted by a disturbing sight – *blood*.

Small speckles splattered the pavement below me. I put my foot on a droplet and drew back; it smeared, fresh. Feeling this was somehow fateful, I followed the trail.

It led me to stop at a place I usually hurried past, a building I feared on Cavan's Main Street. The Surgical.

Its very name was sharp, conjuring images of blades slicing into human flesh and other invasive instruments which hurt before they heal. This, combined with the building's cold blue/grey façade and the recess in which Our Lady the Virgin Mary stood with outstretched arms, created a sinister feel and presence that belied the care and healing this hospital offered. To my eye, it was more a haunted house than a hospital.

Previously, when I'd rush past the open double doors, I'd take a fast and furtive glance in, shuddering at the sight of a cage-like door that opened up into a vast elevator. Never did I want to be shut into it and ascend to whatever horrors awaited above.

My thoughts turned to the unfortunate whose blood had been spilt. A sound halted me, coming from within the confines of The Surgical. A confused commotion of noise and motion, amidst all of which I thought I heard a familiar name but couldn't be sure.

Walking back, I hovered at the entrance and honed in. Amidst the noise, I heard the familiar name again, and this time I was sure – "Dermot."

A female voice said, "Dermot," with a soothing sound, making it the only word audible amongst the clattering chaos of noise filtering out from the hospital onto the street.

My blood ran cold – the blood – it was my brother's – Dermot's blood smeared Cavan's Main Street!

Shocked concern coursed through my body, and facing my fear, I raced through the open door. The trail of blood stopped at the dreaded elevator. My brother had been taken into this space to ascend for God-knows-what. But what had he torn, what had been damaged? Looking left to right, I muttered, "Please, God let him be alright, I know I said his life was better than mine, but I didn't mean it."

Seeing a stairwell to my left, I bounded up until I reached a landing. Standing in the empty space, I listened; all was quiet. The smell of antiseptic surrounded me – the smell of sickness.

Instinctively, I rushed a second staircase. It led to another landing. Again, all was quiet, with the smell of sickness all-pervading. A double door opened into a bright white ward with rows of metal beds, on which men, some laying, some sitting, looked in my direction.

Knowing I was intruding, I stepped out of their sight, slipped, and stumbled backwards. The wall stopped my fall. I steadied and looked at the object I'd slipped on – my every hair bristled.

Picking the thing up, I studied it closely and was left in no doubt – it was the sole of Dermot's training shoe.

Or rather part of it, it was ripped, chewed up and soaked – *in blood.*

Chapter 28: The healing

It was definitely Dermot's trainer; I recognised the popular brand's colour and shape still evident on the side of the mangled sole. Putting my pistol on the floor, I held the pen in my left hand and Dermot's sole in my right.

Looking from left to right, I noted the chewed top of the pen and compared it to the bottom of Dermot's shoe, also chewed. The thought of a possible correlation between the two put me right back on that coaster.

I felt myself ascending, filling with fear. And not having Dad to lean into, panic rose, making my body shake.

There was a small recess in the wall, and I shuffled into it. Leaning back, the small space contained my tremble. I squatted on my hunkers, put my head between my knees and waited, hoping the shake would soon leave me.

A 'crunching' sound interrupted my shake – I knew what it was. Looking up, I saw a black shoed foot on my pistol, its holy ammo pooling outwards towards me from the broken barrel.

"Gerard is this yours?" asked my Uncle Jim, Aunt Margaret's husband. He held my crushed pistol out to me.

I took it, "Yes, it's mine."

"I've stood on it, don't worry, I'll buy you another," he said, a look of remorse on his face.

Jim was a kind man, always cheerful with a sunny disposition. Seeing his guilt, I at once shot to his defence, "Don't worry, Jim, it's my fault for leaving it there." His appearance soothed me, and my shakes abated.

As I stepped out of the recess, Jim was bathed in light from the window, which illuminated his deathly colour, "Jim, aren't you well? Is that why you're here?" I asked. He shook his head, "I'm a bit shook," he replied. The resonance I had in his response spoke to me, "I was too, I was shaking in that corner cos I stood on this, and you stood on my pistol," I said, handing him Dermot's sole.

He took it from me, I noted a slight tremor in his hand, "Dermot's had an accident alright."

I couldn't contain myself, "Is he dead?"

Jim's slight smile eased me, "No, he's not."

"Is he damaged?"

"He is that. How badly we won't know until the Doctor tells us."

"What happened?" I asked, eager to know everything.

Jim pointed over to a wooden bench by the window, "Let's sit down."

"What's happened?" I repeated, anxious.

Jim sighed a mix of frustration and guilt, "I was off to work on the Honda. Dermot heard the revving, and didn't he jump on the back of the bike when I took off – his foot caught the spokes." He lowered his voice, "They ripped off his heel."

I jumped up, "Why'd they do that?" I asked, taking off into the ward to find my footless brother. Jim grabbed me, "Not the doctors; the spokes of the wheel ripped off his heel."

I sat back down, "Will they chop off his foot?"

Jim let out a noise, like a hiccup, "Sweet Jesus, I hope not," he whispered, worried.

Instinctively I made to comfort him, "It's not your fault, Jim, you know what our Dermot's like. He's always jumping on the back of anything with an engine."

He nodded, "No matter, he's in some pain, I feel for the fella."

The sound of approaching footfall interrupted our conversation and we stood to meet it.

In a sparkling white uniform, it was a nurse with a matching box-like hat pinned to the ball of her head. She scurried hurriedly towards us; her pace and pained face caused Jim and I to exchange worried looks.

"It's Jim, is it?" she asked, not noticing me. Jim's face tightened with apprehension. There was a little watch pinned to her chest. She lifted it, looked at it, then turned her head to look back into the ward.

"Well?" said Jim.

She shot back with a nervous smile, "Yes, sorry," she looked at me, "is this Dermot's wee sister?"

Jim put his arm on my shoulder, "It's his brother; he needs a haircut," he said, his words and gesture designed to spare my feelings.

The familiar flame sparked my face, causing it to heat and redden, shimmering in shame; I looked at the floor to hide it. She gave no apology for misgendering me. Instead, she asked, "What's your name?"

"Gerard," I said, gazing at my shoes.

"Alright, Gerard, you sit down there while I take your uncle Jim in to see Dermot," she said, her manner abrupt.

When I looked up, they were gone, leaving me paddling in a pool of dread and shame.

I dreaded the idea that Dermot's damage was connected to or caused by Maria's possession, while my shame for being mistaken for a girl was laced with anger. And although the mistake was hers, the anger was once again, for myself. Dermot's boyhood was never questioned, let alone mistaken; it was a source of great shame that mine was. It felt like I was faulty, and I wondered if I could be fixed, like the way I hoped Dermot was being fixed somewhere within the Surgical.

I didn't sit down as she told me to. Instead, I stooped and picked up my broken pistol. Examining it closely, I saw with care and skill I'd be able to repair it with glue and Sellotape. I wrapped it in a dirty tissue and placed it in my pocket. Looking at Penman's pen, I knew I could do the same with it, so I nestled it next to the pistol in my pocket.

Repairing the pen and pistol gave me a purpose that supplied some respite from my personal turmoil and Maria's possession. I had an affinity for broken things, even ones beyond repair. It gave me comfort to keep the lost and broken with me.

......

Every minute stretched like an hour while I sat waiting for Jim to return with news about my brother. Becoming fidgety, I began to jump up and peer into the ward every few seconds. But all I saw were bemused men looking at me oddly from their sick beds.

An oddity, that's what I was to them. But right then, I didn't care, for I wanted to know how Dermot was. With every passing minute, I imagined the worse for Dermot's heel.

So, when Jim eventually appeared from the ward, my relief was acute, "Is he alright?"

"Well, he could be better."

"What does that mean?"

"They've stitched his heel up, but the healing will come from him having to sit still for a good while; you know Dermot, that'll only happen if we tie him to the bed," he said, with a smirk.

Happy he was fixed, positivity lifted me, "That's alright, Jim, he'll keep still for a few hours."

"We're talking days, maybe weeks, Gerard." He changed tack, "Now listen, I have to go and ask Michael to come in and collect him, then get off to work; I'm already late." He dropped to my level, "I've had a bit of a scare there and wouldn't like to be carrying you back on the bike. Will you mind waiting for Michael for a lift back to your granny's?" he asked.

"Yes," I said, not wanting to burden him anymore.

Jim let out a relieved sigh, "Good lad, and we'll get Kathleen to give that mop a good shearing," he said, rustling my hair before disappearing into the darkened stairwell.

......

Outside I breathed in great lungsful of air, wanting to purge myself of the antiseptic odour, the Surgical smell.

Needing to immerse myself in somewhere atmospherically opposite to the hospital, I walked the few yards to Hickey's sweet shop. I felt the few pence in my pocket and opened the door.

The magnificent Betty greeted me with gusto, "Gerard, lovely to see you." Her manner at once lifted me. "What can I get for you?" she asked, moving slightly aside to give a full view of the glass jars filled with every kind of sweet delights that lined her shelves. At that moment, all my woes fell away, and I literally became the kid in a candy store, eyeing an array of treats as colourful as Betty Hickey herself.

Eventually, my eyes rested on the jar that contained pale, powdery pink spheres, "Can I have this much worth of strawberry bonbons, please."

Betty twisted the top of a white paper bag, brimming with bonbons, "Now," she said, handing them to me. And the kindly tone in which she said that one word said a multitude to me, "Thank You," I said, in response.

Turning to leave, Betty called after me, "Gerard, come here to me." She put her arms on the counter and leaned towards me, her head level with mine as she said, "Will you do me a favour?"

"Yes," I said, happy to help Betty.

"A wee birdy tells me you don't like your hair; well, I'm telling you it's beautiful – don't ever cut it too short." She gave me a lollipop, "Do you know the story of Samson?" she asked.

"Yes, I read it in our Bible in Manchester."

She smiled, "Well, you know so, that head of hair's your strength."

I didn't answer. All I gave was a confused smile – I considered my hair my greatest weakness.

......

Outside I took heed of Betty's favour. I was prepared to endure being mistaken for a girl – *if it would give me strength.*

Chapter 29: The purge

Uncle Michael's car cruised to a stop outside the Surgical. I greeted him, "Thanks for coming Michael, Dermot's alright, but he's to keep still, so his heel heals," I said. He wore his white work gear, speckled with chicken's blood, "We'll tie him down, so," he said, slamming the car door shut and striding towards the hospital.

As he walked into the building, I noticed his wellington boots – pristine white feathers stuck to the black rubber, fluttering gently in the breeze. It looked like Michael was being escorted into the hospital by angels – it was an oddly beguiling sight, indicative of a good sign? I hoped so.

......

Dermot bounced out of the Surgical, his right foot bandaged and bound tight to his knee. "These are brilliant; I'll be able to jump massive ditches with 'em," he said, taking giant leaps on crutches he already used with an Olympian deftness. He turned to me, "Look our kid, I'm Iron Man," he said, bounding along the pavement like the Superhero.

Michael shouted, "Come on, Dermot, quit the showing off. I have to get back to work," he made no attempt to hide his annoyance at Dermot's wilfulness. This very trait had brought him to the Surgical.

......

"Let me do the gears," said Dermot, testing Michael's patience as he drove us both back to Granny's.

Michael flicked at Dermot's hand as it reached for the gear stick for the umpteenth time, "Quit that, you'll have me stall."

Dermot's head shot up, "STOP!" he shouted, making Michael jump, "Feck sake Dermot, one accident's enough for the day that's in it," he said, continuing on.

"I wanna get off at John's; we're going fishing," Dermot insisted.

Michael remained resolute, "You're not. The nurse says you've to keep that foot off the ground till it heals."

"I won't put it on the ground, I promise," said Dermot, his words almost, but not entirely, pleading.

When Michael sped past John's house, Dermot's voice rose, "Come on, Michael, stop being a div, let us out," he shouted, fidgeting restlessly.

"I'll let you out at Mammy's." Michael braked, "Now don't be annoying me, you've put Jim and me out, so behave yourself and do as the nurse says," he said, steering the car into the side of the house.

Pulling on the handbrake, Michael turned to me, "You're the only one with no ailments Gerard, why don't you go out into the sun and look for that ghost of yours," he said, flicking open my door.

I jumped out, leaving Dermot's protests behind me. A few yards away, I looked back to see them both still in the car, gesticulating wildly. Not wanting to see my brother's melt down, I turned away and took off into the woods towards my oasis, the clear lagoon.

......

Wandering amongst flora and fauna of the woods, I thought about how I'd earlier berated myself for self-shackling while longing for Dermot's freedom. Now I was physically free, while Dermot was shackled by injury. I felt sad for him. Dermot was a free spirit; imprisonment would torment him, drive him mad. My authoritarian inner voice shouted, *'That's the Devil's work, Gerard.'*

The soothing sound of the waterfall welcomed me to the clear lagoon, but a sharp pain shooting down my leg caused me to stop and shriek, "OUCH!"

I'd been jagged by Penman's pen, again. I stood and waited for the pain to ebb a little before removing the pen and pistol from my pocket.

At the lagoon, I rubbed the top of my inner leg with my right hand and stared at the pen in my left. I sat cross-legged on a mossy cushion studying the pen I felt had a purpose other than writing, but I didn't know what.

I noticed the end Maria chewed was serrated, almost symmetrically, like a carving knife. I realised Penman's pen had become a tool for destruction, a pain-causing weapon. Conversely, my pistol was a tool for good, a broken device – useless.

It was clear to me the modification of these items was far from an accident. No, they were altered by design, by the Devil himself.

Needing a distraction, I took the bag of bonbons from my pocket and popped one in my mouth. Enjoying the initial sweetness of the strawberry powder, I began to ponder the place I was in, the clear lagoon. This space was the genesis of Maria's change and my resultant turmoil – I silently prayed for answers to my anguish.

Chewing the bonbon, its sweetness opened a memory that spoke to me. The recollection swiftly turned to revelation – a reason these misfortunes were being bestowed upon my siblings.

The bonbons bought from Betty recalled the ones I'd bought from Marjorie as a ploy to steal the penny black-jack to acquire my confessional sin. Subsequently, I remembered the lie I'd told in confession when taken off guard by the Priest, "And...?" he'd asked, unhappy with the singularity of my sin. "I swore at my mam," I'd lied.

My inner voice returned to goad me, *'How stupid are you, Gerard, thinking a week of repentance would get you off the hook. You never swear, never mind swearing at your Mam. Mind you, Gerard, that was the mother of all sins, and now your brother and sister are paying for it.'*

Guilt pushed me onto my knees, and I prayed an Our Father, a Hail Mary, then quietly pleaded, "Dear God, please don't punish Maria and Dermot for my sins." I sat on my hunkers, my focus on Penman's pen, while my inner voice spoke with a firm authority, *'Punish yourself with it, Gerard, that's its purpose, to inflict pain on you to purge your brother and sister of theirs. Go on – do it!'*

I stroked the serrated edge with my thumb, the slight jag of sharpness a preview of the pain it could inflict.

Pain – perhaps it was the answer – my pain might purge my sister of her possessor and heal my brother. Listening to my inner voice, I outstretched my right arm and studied its inner. The translucence of my white skin highlighted the delicate blue veins. I lifted my arm and homed in on these intersecting lines, a rushing network pulsing with life-blood.

Instinctively I pulled my eyes away and placed the serrated pen-edge on my inner arm.

I put my head back, closed my eyes, pushed the sharp end into my skin, inhaled deeply and pulled the pen. Searing heat coursed through me as my skin tore. Only when the pain became unbearable did I lift the pen and throw it at my feet.

When the searing heat gave way to the throb of pain, a strange thing happened. My warm seeping blood seemed to soothe not only the pain but myself as well. The physical pain slowed the torrent of turmoil in my head, and I sat to savour the salve of the ebbing pain.

Watching my blood trickle, I thought of secrets. The old lady in the shop spoke of secrets, Maria had a secret, and now I had one. When the crimson rivulet reached my wrist, I plucked a leaf and let my blood pool into it. Plucking more leaves, I used them to swipe up my arm and pressed them against my self-inflicted wound to curtail the flow as my inner voice spoke once more, *"Suffering, that's your way out of turmoil, Gerard. But don't tell anyone, keep it a secret."*

.....

Having pressed the leaves into my wound for a count of sixty, I removed them. The blood flow stemmed, and I was surprised to see such a small wound, given the pain it caused. I placed the leaves back on my inner arm, words popping into my head. They were the ones spoken by the old lady in Connolly Brother's shop, *"He's spoken about the third secret, that's not right."* Her words sparked a reaction in me, and I said aloud, "This secret's wrong; I won't do it again – but I can't be sure I won't do it tomorrow." I Put the pen back in my pocket and decided to return to the house to repair my pistol.

"Gerard, who're you talking to?"

I spun around to see Maria staring at me with a look of concern, "No one," I said. She moved forward, "You were mumbling something; I saw you." Emotion surged through me, and I wanted to spill everything, tell her the truth of the turmoil I was in.

But instead, I shrugged, "I was singing to myself."

"What were you singing?" she asked. One of our Saturday night songs came to me, "Beg, Steal or Borrow." Maria and I had watched the New Seekers perform in the Eurovision Song Contest and were bereft when their song didn't win.

She smiled wide and walked towards me with open arms, singing, "I, look at you, and I see what I've been looking for...." She embraced me, "I've been looking all over for you," she said, hugging me tight.

Her hug soothed me and gave me something else. She drew back and swept her hair from her face, "Look, Gerard, it's definitely going, isn't it?" My heart leapt when I saw the stye had shrunk considerably, the angry redness almost completely gone.

And right then, standing in the clear lagoon with my sister, the something else in her hug revealed itself. It was my success – *I had exorcised the demon from Maria. Or at least I hoped I had.*

Chapter 30: The Regression

I couldn't be sure whether I'd exorcised my sister of her demon, nor was I sure if the tall-man was her possessor. But what I was sure of – Maria's stye was most certainly retreating.

Sitting with her in The Clear Lagoon, the sun created a dappling discotheque of light around us through the trees. At this moment, I felt a serenity counter to the suffering that led me to self-inflicted pain.

Maria thrust her head in front of mine, "Look, I reckon it'll be gone in a day or so, what do you think?" she asked.

I peered at the eye I previously feared. I saw its retreat, the evil made redundant. I sat back and smiled, "Milly's cure definitely worked. That'll be gone in the morning," I announced triumphantly. My own part in this exorcism would remain secret.

Maria jumped up and clasped her hands skyward, "Thank you, God," she prayed. When she sat back opposite me, I saw she radiated joy, "I'm so happy it's going; it was really scaring me that stye was." I wanted to say how much it scared me, but I wouldn't spoil her moment.

Maria's smile turned to a cheeky smirk. She looked around, then back at me, "Can I tell you a secret?" she whispered.

My heart soared; this was it; all was about to be revealed. I could barely hold my breath, "Yes," I said, my chest heaving in anticipation.

"Promise you won't tell anyone."

"I promise," I said, with no hidden digits crossed.

She paused, and sensing she was struggling to say the secret, I nudged her, "Go on then, tell me."

She lowered her head sheepishly, "I really fancy the Boy with Bruce Lee hair."

She looked at me.
I stared silently back.
Her face filled with expectation as she awaited my response.

But my response was one of disappointment, for her secret didn't satisfy my desire for revelation. And more so, I didn't quite understand it. So, after a short pause, I asked, "What does that mean?"

Maria's face became reflective, it was clear my question had given her ponder. Eventually, she smiled, "It means I really like looking at his hair, his eyes, his smile. I like listening to the way he talks, the way he sounds. I like how he speaks to me." She paused, stood up and let out a big sigh, the end of which turned into a song, sang with an arms wide, swirling, twirling flourish – "I like how I feel when I'm with him."

I knew all of these things, and above all, I now had a sense of Maria's secret. For I'd felt these things myself, not for the boy with Bruce lee hair, but for others my own age. I now understood the bravery of my sister in revealing her 'fancy' to me.

A nervous smile flickered across my face. "I Promise I won't tell anyone," I said while making a promise to keep my secret 'fancies' to myself – forever.

But more so, I knew this wasn't her big secret. Maria wouldn't write to mam privately to tell of her fancy. No, something else had happened, and I was well aware it was a secret she wouldn't reveal to her little brother.

Maria threw her arms around me, "You're the best little brother; I love you so much," she said, squeezing me tight. Releasing me, she rose on her tippy-toes, placed both hands over her heart and began to sing again, "The first time, ever I saw his face, I felt my heart race and race…."

……

Maria continued to sing in an almost trance-like state. I held out Penman's pen, "You left this in the Newsagents."

She stopped abruptly and took it from me, "Did I?"

"Yes – what were you in there for?" I asked.

"Stamps, but they don't sell them – I can't remember leaving the pen on the counter."

When I took it back from her, she noticed my wound, "You've cut yourself," she said, grabbing my arm and examining it closely.

I pulled back, "I didn't cut myself, a thorn cut it." I lied.

She smiled at me, "I know you didn't cut yourself, but you have to be more careful. I don't want you ending up in the Surgical like our Dermot."

I was reminded how my little self-inflicted cut was nothing compared to Dermot's big injury. I still felt his accident was possible retribution for my sin, "Is he resting it like the nurse said?" I asked, hoping Maria might assuage my guilt with her answer.

"Course he isn't, but he'll be alright, you know our Dermot, he always bounces back," she said. The confidence in her response reassured me a little.

Maria looked up, her eyes squinting at the sunlight that managed to penetrate the trees, "It's a lovely day. Let's go for a walk. It's always so dark in here."

We walked in silence, our feet springing on the spongy forest floor. Maria was right; the woodland was always dark, but it was a darkness that I knew, a comfort wherein I could blank out the world and be myself. This cloak of comfort gave me an urge to talk, to tell Maria my truth of her stye and my part in it, to give sound to the strange feelings I'd had on the concourse of St Patrick and St Felim's Cathedral, to wonder aloud about men in makeup, to ask of secrets; and the adult inner voice that startled me so much.

But as we cut through the trees, we were blinded by the sudden onset of sunlight and instinctively stopped to allow our eyes to become accustomed to it. And when mine did, I felt immediately exposed by the light and shut away all thoughts of giving voice to any self-expression.

Conversely, Maria's reaction to the light was completely at odds with mine. She thrust her arms out, raised her head to the sky and burst into ebullient song, "The hills are buzzing with the sound of bird-song, with songs they have sung for a million years. The hills fill my heart with the sound of love-song…."

I watched as she sang and spun down the vivid green meadow,

wishing I could be as free as she now was. But instead, the hills filled my head with a dull dread that weighed heavy on my heart. I sauntered down the meadow mournfully to join my newly liberated sister.

......

Maria finished her performance and slumped on the grassy carpet as I arrived by her side, "Why didn't you join me? You love that song," she asked, recovering her breath.

I shrugged, "I'm a bit tired." Then wanting diversion, I asked, "Did you ask Mam if I can get the Sea Monkeys when we go back to Manchester?"

"Course I did," she said, pulling me down to sit with her.

I homed in on her face, startled.

Maria reacted to my startle with a hand on her mouth, "Oh my God, what is it now, Gerard?"

"You know what, the stye's gone even more from the last time I looked," I said, amazed by its rapid retraction.

She beamed and tapped my knee, "You scared me then, with that look on your face."

"Sorry."

She rubbed my knee, "Orr, no need to be sorry, you did nothing wrong."

I lowered my head, "I did."

"What have you done?" she asked, concerned.

"A really bad thing."

Her finger found my chin, and she lifted my head. The concern in her face made my lips quiver, and with their tremble came my tears.

When she folded me in her arms, I released a great tsunami of worry, which soon soaked her t-shirt.

She gently rocked me, and when my tears abated, she said, "Gerard, I know you, whatever you've done, I know it won't be that bad."

"It is," my words stifled in her sopping t-shirt.

She gently prized me from her, "You can tell me you know; it might make you feel better," she said, her words gently coaxing, her hand wiping my tears.

A gulp fell from me, followed by, "I lied to Father Carey in my first confession." The release I felt from saying this aloud was cathartic, and I continued, "I even stole a Black-Jack to get a real sin, but when Father Carey asked me for another one, I told him I swore at Mam, which is a massive lie...."

...I abruptly stopped when I saw Maria's shoulders gently heave, "Why are you laughing?" I asked, confused by her reaction to me confessing my crime and sinful lie.

But her laughter escalated until she too was crying – a sopping, snotty guffawing. Eventually, her mirth subsided, and she wiped her nose with the back of her hand.

"Why is that funny?" I asked, confused.

She mopped the mirth from her eyes with her hands, "We all tell fibs in confession, especially when we're too young to have real sins – I'm laughing at you robbing a toffee to get a sin." She looked up, "And you know what, I bet you gave God a good giggle, too," she said, standing up.

Maria took my hand, *"Come on, let's go for a walk and talk,"* she *said, guiding me further into the vivid green of the meadow.*

Chapter 31: The talk

Maria's reaction to my first confession was revelatory to me. And as we walked, I talked further of my fear of God's retribution for my confessional sin. Yet I was mindful of my boundaries; I couldn't go near my thoughts on her potential possession.

I listened intently to Maria's words as we walked Cavan's sun-soaked hills and valleys. "You know what, Gerard, God's good. We shouldn't be scared of someone who's good. That's why I don't get the God they teach us about in school."

She stopped to pluck a daisy, placing it behind her ear, "Does this look nice?" she asked, using her hair to secure the flower.

"Yes, I like it."

Brow furrowed, she continued, "It makes me sad to think of you fretting about something bad happening as punishment for doing something silly. It's all so wrong what they tell us, and the real God knows it is." She spoke with an authority that enlightened me, and I felt myself lighten.

But only a little, because as I spilled some fears to Maria, I remained reserved about revealing too much of myself. So, when I felt she was veering too close to self-expression from me, I steered us away from me and towards others. "You know what, I know they're all scared of God because I heard this woman in Connelly Brothers whispering to the shopkeeper about the Pope telling, 'the third secret.' And she seemed really scared about it; then I saw her praying the Rosary with

Milly and a man at the Cathedral after mass – do you know what that secret is?" I asked.

She thought for a moment, "Ah, you know what, it's probably to do with that apparition of Our Lady in Fatima when she appeared to them three kids."

"What does a partition mean?" I asked.
Maria chuckled, "Apparition. It means Our Lady appeared to three children in Fatima and gave them messages, secrets about what's going to happen in the future."

I felt my skin prickle as Maria proceeded to give me further insight into the secrets that had so troubled me. "Sister Mary at school told us about how the Pope let the third secret slip. She was right scared about it."

I gripped her hand, "What is the third secret?"

"I don't know, Sister Mary didn't know, didn't even know what the first two were," she said, her answer taking the edge off my excitement.

But still, I felt more enlightened. I'd thought The Rosary Praying Trio I called The Guardians of The Congregation were key players in my dark narrative. Now I knew their prayers were for secrets unrelated to my story; it made me relax some more. I had misread their intentions just as I had the Penman's – I was now getting answers.

There was one more thing I needed to know, the big one, and while we continued our journey to nowhere, Maria brought him up. "Have you any idea who the ghost is, the tall-man?"

Although I thought he was the demon that possessed Maria, I still

211

didn't know who he was.

I sighed, "No." Then I tugged her hand to stop, "But I know he's not 'fierce' like the boy with Bruce Lee hair said he was."

Maria looked intrigued, "You've said that before. When did he tell you that?"

"When I met you both that day in the farmyard, I asked him if he knew who the tall-man was, and he said, "*No, but I know he's a fierce tall fella,*" I explained.

Maria chuckled and resumed our walk, "He didn't mean he's *fierce* (her voice deepened as she said the word). He means he's very tall; you know how in Ireland they use some words different to us."

I matched her chuckle, "Like how Granny calls shopping, messages?"

"Yes, by fierce tall he meant, very tall." She smiled at me, "It's so sweet how they do that, isn't it?"

"I don't think it's sweet. It muddles me up, like when Town Granny asked me if I wanted a mineral, and I didn't know what she meant."

Maria nodded in agreement, "I know what you mean. I didn't know a mineral was pop when I was your age, either – I still think it's dead good the way they use some words, though."

When we reached a valley, we sat down. Maria pulled a clump of grass, then opened her fingers to let the fronds fall through, "Have you any idea who the tall-man could be?"

She continued her grass pulling routine while I wondered, "Take your time, think about it," she said.

Watching the fronds of grass tumble through Maria's fingers, thoughts tumbled through my mind, and I said them aloud, "I've got no idea who he is, but I know what's up with him. He's lost, and he's looking for something; he doesn't like himself because something's wrong with him, and that's why he's not got into heaven yet."

Maria paused her grass pulling, "Orr, he sounds dead sad and lonely – what's wrong with him that he can't get into heaven?"

I tilted my head, "I don't know."

Maria matched my head tilt, "What do you think's wrong with him?"
I head-swivelled, "Don't know."

Maria pondered, "Well, you can't *not* get into heaven because something's wrong with you; God's not that mean."

Then to my shock, I realised I was possibly talking about myself, so I was happy when a thought popped into my head, diverting me from any self-revelation.

My back stiffened, and I sat upright, "Do you know what, I think I've got an idea who the tall-man might be." I said, excited by the idea that was gradually presenting itself to me.

Maria sat up with me, "Come on then, tell me." Her excitement matching mine.

My words flowed, "Right, I think I've got it – the woman talking in the shop about secrets put me off a bit because I made up in my head what the secret might be. But she was talking about the partition in

Fatima, about Our Lady appearing to them kids." I paused to collect my thoughts before continuing,

"So right; Dad was a kid when he saw the tall-man." I focussed intently on Maria for my big reveal, "So, I think the tall-man was Jesus who was doing a partition to Dad." I held out my hands to invite Maria's reaction to what I considered a brilliant theory.

She stared at me, slightly open-mouthed. I stared back – waiting for her to remark on the genius of my thinking. But, she burst out laughing.

My disappointment in her reaction made my hand tap her knee defensively. "Don't be horrible, you; it's not that stupid. If Mary can appear to kids, so can Jesus – and Dad's so good it makes sense Jesus would want to meet him," I reasoned.

"You're dead right about Dad being good, but I honestly don't think Jesus appeared to him – Dad would've told us if he thought he saw Jesus, but he told us it was definitely a ghost."

She stood up and took my hand, "I think you have to keep looking." Pulling me to my feet, she said, "You'll find him; eventually, it'll just take time." She led me up the hill and out of the meadow.

……

Ambling silently along quiet country roads, a familiar tightness took root in the pit of my tummy; time was something I didn't have a great deal of. The summer was moving on, and soon Mam and Dad would be over for our final week. I really wanted to discover the identity of the tall-man to make Dad proud of me.

With Maria finally free of her possessor, a renewed determination to discover the tall-man's identity grew within me.

......

That night, Dermot's bandaged foot rested by my head, filling my nostrils with its antiseptic smell as we lay head to toe in the narrow bed we shared. His breathing matched my uncles, all three of them sleeping in sound harmony.

I lay wide awake, my whirring mind denying me sleep. I reflected on the day's revelations. What really buoyed me was Maria's idea of God. It tempered my fear of him and made me question the perception the Priests had given me of him. I thought how I'd initially thought the tall-man was the Devil possessing my sister, and how that led me to think he could be Jesus appearing to Dad.

Despite Maria's laughing dismissal of my theory, I still felt it had credibility. And this thought led my leg to leave the bed and my foot to touch the floor.

Deftly I crept downstairs and out into the blackness of the night. Being bare-footed, I turned to go back for my wellies, but I didn't. I liked feeling the ground beneath my feet; it guided me. I walked the warm concrete, using the wall of the house to guide me.

When I reached the end of the wall, my feet felt the prickle of parched grass and dry, thirsty earth beneath. The only noise was the soft trickle of the stream, and I followed its sound.

I held my arms out, and when they found the gnarled wooden bannister, I guided myself down onto the top step that led to the stream. I sat and looked up at the inky black sky with its immense expanse of twinkling stars. I began to talk in a low whisper, *"Jesus, are you here?"*

Chapter 32: Jesus

Now, Despite Milly telling me I was special, I knew I wasn't special enough for Jesus to talk to me. No, I had to look for his answer. So, I looked skywards for a sign in the stars.

There were millions, but I focussed on one that moved. My stare was intense, and when it blinked at me, I jumped up, "Is that a yes, Jesus?'

The blink turned into a flurry of flashes that, to me, said, "Yes. Yes. Yes!"

I jumped up, energised by this positive response, "Are you the tall-man? Did you do a partition to Dad when he was my age?"

My heart swelled with hope as my head strained backwards, awaiting his response in the stars.

But the star's flourish returned to a slow blink until it ebbed and flowed away from the night-time sky. I lowered my head and whispered, "That's a no, then."

I sat on the stone step, sinking into its mossy cushion. The only sound was a soft swash of the stream as it flowed toward the rush of the clear lagoon. Its swooshing melody soothed me, a cloak of calm enveloped me, and I felt a physical warmth.

"Tell me about the ghost, Dad," I whispered. My words carried on the stream, transporting me back to a dusky evening in Manchester. Dad had finished his evening meal and was enjoying his cup of tea when I asked him the question for the umpteenth time.

He lifted his cup, then put it down as though interrupted by a thought, "I've told you about him several times," he said, disappointing me.

"Tell me again, please."

"Will I tell you something about him I've never told you before?"

My heart raced, "Are you going to tell me who he is?"

"No, I don't know who he is."

Eager to hear more, I said, "Go on, tell me something new about him." I crossed my legs on the chair, ready to hear a new aspect of Dad's ghost story.

He took a swig of tea, "I was never afraid of him when I saw him. He never put a fear in me."

My legs flew from the chair, "You saw him more than once?" I asked, astonished by this new revelation.

"Indeed, I did. On cold nights his shadow followed me round the farm while I swept the square and closed up the buildings; I'd talk to him so I would."

"Did he talk back?" I asked, intrigued.

"Not at all, sher, that's why he was good company for a wee lad like me-self, he listened."

"What did you talk to him about."

"Ahh, anything and everything."

I wanted to push him further about his relationship with tall-man, but Dad drained his cup and stood up, "Don't you be afraid of ghosts, and don't you ever be afraid to talk to Mammy or me, do you hear me?" When I nodded a yes, Dad said, "Good lad," and left the kitchen, leaving me wondering what he meant.

......

A splash from the stream took me back to my present. Tadpoles on the cusp of transition sprung through the stream's surface for gulps of air; the sight of them mesmerised me.

These tiny creatures fascinated me. They intrigued me with their ability to change from one thing to another. I slid further down and leaned in; my head created a black reflection in the stream, stopping the froglets from doing their breath jumps. I leaned back to allow them to resume their jumping gasps.

Change – it marked my summer. Even though I knew my sister was no longer possessed, I was in no doubt Maria had changed. But unlike the tadpoles, her change wasn't physical; it was a transition I couldn't see nor fathom.

I edged back up a step, put my elbows on my knees, rested my head in my hands and sighed. My sigh sounded loud in the night silence, and I looked back to make sure I'd not woken anyone in the house.

I hadn't, so I spoke quietly, "It wasn't that loud. Stop being silly," I whispered, admonishing myself. Silly – the word spoke to me. Of course, Maria was right; the tall-man wasn't Jesus, such a childish thing to think.

That thought gave me insight into an aspect of Maria's change. I was still childish; she wasn't. She knew for sure Jesus hadn't appeared to Dad, and her knowing talk of God seemed to come from a grown-up rather than Maria, who still wasn't grown-up.

Feeling deflated, I stood, looked to the sky and spoke to Jesus, "Sorry for thinking you did a partition to Dad, I was being silly," I whispered.

When the twinkling stars combined with Maria's insights, I felt lifted. I realised Jesus wouldn't judge me. There'd be no retribution, no punishment; I need not cause myself pain for my silliness. I smiled, and my inner voice spoke with an encouraging tone, 'Whatever Maria's change is, Gerard, I think it might be a good thing.'

I quietly sauntered across the crunchy grass onto the warm concrete and slipped quietly back into The House in The Hollow.
......

My stealth was so adept, I slipped back into bed without stirring a soul. I lay next to my brother, his sleeping breaths in sync with my uncles.

And although I was with company, I was still alone with my quandaries and questions.

Yet, I was comforted by my new relationship with Jesus and felt a new motivation to find answers. And with my head resting on the pillow, I felt myself sail into something rare – an unencumbered, replenishing sleep.

......

Chatter from downstairs woke me. I lifted my head, ruffled my hair, and listened. It was Maria and Dermot, talking excitedly about the day ahead. I dressed quickly, not wanting to miss their chatter.

My arrival diverted them from their talk. "Here's sleepy head, you know what our kid, you'd sleep for England and Ireland you would," said Dermot, buttering a slice of soda bread.

I didn't answer because Maria's appearance rendered me speechless. She'd literally changed overnight – from pretty to beautiful.

Her hair was sleek, with a shine I'd never previously noticed. Her eyelids were swathed in a shade of delicate green, and her lashes fluttered long and black while her lips glistened with a pink gloss.

Maria touched her face, "What you staring at?"

"You."

"Why?" she asked, worry clouding her face.

"You look dead different," I said.

She thrust a hand through her newly glossed hair, "Different good or different bad?"

I smiled, "Dead good, you look really nice."

She smiled, "Orr, thanks, Gerard, you know I value your opinion."

Dermot chipped in, his words muffled by mouthfuls of bread, "Eh, I said you looked a bit of alright, don't my opinion count?"

She laughed, "Course it does," she said, standing up. That's when I noticed she was wearing the dress, the one she'd displayed in Betty Hickey's shop, the miniature wedding dress.

I couldn't take my eyes off her – she reminded me of a bride, a beautiful modern-day bride.

She walked past me, and only when her hand reached the door handle did I find words, "Where are you going?" I asked.

"For a walk."

"Right," I said, frustrated by my one-word answer.

Maria smiled, left without a goodbye. And now, I knew I had to let her go without further question.

Dermot slurped his tea, "She fancies that lad who works on the farm," he said, draining his cup.

"I know."

"How'd you know?"

"She told me."

"Blimey, she tells you more than me then."

"If she didn't tell you, how'd you know she fancies him?" I asked.

"She goes dead daft around him, and she spent ages doing herself up this morning. It's dead obvious, our kid," he said, grabbing his crutches.

I raised my voice, "Where are you going?"

He leapt to the door in one swoop, "Out."

"NO! You're supposed to be resting your heel, the nurse said so," I implored.

He flicked open the door, "Stop being a soft-arse, me heel will be alright," he said, the door banging behind him.

......

I stood in the centre of the room, listening to the clattering of pots and pans as Granny cleaned the breakfast utensils to make way for dinner preparations.

Not wanting to disturb her, I tip-toed to the table and took a piece of currant soda bread. I looked at the picture of Jesus, smiled at him, and left the house.

I munched my breakfast, ambling aimlessly down the road.

Chapter 33: Amble

I ambled off-road into a field that led nowhere I knew of – unchartered territory. Walking its green pasture, a weight lifted. The burden on my shoulders lightened a little. It didn't lift entirely, but enough to ease my previous pressures.

Thoughts of Maria's possession by a demon seemed less likely, and I deduced Dermot's accident was most probably that, not some retribution for my confessional mishap.

At the peak of this new pasture, I sat cross-legged and looked out over the undulating hills and valleys. The morning was still and warm, the sun hidden behind a hazy grey, but for me, it was the most beautiful day.

I'd grown a little, not in stature, but in myself. Maria's talk had somehow freed me from the torment of my tumultuous mind.

I was a boy, a child still, but sitting on that hill, I was growing up. My legs instinctively unfurled, and I lay back, threw my arms out and stretched all four limbs, letting out that expulsive sound of new-day rejuvenation.

Sitting back up, a thought struck me; I missed my sister Maria, yet at this moment, I didn't yearn for her. She'd moved away from me, I was losing her, but I hoped she'd come back to me – one day.

I suspected when that day arrived, our worlds would be different. But whereas previously I'd have fretted about that change, now I didn't.

It was a weight I wouldn't lift, not on this day.

I lay on the pasture and fell into a peaceful slumber.

......

The sun woke me; it burst through the grey onto a canvas of vivid blue; scorching my face.

Leaping up, I felt energised and wanted to talk with someone. And my newfound liberation drove me not toward Maria but forward to my favourite new friend.

I raced down the pasture, my stumbles turning into effortless forward rolls as I tumbled towards sweet apples plucked from trees, a grass-covered donkey, and insights picked from a brain I now treasured – my old friend, Johnnie.

And I knew what I wanted to talk to him about – sisters.

I hoped he had another letter from his sister, Evelyn, for me to read aloud to him, which would give me a reason to ask about this brotherly-sisterly thing that connected us both.

......

Wanting to avoid passing Auntie Margaret and her intrusive need for news, I followed my instincts and took a route over the fields I felt would lead me there.

As I continued on, the terrain remained unfamiliar, and I considered returning via familiar fields. But I became aware of my senses, or at least one – smell. The acrid smell of old smoke filled my nostrils, and like a dog, I followed the familiar scent of my friend, Johnnie.

The smell led me into woodland, which became ever denser as the smoke odour intensified. Suspecting I was on the right track, I carried on. I'd become expert at battling bramble and thorns and was able to navigate their skin-tearing tangle with only the odd scratch.

My eye was caught by a blackened plume snaking up into the blue sky. I smiled, "Well done, Gerard, you found Johnnie's place," I said to myself, proud of my orienteering skills.

Ahead, I saw what looked like a clearing and made slowly towards it, the acrid smoke stinging my eyes.

And then, right before me, was a house that stopped me and made me instinctively mouth the word, "WOW!"

It looked like the fictional haunted houses familiar to me from films and comics, and now I was standing in front of a real-life-one – fact. It didn't frighten me; it fascinated me.

I stared at what was once a fine house, but time had blackened its walls. Through cracks, great swathes of ivy snaked over every surface, slithering into every nook and cranny, threatening to consume the house entirely. There was a sentry-like doorway with a heavy wooden door that carried a rusted circular knocker. Four sash windows below and five above were completely black, like intentionally painted blackouts.

It dawned on me that maybe this wasn't Johnnie's, as clearly this house and its overgrown space hadn't been inhabited for years. Yet the smoke told me otherwise – it plumed from the chimney. Somebody lived here, was here; and I turned to go back lest I'd stumbled upon and was trespassing on a stranger's homestead. But while readying for the first barrage of barbed-brambles, a sound stopped me, "Hee-haw." The donkey's call.

"Johnnie's donkey"? I asked myself. The odds were, it was – so I turned back.

Tentatively, I walked towards the gable of the house, stopped, and listened. All was quiet save for the birdsong. I couldn't rudely walk around the back, so I took a deep breath and said, "Johnnie, are you there? Can I come around?"

His response was swift, "Ah young Smith, tis you, where are yee?"

I smiled and walked around, "I'm here."

Johnnie sat on a rickety three-legged stool, milking a cow. He turned to me while continuing to pull and squeeze the cow's teats, "Yee came to visit me?"

"Yes, is that alright? I can go if you want?"

Slowly he stood up, his bones audibly cracking and creaking, "Tis a sad man who'd refuse a-bit-a-company," he said, lifting the bucket, and shuffling forward.

"Come on in, and I'll make some tae," he said, ushering me to follow him. The back door was little more than a rotting gate, and a little piece from the bottom broke off as he pushed it open.

My heart began to jog a little with the apprehension of going inside, but I carried on, regardless. I stepped into pitch blackness, "Johnnie, where are you? I can't see anything?" I said, not panicked, more confused.

I heard him fumbling in the dark, "Hold on now, don't be freckened; we'll have her lit in no time." There was a rattle and rip as a match burst into flame and hovered over a single candle, "Now there we have it, light."

The candlelight shone bright, illuminating the tiny space in which Johnnie lived. Weeds and grass grew up through the cracked concrete floor; hordes of newspapers piled up and down like enormous stalactites and stalagmites in an ancient cave; a metal kettle rested on dying embers in a recess, and in the middle of the room, a tiny wooden table on which sat: tin mugs, a chipped jug, bent cutlery, and a single bag of sugar – I'd never seen a dwelling like this in my life.

I looked around, searching for signs of home-comforts in the corners that the candlelight couldn't reach. But I saw no shapes that would suggest couches nor armchairs on which to slouch after a long day. Johnnie kicked the embers with his boot, which stoked up the flames, "Sit down," he said, picking up the kettle and shaking it.

"Where?" I asked, seeing only one wooden chair.

"On the chair," he said.

"Where will you sit?"

He made for the door, "Ah, you can see I'm not used to much company, I'll sit on me milking stool."

Alone, I became aware of the odour, a smell of concentrated burning so strong that it smelt like I was in the aftermath of a forest fire. I moved to the chair that wobbled precariously when I sat on it. All my senses were engaged with a heightened wonderment about how a human being could live like this. Yet, I had no feeling of judgement. I wasn't blaming Johnnie for living amongst decay and detritus; instead, I wondered – why?

'Why does Johnnie live like this?' I asked myself. It was obviously his choice; he could clean the house up, throw out the papers and other rubbish, fill in the cracks, paint the walls – yet he chose not to.

I knew it was a question I mustn't ask Johnnie, so when he returned, I jumped from the chair, "You sit here, I'll sit on the stool," I said.

"Not at all, you're the guest. It's only right you have the good chair," he said, returning to the kettle.

He touched the kettle, "Ah, she's ready enough." He picked up a mug, peered into it and slopped its contents onto the floor before repeating the process with a second mug.

Above the recess was a mantlepiece from which Johnnie took a small pan, it was buckled, and its handle wobbled when he put it on the table. Next, he took a box from the mantlepiece, stuck in his hand, and threw tea leaves into the pan before picking up the kettle and pouring water into it. Without thinking, I asked, "Haven't you got a tea-pot?"

His hand shifted amongst the cutlery, and finding an old bent spoon, he stirred the pan, "That's me tea-pot," he said.

He continued to stir the small pan while making a series of high-pitched whistles. I sat and said nothing while he poured the tea into two tin mugs, pushing one to me. He continued to whistle, scooping huge mounds of sugar into his mug. Taking another mug, he scooped milk from the bucket by his side and poured some into his mug, all the time whistling. He handed the spoon to me, which I took, sprinkling a spoonful into my cup and stirring. Johnnie looked aghast, "Is that all the sugar you're taking?"

I nodded, "Yeah, I take one," I said.

He stirred his own, which now resembled syrup, "Sher that'll not sweeten it," he took another spoon and heaped my mug with sugar, "There you have it, that's a good mug-a-tae," he said, resuming his whistle.

His whistle stopped, and Johnnie looked up, "Ah, here he is, come on in," he said, looking toward the door. My head shot around, but nobody came in. Instead, I felt a tickling sensation up my leg. Turning back, Johnnie spooned a heap of sugar into the middle of the table, "There yee are wee man, enjoy that." I jolted; it was a mouse – a fat mouse.

I couldn't look at the mouse, my focus was on Johnnie. He grinned a wide toothless smile as he looked lovingly at the sugar-plump creature gorging itself on even more sucrose. Eventually, he reached his finger towards the animal, "That's enough now; it's fatter yer getting," he said, pushing the mouse away. The mouse wobbled rather than scurried away, and to my horror, Johnnie scooped up the remaining sugar and put it back into the bag.

I couldn't drink tea containing mouse-spit sugar, and with Johnnie distracted by his fat friend's departure, I discreetly poured the liquid onto the floor underneath the table.

He looked back to me, took a slug of his tea, and said, "He's great company, he'd talk to yer if he could."

A wave of sadness washed over me at the thought of an old man having a mouse for a friend.

Johnnie cradled the tin mug and took sips from the syrupy liquid with lip-smacking relish.

My curiosity got the better of me, and I asked, "Is your bedroom upstairs?"

He took another sip, "This is my bedroom."

I looked around, wondering how I'd missed it, "Where's your bed?"

He stared into his mug, "It's wherever I lay my head."

I was on a roll and couldn't help myself wanting to know more, "But this house is massive, I saw the front, it's got front rooms and an upstairs and everything."

He put his mug down, "This room does me grand; the house is too big for one man."

His demeanour became mournful, and he pointed to a place in the darkness, "I haven't been through there since Evelyn left."

Following his point, I made out the shape of a frame, "Is that a door?" I asked, straining to look.

"It is, a locked door; sher, I wouldn't know where the key is, or any of the keys, they're all long lost somewhere."

His toothless smile returned, "Will I show you something?" I sat up, hoping he would show me into the main part of the house, which I was dying to see. But he put his hand inside his jacket, "Didn't I get another letter from Evelyn."

He handed it to me, "Will yer read it out to me?" he asked, his hand shaking with what I took to be excitement.

"Course I will." I took my time to decipher the words before I began – *'Dear Johnnie, How are you? We are both well. We had no summer weather, only the heatwave. How are Jim and Margaret? Tell them I was asking for them. You have an envelope. Do write soon.*
All the best, Evelyn.'

I was struck by how short it was, the content basic with no real expression of love. But when I looked at Johnnie, he obviously loved every word; he was grinning from ear to ear. He thrust his hand back inside his jacket and produced an envelope, "Look, do yer see this, didn't she send it over to me so I can write back to her, she wants to hear from me, so she does," he said, gleefully.

I handed him the letter back, "You can tell her that my Auntie Margaret and Uncle Jim are both alright," I said.

He took the letter and put it safely back, "I will surely," he said.

In truth, I was disappointed in Johnnie's second letter. I found it emotionally cold, and it gave me nothing with which to connect with Maria. So, I decided to return to my quest and asked, *"Johnnie, do you believe in ghosts?"*

Chapter 34: Ghosts

Johnnie raised an eye, "Who doesn't believe in ghosts?" he asked.

My interest piqued, "Some kids in my school don't."

Johnnie drained his syrupy tin mug, "They'd be freckened childer, is all." he said.

"Do you think they're lying?" I asked.

Johnnie stared past me, "There's no harm to be had in a ghost."

Ignoring that he'd not answered my question, I asked another, "Have you ever seen a ghost?"

"I haven't, but I've felt many."

"What, like you've touched ghosts?"

He chuckled, "Not at all; I'd feel them like you'd know they were there in the room with yer." He pointed to the door, "That's why I do never open that door, too many ghosts are in them rooms. I feel safer here," he said.

Confused, I asked, "You said there's no harm in ghosts, what are you safe from then?"

He paused, looked around the small cave-like space and said, "The years gone by, they do give me the lonesome."

"What does that mean?"

He lowered his head, "I don't know meself, all I know is I don't get the lonesome here, so I'm happy enough." He lifted his head and took up the pot, "Here, have another drop."

"NO!" I shouted, shooting my hand up. Johnnie jolted, "You're a flittery wee fella. I've never met the likes of yer," he said, with a toothless grin.

Immediately I regretted my reaction and lowered my voice, "Sorry."

He poured himself another mug and heaped in the sugar.

Wanting to keep the talk of ghosts alive, I continued, "The College Farmyard's haunted; my dad used to see a ghost there when he was my age." I sat back, waiting for his reaction.

He stirred his syrup and pondered, "I'd say there's many a ghost up there, alright," he said, taking a slurp.

"Why?" I asked. My anticipation of having some kind of tall-man insight made my heart race a little.

I studied his face; he lifted an eye, "The big school must be near a hundred years old, that's a long time gone by." I waited for him to say more, but instead, he took another slurp, so I jumped back in, "What do you mean by that?"

He settled his mug down, "The longer the past, the more there's ghosts."

I changed my angle, "My dad said the ghost followed him around the farmyard." At this, Johnnie nodded his head with what looked like knowing.

"Do you know who it was?" I asked, certain I was on the cusp of some revelatory route to the tall-man's identity.

"I'd say it'd be one of the long-gone Bishops or Priests, looking for boys stealing the apples to give them the fright," he said.

I deflated and disagreed, "Dad wasn't stealing apples; he was working, sweeping up and stuff."

Johnnie drained his mug and licked his lips, "Then that ghost liked spending time with a good gossun, so," he said, with an affirmative nod.

'Gossun' I knew that word. Dad often used it with me, like when I'd give him the newspaper from the shop, he'd take it and say, "Good gossun."

Johnnie's use of it made sense, and I smiled, "Dad called the ghost, tall-man. Do you know any dead Bishops or Priests that were tall?"

My question made Johnnie laugh and spittle, "Sher holy-men come in all shapes and sizes, I wouldn't know the heights of ones past."

Despite the fact I didn't have an answer, I felt I had information that could lead me to identify the tall-man. And sitting at the rickety table with Johnnie, my mind began to turn and think how I could best use this intelligence.

"Heat," said Johnnie. His voice pulled me from my thinking, "What?" I asked.

He patted the lapel of his aged jacket, "The heat," he said.

"What about it?"

When he smiled, I was struck by something; he still had a nice smile even though he had no teeth.

"Evelyn, she never liked the heat," he said. I realised then he was referring to her letter. He continued talking through his toothless smile, "She'd hide away from a hot day." He nodded towards the beam of sunshine streaming through the rotting back door, "She'd not like that day one bit." He pointed upwards, "She'd be in the room above with the drapes closed and her nose stuck in a book."

I followed his finger upwards, my eyes halting at the low ceiling. I wanted to be up there, exploring the rooms beyond the hovel in which I sat, and feel the ghosts that Johnnie spoke of.

I scanned the space, "What room of the house is this?" I asked.

Johnnie, his hand still on his lapel, answered, "Mammy washed the spuds, vegetables, clothes, pots in here, it was mammy's wee room; that's why I do like being here, this is all the house I need."

His left hand fished in his lapel pocket, and he pulled out a folded piece of paper. His right hand slipped into his jacket pocket, and he took out a pencil that was paired down to a mere stub, "I must write back to her, or she'll be vexed with me. I'll do that today."

"What will you say?" I asked, immediately regretting my intrusive question.

"I'll have a walk over the fields with the donkey and have a think about that," he said, putting the pencil stub back in his lapel pocket.

Feeling it was time to go, I stood up, feeling a familiar jab to my inner thigh, "Johnnie, your pencil's nearly finished, do you have a pen?" I asked.

He swivelled his head, "Ah now gossun, I'll not be writing much now, I'll get another letter out of that stub yet."

I pulled out penman's pen and handed it to him, "Here, have this, you'll get loads and loads of letters from it," I said, happy to hand over the pen.

Johnnie took it from me, holding it close to his eyes. I watched his face curl and crumple with a whole range of emotions as he delighted in the pen, "It has a boat in it," he said.

"Tip it up," I said.

Johnnie slowly tilted the pen; his eyes widened at the sight of the boat moving forward, "Jeepers, would you look at that? It's sailing." He continued to swivel the pen, laughing like an amused child.

I enjoyed seeing him happy, "You can keep it."

He looked at me, "Not at all, I'll give it back to yer before ya go back over the water."

"No, you can have it. I can buy another one on the boat home."

He looked at me quizzically, "Who sells these things on a boat?" he asked.
I smiled, "They sell them in the shop."

He tilted his head, "They've a shop on a boat?"

I nodded, "Yep, and pubs, restaurants, slot machines, and loads of bedrooms."

He stared back at the pen, "Isn't that a holy terror."

'Holy-terror.' By now, I'd learned enough of the Irish lingo to know what Johnnie meant was, 'Isn't that amazing.'

"Have you never been on a boat, Johnnie?" I asked.

"Not at all, and you wouldn't get me on one either." This was Johnnie's world, and he wasn't going to leave it. And I found warmth in that thought; looking around his dark and tiny place, I felt the same sense of safe I found when I'd cocoon in small spaces.

I pulled myself from those thoughts and sidled towards the door, "I'm going now Johnnie."

He looked over at me, "Will you call again?" He asked, with a tone that carried a little yearning.

Feeling like I was the grown-up and Johnnie the child, I reassured him, "Course I will."

He held up the pen, "You can show me how to use this contraption," he tapped his lapel, "I'll use the tool I'm used to, to write to Evelyn."

At the door, I stopped and stared at a sight that belonged in my Eerie Comic. The candlelight bathed Johnnie's face in its glow while his body disappeared into the darkness. From my short distance at the door, his face looked like it was disembodied, flickering, and floating in the dark – *like a ghost.*

Chapter 35: Tall men

I was happy to have passed on penman's pen, from one kind man to another – a winning relay. The joy it had given Johnnie cancelled out the pain it had given me. I wandered back into the woods with a spring in my step.

The tree foliage above gently shimmied in a light breeze, and needing shelter from the hot sun, I welcomed its parasol. Sitting on the crunchy ground, Johnnie's voice returned to me, "Heat," he said. I smiled as I realised I had the same aversion to heat as his sister, Evelyn. While she hid from it in her room with a book, I hid from it in the woods, with my thoughts.

As they ebbed and flowed through my head, I tried to read them. But like the pages of a book blowing in the breeze, I couldn't focus on anything to catch a coherent narrative.

But one thought from Johnnie fluttered and caught in my breezy mind, "The longer the past, the more there's ghosts."

I wasn't cold, yet I shivered and stood up to shake away the shiver. Johnnie's house returned to me, and I saw its aged walls clearly. It was ancient, from a distant past. The walls dissolved, and I was back in that little room looking at Johnnie's smiling face floating in the darkness. The image of his face vanished, and I looked at him on the first day I met him in the orchard. He stood next to an apple tree, and though he was old, he wasn't stooped. No, he stood erect and straight as he plucked an apple with ease from a tall branch.

To give credence to the thought tumbling over my head, I articulated it aloud by asking the trees surrounding me, "Is Johnnie a ghost? Is he the tall-man?"

They answered with a collective rustle, a sigh that said nothing. I stared in the direction of Johnnie's old house and answered my own question, "I think he is – I honestly believe the tall-man's visited me the way he did Dad."

......

I'd wanted to keep my friendship with Johnnie secret, but now I had a desire to talk to Maria about him. Knowing I couldn't, I ran through the woods to escape the mournful thoughts that were beginning to creep up on me.

Such was my rush; I was careless with the barbed bramble and acquired some nasty scratches. When I saw the clearing that led onto the lane, I slowed and let the sadness catch me.

Grabbing a bunch of leaves, I attended to my scratches. When I looked back up, I saw the man-in-makeup pushing his pram with his sisterly friends walking towards me – The Three Wise Women. The sight of them salved my sadness, for I really liked these people; I felt at ease with them. And when they neared, their waves and wide smiles told me they felt the same about me.

"And where've you been galivanting?" asked the man-in-makeup.

I didn't know what he meant, but I knew I now had someone to talk to, "I was visiting my friend, Johnnie."

One of his sisters nodded down at me, "You've the wee legs nearly torn off yer, you need to be careful coming through them woods, there's thorns that could open a vein if one caught yer," she said.

Her words were delivered with such care that I felt the need to reassure her, "I will, I promise," I said, pushing the thought of marauding thorns slicing my throat to the back of my crowded head.

She nodded, "Good Gossun."

I noticed the man-in-makeup wasn't wearing as much makeup, "Mind yourself," he said, pushing his empty pram forward.

"Wait a minute!" I said, my voice raised.

"What for?" he asked. All three of them looked at me quizzically, and I felt the familiar self-conscious flame heat my face.

"Nothing, sorry," I said, lowering my reddening head.

"No, what do you want us waiting for?" he asked, with his eyebrows raised.

I lifted my head and forced out the question, "Do you know Johnnie, the old man with the donkey?"

They glanced at each other with interest; Makeup-Man answering, "We do see him sometimes and say hello, but we know nothing of him – is there something we should know?"

I shrugged, "No, that's it, that's all I wanted to know." There was disappointment in his smile, "And I thought you had some scandal for us." The three turned in unison towards the dump – true friends on the way to their treasure trove.

Turning to walk away, I stopped and looked back, lingering to look at the three of them as they dwindled in the distance. Under the high sun, their figures shimmered. And in this celestial like haze, I noticed the man in the middle's height – Makeup-Man towered tall amidst his sisterly friends.

Only when they disappeared into the distance did I turn and dawdle away with Makeup-Man's tall image still shimmering in my mind – *like a ghost.*

......

Berries grew abundantly on the hedges that surrounded me; I paused and plucked one. Not knowing what kind of berry it was, I popped it in my mouth, wincing at its initial bitterness, which gave way to sweetness. I pulled more and sat by the lane-side to enjoy mother nature's pre-prepared lunch.

The heat of the sun on the back of my neck brought me back to Evelyn's letter, 'We had no summer, only the heatwave,' she'd written. Her reference to the summer in the past tense made me sit up. Such was the tumult of my time in Ireland that I'd lost all concept of time. Was summer nearing its end and my return to Manchester imminent?

All thoughts of Johnnie being a ghost and the tall-man fell from me, replaced with a sense of loss. I'd lost my summer to demons and darkness. But above all, reality hit me – I'd lost Maria.

My sister had left me for another life. A life of 'fancies,' where Dermot said you act "dead daft" around lads. A life I didn't understand because it was so far away from me – and I couldn't catch up.

The weight of sadness leaned on me; I began walking to shake it off. But sad followed me to a stream where I gave into it, allowing it to push me down.

I watched Minnows being swept along in its gentle current; their presence made me acutely aware of an absence – there were no tadpoles.

No, they'd changed and hopped away from the stream to live in another land. Like my sister, Maria.

......

Above me, clouds sailed by like great galleons in a blue ocean. Alone in a field watching the sky, I felt secure and safe from sadness. And once again, Johnnie's words spoke to me, "I don't get the lonesome here, so I'm happy enough."

I understood him now. I felt safe and happy being alone.
I wasn't lonely. I felt comfortable, wrapped in alone's cloak.
Away from the world and all its chaos.
Chaos, I created myself with my fretting.
If I didn't see Maria, then I didn't have to deal with the ache her change gave me.
If I didn't see Dermot's high-energy jumps and tumbles, then I didn't have to worry about him damaging his heel further.
Alone in a field, I wouldn't feel the shame of a stranger's judgement.
Staring at clouds, my mind wouldn't make up catastrophic situations from adult whisperings.
Lying on warm grass, I didn't have the tormenting questions about St Phelim and St Patrick that I had when sitting in their Cathedral's pew.
Looking at the sky, I wouldn't feel the searing pain of 'goodbyes.'
Alone in this field, I had no Devil to deal with.
No God to kneel for.
No Priests to be fearful of.
No sins to collect and confess.

No inner voices to goad me.

No awkwardness to heat my face.

Instead, I had calm and clarity.

And in the freedom of alone, I said to the sky, "Johnnie's not a ghost. He's me when I'm old."

Right then, I wanted to be Johnnie.

But a boy version of him – alone, yet safe from, *"The lonesome."*

Chapter 36: All alone

I had a long wait to have what Johnnie had, the safe lonesome I coveted. I longed for adulthood, to be free of childhood with all its unknowing constraints.

A thought hit me with an almost physical slap, and I stood up. Boyhood didn't suit me; I didn't know how to wear it. I checked myself over and saw my shorts were too long; I pulled at my t-shirt, which was a little too small. I hitched up my socks and realised I did this constantly as they were a shoe size too big. My clothes never fit me properly.

My clothes were like me – ill-fitting.
Not only did boyhood not suit me, but it also didn't fit me.
I didn't fit in with the boys at school. I fitted in with Johnnie, Betty Hickey from the sweetshop, and the man-in-makeup with his sisters.
I yearned for adulthood, so I could finally find my fit.

Realising I was beginning to pull myself into the darkness of self-dislike, I ran down the hill to distance myself from the debilitating feelings.

......

At the bottom of the hill, I collapsed in a heap of breaths. My sprint had helped because as my breathing resumed to normal, I felt a semblance of whatever normal was. Picking myself up, I was hit with a different pang – hunger.

A yearning for buttered soda bread and sweet tea drew me in the direction of the house in the hollow.

......

At the peak of the road, the house halted me. It was its appearance – it looked different.

But I couldn't figure out what the difference was. When I looked at the sky the sun's position told me mid-afternoon was giving way to early evening. I'd been out for hours, which the hungry roar of my belly confirmed.

When I looked back at the house, I saw the difference, the chimney was dormant – smokeless.

I'd never seen the house not smoking. A snaking sooty plume from the chimney was a constant that sustained the household.

Assuming the fire had been distinguished to carry out some kind of repair work, I continued down the road.

......

On the road, I noted the stillness; there wasn't even a tremor in the trees. My pace shifted a gear into a power walk, which drove into a jog and up into a sprint.

I stopped at the door, but my heart didn't, it raced, pounding so hard in my chest that I feared it might bust.

Slumping on the step, I rested my head on my knee and waited for my heart to slow. When its thumping in my ears stopped, I stood up. The front door – it was closed.

The door into the tiny hallway was always open, welcoming. This door was a stranger to me, I knew it was there, but I'd never met it face to face like this. Unlike the flimsy inner door, this was a heavy, thick wooden door, strong and handsome.

This door was security, a guard. I placed my hand on one of its panels and traced it down to the circular metal doorknob. My hand enclosed the knob, but I paused for a moment as my heart quickened its pace again, this time pushed by creeping anxiety rather than physical exertion.

I tightened my hand around the doorknob, took a deep breath and turned it. Relief waved over me as it clicked; the heavy door released itself from its frame – I wasn't locked out of my haven.

Tentatively I pushed the door and peeked into the tiny hallway, "Granny!" I didn't expect a reply, for Granny would be in the scullery and wouldn't hear me. I said it to ease me in, a reassurance to push the door to its rightful place against the wall and return the house to its accessible norm.

The hallway looked the same. In front of me was a small window, the view into the room obscured by a net curtain. Above the window, Jesus stared down at me, his warm eyes welcoming me in.

Standing in the doorway, I held his stare and looked at him differently. My feelings for him had changed. The sight of him no longer induced creeping anxiety. Maria's talk had altered my perception. I believed her perspective of him as a kind man, rather than the Priest's preachings of a vengeful deity. I waved at him – Jesus was now my friend.

Feeling freer, I entered the house and shouted, "Gran!" There came no reply. She was always in the house at this time. I feared she'd been taken ill and so moved to the stairs, "Maria!" No reply: the house was empty. I'd never been on my own in this house, and I didn't like it.

Being voluntarily alone was preferable to having all-alone imposed on me.
Standing in the middle of the empty room, I wondered, 'Why?'

"Where is everyone?" I asked no one.

Putting my foot on the first stair, the creak in the silence was a piercing screech making me flinch. I jumped up the stairs and into Granny's bedroom. The two double beds were neatly made. Into my uncle's bedroom, and all was the same, beds made without a crumple. The house was vacant.

I walked back through the rooms, my footfall creating a racket from the floorboards, the sound amplified by the empty house.

The rackety boards and screeching stairs unnerved me. Descending the stairs, it sounded like the house was crying. I jumped down in haste to stop its weeping.

Standing in the centre of the small main room, the heart of the house, it was without the beat and bustle of the life-blood that flowed through it.

I couldn't stand still. I needed to know where everyone was, what had happened to empty the house? I strode towards the scullery, halting when I saw a note. It was on the kitchen table, waiting for me. With a trembling hand, I picked it up and read – *"Gerard, where did you disappear to? We waited for over a half-hour, we had to leave without you, sorry.*

Maria XXX"

My legs weakened and wobbled. I made it onto a chair before they gave way on me. I read Maria's note again and again. On my third read, I crumpled the paper and put it in my pocket. I couldn't believe it; Maria and Dermot had left Cavan without me.

It made sense, that's why Maria had worn her new dress and made herself up – for the journey back. Yet, it didn't make sense because Mam and Dad usually returned for our final week to make the return trip with us.

Glancing from wall to wall, I knew I'd overslept and missed the boat; and my amble had almost made the household miss an event. My head was woolly without a clear thought.

I needed to get out and look for people. Pausing in the hallway, I looked at the outer door and realised I had to leave the house as I found it – closed.

The door was heavy, as was my heart as I pulled it shut. Instinctively, I turned away and ran across the road and up the tree-lined lane towards the farmyard.

Again, I was stopped by the stillness and silence. This time was usually a quiet one on the farm, but it was never without some bustle.

In the middle of the sun-filled silent space, I had a strong sense of spirits.

Without physical persons milling about the place, I sensed soul's past wandering through the empty space.

A gentle breeze caused a slight tremor in my t-shirt, then it was gone, and stillness returned. I looked behind me but saw no sign of the ghost passing through me.

And I was sure it was a ghost; because Johnnie had given me clarity, "The longer the past, the more there's ghosts," I said aloud.

Looking around, I now saw this farm was old. Age was beginning to wither many of the buildings; in parts, they broke and crumbled

They looked like old people holding onto life because their work was not yet done. This place had a long past, and now I could clearly see it.

The stillness was once again broken by a soft breeze. As it passed through me, I swiftly turned and yet again, I saw nothing. But Johnnie's words returned to me in his answer to my asking him if he'd seen a ghost, "I haven't, but I've felt many."

I wasn't seeing ghosts, but I knew I was feeling them in this aged place.

Feeling the tremor of another breeze, I waited for it to caress me, and when it did, I held out my hand to catch it and said, "Hello."

Like the others, it passed through me, but I was startled by a voice, *"Wee fella, what're you looking for here?"*

Chapter 37: The Show

I spun around to see a man exiting one of the buildings to the left of the farm and walking towards me. I mumbled, "Erm, no one, nothing."

Yet I relaxed when his smiley face told me he was a friendly man. He was unfamiliar to me, and his appearance didn't fit with the farmyard environs. Although he wore wellington boots, the rest of his clothing was smart: a crisp, short-sleeved white shirt tucked into black trousers tucked into wellies; and to top off his gentlemanly image, he wore a blue flat cap. He looked more teacher than farmer.

He stopped and looked around the space before focussing on me, "Isn't it fierce odd to see the place so empty and quiet?" "Yes, it is."

He walked towards one of the right-hand buildings and knocked on the door, his rap causing it to sigh slightly ajar, "Hello, is anyone there," he said, with a raised voice. When there came no reply, he sidled inside, the door clicking closed behind him.

This man had asked me who I was looking for, and now I wondered who he was looking for? The familiar cloak of fear began to creep up on me, and I lowered my head and asked myself again, "Where is everyone? What's happened?"

The place darkened, and I looked up to see a black cloud obscure the sun. A breeze bristled, and without the sun's heat, it shivered through me, cold and unfriendly. I wrapped my arms around myself to warm up against the arrival of these different spirits. The shift in light changed my surroundings, and I looked around to identify what the difference was.

Instinctively I whispered, "It's dying." The dim light highlighted the old age of the farm, I felt the place slipping away from me, and I wanted to save it, but I knew I couldn't.

Time was taking the farm away, and nobody seemed to care. The place was alone and abandoned in its time of need.

The creak of an opening door distracted me. It was the man; he looked skywards, "There's rain on the way." He strolled towards me, "But thank God it held off for the show."

His words crept up on me with a mix of dread and disappointment. He stopped, leaving a comfortable space between us, "What has you up here? Why are you not at the show?"

Clarity came over me, Maria's note, the closed door, the emptiness, it all made sense now – they were at the Virginia Show.

"I forgot about it," I said shamefully.

He began to laugh, "Ah-here, how could you forget about the Virginia Show? Isn't it the highlight of the Summer?"

I stared ahead, *"My sister's changed, and I miss her, so I went for a walk and had a lie down in a field and fell asleep. Then I woke up and went to see my friend, Johnnie, to talk about sisters, but we talked about ghosts instead."* I gulped, then started again, *"Then I came back here because I'm looking for a ghost that my dad used to see when he was a boy. But I didn't see it, I felt it, like the way Johnnie feels ghosts."* I said all of this in my head; breaking my stare, I looked at the man, who looked at me, "You're a wee man of few words; how could you forget the show?" he asked again. The words wouldn't come, so I just shrugged my shoulders.

He shook his head, "It's the hooley of the Summer, and you're stuck up here on your own. You should be enjoying the show with the other children."

A word he said was lost on me, "What does hooley of the Summer mean?"

He glanced at his watch, then back to me, "The best part of it, its big finale, the final farewell." His head tilted to the sky, "You'd already notice the evenings drawing in, the temperature dropping." He winked at me, "It'll be no time till you're writing to Santy."

My head began to spin at the enormity of what he was telling me. The Summer was almost over. This meant Mam and Dad would soon arrive to accompany us home – and I'd not found out the identity of the tall-man.

Desperately, I spluttered, "Have you ever seen the ghost that haunts this place? He's tall?"

Clearly, I amused him again as he threw his head back and laughed, "It's not ghosts that haunt this place, it's the living you should be looking out for."

"What do you mean?" I asked, intrigued.

"Nothing for you to be worrying your young head about." He smirked, "Before I go, let me ask, were you up here looking for the ghost?"

"Yes, I was," I said sheepishly.

252

"Well, I hope you find him; it'll make up for you missing the Virginia Show."

I watched him walk back towards the avenue. He seemed to grow in stature the further he walked away. A breeze passed through me, I turned with it, and when I looked back the man was gone.

Vanished – *like a ghost.*

I remained rooted to the spot, like in a dream where I wanted to run yet couldn't. The breeze picked up, it whipped through me, and this time I felt its chill. I shivered under a darkening sky. Looking back around the space, I could see clearly now – the Summer was getting old.

My tummy tied itself in knots. Not only had I missed the seasonal highlight of the Virginia Show, but I'd also lost my sister – and I'd lost my Summer to a failed quest.

Mam and Dad would soon arrive, they'd see Maria's change, her blossom into beautiful, they'd laugh at Dermot's exploits and his bravery in the face of injury. And when Dad would ask me, "And what did you get up to, son?" I'd have to answer with my failing, "I was looking for the ghost of the tall-man, but I didn't find out anything."

I couldn't tell him my truth: my foolish belief in Maria's possession, my sadness at losing her, and above all, the strange feelings I'd had around The Cathedral. I had to pull the shutter down on my Summer.

My Summer wasn't normal, especially for a kid. My feet felt heavy, but I managed to move them and shuffled myself forlornly away from the farm and back towards the House in The Hollow. Reaching the top of the lane, I stopped and spoke to myself, "You're not normal, Gerard, and everyone knows it."

The dread knots tightened, causing me physical pain that made me wince and clutch my tummy.

Needing to sit down, I saw the concrete stump by the slaughterhouse. Sitting there, I became aware of the faint metallic smell of blood, which brought me back to the beginning, when my summer was young. Staring at the stark concrete building, I reflected on its function as a place of finale, wherein life is ended. Yet, it was right here where my story began.

This place was the genesis of my Summertime tumult. An urge to distance myself from the memory made me stand up, and I walked towards the row of buildings to the left of the farm.

These buildings were unfamiliar to me. Tentatively, I opened the first wooden door I arrived at, the same one the smart man had entered, "Hello." When my greeting echoed back at me, I entered. It was a long space, with individual concrete stalls designed for the containment of single animals. Each stall had fresh straw on the ground, ready for new inhabitants. I noticed something midway down, and I went to it. A coat hung from the corner of one stall.

Nothing unusual in that, except there was. The coat was long, made of thick black cloth. And rather than hang, it bonded stiff and hard, melded into the concrete. The coat was old, from another time and place. I reached out to touch it but immediately withdrew my hand. It felt disrespectful to touch a coat that hadn't been touched in years.

I wondered why the coat had been left here and by whom? Feeling uneasy, I left the building, pulling the door shut behind me.

Back outside, the cloud cleared, showing the sun sailing towards evening.

Time was literally flying, and without any more distraction, I made my way back to the house.

……

The main door was still closed. They'd not yet returned from the show. I sat on the step and rested my head in my hands – *I'd missed all the fun.*

Chapter 38: Homecoming.

A distant rumble raised me to my feet. Few cars travelled on the road, and I recognised the sound of many engines. The roar in the acceleration of this one told me it was Uncle Michael's car.

I braced myself. Was I going to be in trouble for missing the show and delaying their departure to it? As the car approached, beads of sweat pricked my forehead. I stood up, ready.

But Uncle Michael's car sped past me. Through the speeding blur, I couldn't actually see who the passengers were.

Standing on the road, the screech of brakes made me flinch. Ahead of me, Michaels's car came to an abrupt halt, the back door flew open. There was a moment's pause before Maria jumped out, slamming the door behind her – the car continuing onwards.

My sister stood in the middle of the road, her white dress in the evening sun glowed, giving her an ethereal look – like an angelic bride.

She began a slow walk towards me, which turned to a gentle canter. Instinctively I matched her speed. We stopped in front of each other. I was hyper-aware of her looking down at me while I looked up at her. My sister seemed to have grown taller while at the Spring Show. A gentle breeze caused wisps of hair to flutter across her face like a delicate veil. Maria secured the hair behind her ears, threw her arms around me, picked me up and spun me around.

Maria actually picked me up. My big sister picked up her little

256

brother. This hadn't happened since I was a toddler. Her picking me up made me acutely aware of the time that separated us.

It felt like this passage of time had crept up, startling me with its sudden revelation – Maria had grown up. She looked like a woman while I was but a boy.

She put me down, "Where were you? Me and Dermot searched all over the place for you?"

I pointed behind me, "I fell asleep in a field over there," I said, feeling guilty.

Maria smiled, "I bet you were daydreaming, weren't you?" she asked.

I shrugged a yes. I noticed a canvas bag over her shoulder, "What did you get from the show?"

She took my hand, "Goodies." Pulling me forward, she said, "Let's go and have a little picnic in the woods while it's still bright."

......

The soft trickle of the clear lagoon lulled me, and I sat cross-legged at a little clearing. Maria sat with me and removed two small bottles of milk as well as two brown paper parcels. She placed the bag in front of us to create a little picnic cloth. I watched as she unwrapped the first parcel, placing a triangle of apple pie on my side of the bag.

Hungry, I gobbled a great mouthful, hardly savouring the crumbly pastry and tart apple filling. I went in for a second bite but stopped when I noticed Maria staring at me, "What's up?" I asked.

"Nothing," she said. I nodded to her unwrapped parcel, "Eat your pie." She swivelled her head, "I'm not hungry; you can have it. It's obvious you're starving."

I peeled the foil cap from my milk and supped the creamy top. Maria chuckled, "You're supposed to shake it; the rest'll be all watery now."

I put the bottle down, "I don't care; I only like the first bit."

"What was the Spring Show like?" I asked.
She cast her eyes down, "Dead disappointing."

"Why?" I asked, putting the second piece of pie down.

When she looked back at me, she said nothing; but I saw her eyes were wet – she was holding back tears.

My hand instinctively flew onto her knee, "What's up? Why are you getting tearful?"

She swiped her eyes, "It's nowt, I'm just being dead daft again," she said, through a sad smile.

"You're not being daft; something's up again, like the first day we were here,"
I turned and glanced behind me, "I think this place has a curse on it."

Maria tapped my knee, "Now you're being daft."

I felt fearful my mind would make up another dark narrative to place Maria in, so I implored, "Please tell me what's up, I'm big enough to know now."

She looked wistful, "He doesn't like me," she whispered.

It was like she was trying to hide her words, but I found them and asked, "Who doesn't like you?" my voice raised. Maria grabbed my hand, "Shhhhh."

I repeated in a hushed voice, "Who are you talking about?"

She looked around, then leaned into me, "The boy with Bruce Lee hair, he doesn't like me."

Taken aback, I paused before a wave of anger pushed out my words, "Why did he say he doesn't like you?" I asked, astonished that anyone would find anything to dislike about my sister.

"Maria sighed, "He didn't say he doesn't like me."

Confusion diluted my anger, "You said he did."

She gently nodded, "I did, cos I know he doesn't like me the way I like him."

She rummaged through my hair, pulling out a couple of sticky-willy seeds, "Sometimes you know what people think about you without them having to say it," she said.

I didn't answer her because I understood what she meant. I'd felt the woman in Hickey's shop didn't like me, even though she never actually said she didn't. I nodded my understanding and took a big bite of pie.

I swallowed and asked, "Is he still taking you to the pictures to see God the father?"

She chuckled, "Yes."

I jumped in, hopeful, "See, he does like you then."

Her face was tight with doubt, "No, he's just being nice." Her mouth flickered with a tentative smile, "He's so nice, other lads would try and get their wicked way before I went back to England, but he's not like that," she said.

I was about to take another bite of pie but put it down, "What's a wicked way?"

She let out a low-level laugh, "Nothing, I shouldn't have said that," she spluttered.

"But it must be something, cos you said it; are some lads wicked?"

She took a sip of milk, "Yes, Gerard, some can be," she took another glug, "but many aren't."

I suspected Maria was talking from an experience that was painful for her, and my experience of this fateful summer told me to pry no further. I slugged my milk and put the empty bottle back in the bag, "Should we go back to Granny's?" I asked, standing up.

Maria remained seated, cross-legged, "Not yet, let's stay here for another while. It's really peaceful."

Back on the ground, I scratched my head, "I never found out who the ghost is – Dad'll be dead disappointed in me, won't he?"

Maria took my hand away from my head and ruffled my hair, "Now you're being proper daft, Gerard. You know Dad only thinks good of the three of us, he'd never be disappointed in us," she said, patting my hair down.

My hand flew back to my head, and I twirled a clump of fuzzy hair while knowing it was myself I was disappointed in, something I didn't want to acknowledge out loud because I didn't know how to – I didn't have the words.

Again, Maria took my hand away from my hair, "You're full of nervous habits." She placed my hand on my knee and kept her hand over it, "You're a kid Gerard, you shouldn't be worrying as much as you do."

I snapped back, defensively, "You're still a kid too. You're not even eighteen yet."

She smiled softly, "I am still a kid. I just don't feel like one anymore." I looked at her but remained silent. Maria opened her arms, "Come here, you, give us a cuddle." I lay into her as she folded her arms around me, resting her chin on my head, "Your hair tickles," she chuckled.
"I bet it does. It's horrible my hair."

She lifted her head, "No, it's not. It's as lovely as you are." She brushed my hair with her fingers, chuckling when she got stuck in a tangle.

I helped her retrieve her hand from my head nest, "See, told ya, it's a jungle," I said, joining her in chuckle.

The sun began to journey down through the trees as Maria softly sang, "Doe a deer, a female deer...."

I tapped her hand, "No, start at the beginning, please."

She gently changed key, "I'll start at the beginning, for you, it's a very good place to start when you read you begin with A-B-C when you sing, you begin with you and me...."

And in the warmth of that late summer woodland, at that moment in my sister's arms, listening to her sweet singing voice, *I felt safe, sound, and soothed.*

Chapter 39: Found

Maria and I were squashed into a pew as the Cathedral struggled to contain its bulging congregation. Numb with discomfort and boredom, I wriggled to give my cramping legs respite. "Stop fidgeting, would ya," admonished a woman to my right, irate with my wriggling interrupting her reverence.

Maria seemed oblivious to discomfort, her head bowed, staring at her knees. I nudged her, "What?" she asked sleepily.

I nudged her again, "Get up, it's Communion time." I stood and stretched my arms upwards, my clicking joints and instinctive grunt amplified by the reverential silence.

Maria grabbed my arm and yanked it down, "Gerard, we're in Mass, mind your manners," she whispered.

Seeing the judgemental looks surrounding me, I said a quiet, "Sorry," and stepped into the aisle.

I shuffled along with the crowd towards the holy host. My head swivelled, searching for familiar faces. I was stopped by a smile on the parallel aisle; it was the boy with Bruce Lee hair. He gestured towards Maria, who continued to shuffle with a bowed head. I tapped her elbow, and when she looked at me with slight annoyance, I immediately pointed over to him. When their eyes met, their beaming smiles lit up the Cathedral.

With my head held high, I marched forward, sure that the boy with

Bruce Lee hair did like my sister, and I was instrumental in making Maria see that, hopefully.

I felt I'd achieved something and thus received my host with a happy relish, letting it melt on the roof of my mouth as I returned to the pew – proud.

Outside, released from the restrictive confines of the Cathedral, I blurted aloud, "Did you see the way he smiled at you? He likes you loads."

Maria took my hand and whispered in my ear, "Keep your voice down."

Disappointment stopped me, and I lowered my voice, "But Maria, he wouldn't smile like that if he didn't like you," I surmised.

"I know, I think you're right," she looked around, "I just don't want him to hear you and know I've been talking about him."

I was beginning to understand something of sorts; Maria had grown and was partaking in the whisperings and secrets I associated with the adult world.

Pulling my hand from hers, I asked, "Don't you want to go and talk to him?"

She grabbed my hand, "Not now. His smile is all the talk I need at the moment," she said, pulling me down a grass verge towards Uncle Michael's car.

I let go of her hand again, "A smile can't talk. Why are you saying daft stuff?"

She quietly chuckled, "I know it can't. What I mean is, his smile made me feel nice, and now I just want to go and enjoy a nice breakfast and think about what to say to him when I see him next."

Sort of understanding her, I continued to the car, propelled by hungry thoughts of great Uncle Frankie's post-Mass-Breakfast-Feast.

......

The house was enveloped in the salty smell of cooked bacon. Granny had already breakfasted and was busy in the scullery preparing the Sunday Lunch.

"Now, enjoy that," said great-Uncle Frankie, dressed smartly in his Sunday suit. Dermot put down a half-devoured sausage.

"And you enjoy your drink in Eddie Gorman's after Mass, Uncle Frankie," he said, stuffing the remaining sausage in his mouth. Frankie put on his cap, "I will surely," he said, heading out the door to his chauffer, Uncle Michael.

Dermot grabbed another sausage and raced to the door, "See-ya-later- alligator."

With only Maria, Uncle Tommy and myself at the breakfast table, a quiet descended, the singular sound our collective munching. Uncle Tommy broke the silence, "So tell us, what had you missing the show?" he asked me.

I took a slurp of tea, "Fell asleep in a field."

"Not for the whole day, surely?"

"No, I woke up and went to visit Johnnie Simons."

Tommy smirked, "What does be going on in that woolly head of yours that you'd forget such a great day?"

I had an urge to confess and spill the torment that marred my summer. But I didn't; instead, I scratched my head, shrugged my shoulders, and said, "I dunno."

"He's a daydreamer," said Maria.

"He is that," concurred Tommy.

Wanting to steer the conversation away from me, I jumped in, "It was dead quiet up at the farm when you were all gone."

Tommy buttered a piece of soda bread, "Sher, they were all at the show."

I butted in, "Except that man."

Tommy put down his knife, "What man?" he asked.

Feeling I'd spoken out of turn, I said, "The posh man."

Tommy's interest piqued, "What did he look like?"

My heart picked up a pace, "He was dressed smart, not like a worker, he had black straight hair all neat, and he had a blue cap on," I explained.

Tommy's eyes widened, "Was he a thin, tallish fella?"

"Yes."

He took a sup of tea, "And what do you mean by posh?" he asked.

My throat dried, so I took a gulp of lubricating tea, "Like he wasn't a farmer, more like a teacher or a man who works in an office." I worried I may have done a wrong thing in meeting the man.

"What did you talk to him about?" asked Uncle Tommy, with heightened interest.

"The weather and how the farm was looking old," I said, looking to Maria for any idea of which direction Tommy's questioning was going in. She looked blank as Tommy continued, "Did this man go into the milking parlour or the slaughterhouse?" he asked.

"No."

Tommy sat upright, "Did he go into any of the buildings?"

I had to think for a moment before answering, "Yes, he went into one of those buildings that run on the other side of the farm."

"And did he stay long?"

"No, just a few minutes. I think he was looking for somebody."

"Did you shake his hand?"

"No."

Uncle Tommy's eyes widened further, "So you never actually felt him, like?"

"No, I never did."

Uncle Tommy drained his teacup and sat back, looking at me strangely. Feeling uncomfortable, I asked him, "What you looking at me like that for?"

He leaned in, "Gerard, I think that fella was looking for you?"

My hair began to bristle, "What do you mean?"

He glanced at Maria, then back to me, "That man you describe died long ago."

I felt my hair stand up and my mouth fall open as Tommy continued, "He was looking for you to let you know you'd found the ghost of the tall fella." Tommy stood up, "Good work Gerard," he said, ruffling my hair before leaving the house – leaving me gobsmacked.

My whole body tingled as my mind went back to my meeting with the man in the farmyard. I felt Maria's hand on my arm, "Gerard, you're shaking."

I stood up, "Do you think it really was him, honestly?" I asked, desperate for confirmation.

Maria smiled and nodded, "Yes, I think you found the ghost, Gerard – Uncle Tommy will tell Dad who the man was. He'll be dead proud of you," she said, shaking my hand.

I pulled away from her, "Do you mind if I go out?" I asked.

Maria looked happy, "Course I don't, where you going?"

"I want to go back to the farmyard to have a look around," I said, bolting for the door.

Maria called after me, "Gerard!"
"What?" I asked.

She smiled, "You're a great ghost hunter."

I matched her smile, "Thanks," I said, feeling strangely good about myself.

......

Outside, I felt a change in the air. Although the sun shone, there was the slightest chill that caused me to run up the lane to the farm – I needed affirmation that I had met the ghost, although how I was going to get that, I didn't know.

On arrival, I immediately noticed the bustle. It wasn't quite as busy as it was mid-week but considerably busier than the previous day. The place seemed to have come back to life in the space of twenty-four hours.

The door to the left-hand building was open, and I was drawn to it, "Hello," I said.

"Who's that?" asked a man.

I walked in, "It's me, Granny Smith's Grandson," I said, by way of introduction, as I'd never met this man before.

He finished throwing straw on the floor, "How-are-ya?" he asked.

"Alright," I said.

His job finished, he readied himself to leave the building, but I instinctively stood in front of the exit, "Whose is that coat?" I asked.

He turned to look at the old coat, "That was a young fella's from long ago, he left it there and never returned. They say he's dead this long time."

I moved away from the door as he walked towards it, *"We do leave it there out of respect," he said, walking out into the farm.*

Chapter 40: Coats

The door slammed shut behind the man, causing me to jolt. I stared at the coat and slowly reached out my hand. I stroked the collar like it were a dog, and words instinctively fell from me, "I hope you're at peace now; thank you for visiting me. I'll never, ever forget you; I promise." My head shot round to the door to check no one could hear me talking to an old coat.

Back in the farmyard, I felt lifted by achievement; Uncle Tommy was impressed with me, and I knew Dad would be, too. Feeling my pocket, I felt the outline of a fifty pence piece, and my joy soared – I could treat myself to a solitary celebration.

Betty Hickey's sweetshop beckoned. Setting off down the farm lane, I began my celebratory feast with blackberries plucked from the abundant bushes that flourished along my way. My ghost-hunting success made them taste sweeter. I arrived at the main road, sweetly satiated and with a spring in my step.

In no time, I made it onto the town's main street. Looking behind me, I realised I'd completed the walk in record time. I smiled to myself and reasoned that I could actually fly without the weight of burden holding me back.

Even though it was Sunday morning, the town bustled as people bought newspapers and post-mass treats. I ambled along, soaking up the atmosphere and making a mental list of what I would buy and eat first.

I made my decision as I entered Hickey's hallowed ground, "Good-Morning Gerard, have you come in on your own?" asked Betty.

"Yes," I answered. And as if reading my mind, Betty sculpted an ice-cream cone, handing it to me without my having to ask for it.

Its creaminess was in stark contrast to the blackberries, and I savoured every lick. "Can I have some strawberry bonbons and a bag of those cinnamon sweets that Granny likes, please?" I asked, placing my coin on the counter.

And it was with a combination of indulgent enjoyment and relief from burden that I blurted out, "I saw a ghost in the college farmyard, I was talking to him and everything…."

But I abruptly stopped when I noticed Betty standing with her back to me in silence. Of course, I'd said too much, been stupid, I'm just a kid who believes in ghosts, and I shouldn't be bothering Betty with my banter. I felt my face begin its familiar redden, and I was about to retract my statement when Betty spun round, her pink kaftan swirling about her,

"I well believe it, Gerard; ghosts only appear to the good amongst us." She placed two bags of sweets on the counter, "And you're very good altogether, buying sweets for your granny," she said, patting the cinnamon bag.

I finished eating my cone, stuffed the sweets and change in my pocket and said, "Thank you, Betty, thanks a lot." I seemed to float on a sea of Betty's validation, and I cruised out of her shop with her words in my sails.

……

Buoyed by my good-boy status, I decided I had to treat both grannies. So, I headed off up the town to the Half-Acre to give Town Granny my strawberry bonbons.

Starting on the hill, I slowed, hoping I'd meet the man-in-makeup. But on reaching the summit and seeing the empty stretch of half-acre before me, I knew I wasn't going to; I resolved to make sure I'd see him before I left for England.

The morning had drifted into afternoon, a fact that stopped me. Town Granny might be having her dinner and could potentially offer me some. This was something I couldn't risk, so I decided to dawdle to ensure I was most definitely on the other side of dinner time before I delivered the bonbons.

Now, I may have been a good ghost-hunter, but what I really excelled in was dawdling. With my head empty of worldly thoughts, rambling idly was one of my favourite things to do. So, when approaching Town Granny's house, I hunkered down and scurried past, eventually straightening as I reached the road to Dublin.

The Dublin Road stalled me. I watched as cars turned onto it, most of them returning to their homes in rural Cavan. Soon, we would all be loaded into Uncle Tommy's Zephyr and turning onto this artery to take us back to Manchester. I felt the first ache of sadness in my stomach, followed by a familiar fear – I was frightened of Goodbyes.

And whereas on the way to Ireland, I had only two Goodbyes to contend with, Mam and Dad's; here in Ireland, I had a multitude. The traffic cleared, and I ran across the road, "The Summer's not over yet," I said aloud to myself, my words lifting me.

I stopped in front of a lake and leant against a fence pole. The afternoon sky had clouded over, rendering the small lake grey and silvery – sad looking.

"Cheer up," I said. I made myself chuckle. I'd progressed from talking to crows and donkeys, to lakes – I really was odd, and at this moment, I didn't care because there was just me and this sad lake, so I could be as odd as I wanted to be.

I felt sorry for the lake, it looked lonely, and it wasn't pretty. Cavan was full of glorious looking lakes situated in lush and beautiful surrounds. Yet this one was sunk in swampy ground on the edge of a main road. I surmised that nobody noticed this lake, nobody looked at it – except me.

It was the ugly duckling of lakes, and I wondered if it would one day blossom into a swan. But there was something else that drew me to this murky puddle of water – it looked haunted. It felt haunted, I sensed the restless spirits sailing above its surface, I heard them rustling in the reeds. And despite all these negatives, I had an affinity with this place; like me, it seemed displaced.

Readying to leave, I looked out at the lake, "I'll be back someday, I promise," I said, waving goodbye. Already, I was rehearsing my goodbyes.

......

Walking back towards Granny's, I stopped by a house that always intrigued me. It stood proud on the cusp of the half-acre and the road into the town centre. I assumed the people who lived in it owned Cavan and must be very grand indeed. But again, as I stood in front of it, I felt it too, was haunted by something I couldn't grasp. A chill travelled through me, pushing me on to Town Granny's.

We usually entered the house from the back, but I felt it best to go via the front door this day, so I skipped down the steps that brought me onto the front of the neat little row of terraced houses.

Milly's house was the first, and I thought about knocking on her door to let her know that her cure of Maria's stye had been successful. But I thought better of it and continued on. Each house had a tiny square of garden separated from the house by the street, and they all had one thing in common, they were all beautifully tended with late summer flowers in full bloom, lending the street a riot of colour.

I stopped to look at them but instead saw Town Granny standing on her doorstep with her arms folded, looking at me.

Walking towards her, I noted she looked a kind of low-level annoyed, which I tried to counter with a cheery, "Hiya Granny."

Her arms still folded, she asked sternly, "And were you going to call into me at all, or were you going to try and sneak past me like you did out the back?"

Wanting the ground to open up, I grappled with explaining, "No Granny, honest – I was gonna call then realised you might be having your dinner, so I crept by to give you time to eat," I said.

Her face softened, and she untied her arms to straighten her pinny, "And where've you been hiding for the last hour?" she asked.

Relieved that my honest excuse worked, I smiled, "I wasn't hiding, I went over to see that lake," I said, pointing behind me.

Her face dropped, "You were at the Green Lake?"

I nodded, "Is that what it's Called?" I asked.

"It is, and it's a danger, I don't want you going over there again, do you hear me?"

Feeling admonished, I conceded, "I won't, promise."

Granny pushed open the door, "Come on in and have a mineral."

Granny disappeared into the kitchen, and I sat on the chair next to the ornamental cabinet that fascinated me. I stared through the glass at all the twinkling trinkets, ornaments, and mementoes, all kept in pristine condition by Granny's weekly polishing. Little porcelain cats and dogs sat alongside religious relics and ceramic saints from a place called Knock. And my absolute favourite, the jewel in the cabinet collection – Wedgewood.

A pale blue saucer stood upright on a stand to best display the raised white filigree around its edge. The cup sat in front of its upright saucer; a trio of figures in white was acting out some kind of scene. I moved to get a closer look, "Don't be touching the glass; I'm only after polishing it this morning," said Granny, her voice slightly raised.

I jumped back into the seat, "Sorry, Granny, I didn't touch it, honest."

She placed a brown bottle on the table and picked up the glass, tilting it to pour the brown liquid in. When she placed the glass down, I saw the brown liquid had a thick white froth on it.

"Come and have your mineral," said Granny.

Getting up, I felt mild shock, "Granny, is this Guinness?" I asked.

She laughed, "Indeed it's not. What would I be giving a child porter for – that's Cavan Cola."

I took a sip. The froth was thick and creamy, and the liquid that seeped through it was comfortingly sweet with a hint of the taste of Drumalee Granny's cinnamon sweets. Which reminded me, I put the glass down and tugged the bag from my pocket, "Here, Granny, I bought you some Strawberry bonbons from Hickey's shop."

She looked at the bag, and I looked at her face, softening and settling into a gentle smile. She picked them up and put them into the pocket of her Pinney, "Thank you, gossun, I'll enjoy them, so I will." She pointed to the glass, "Do you like the mineral?"

Taking another sip, I smacked my lips, "It's dead nice, thanks, Granny."

Her smile subsided, "I do get them in for the three of yous, but sher, I hardly see yous at all."

Feeling sorry for her, I didn't know what to say, so I just drained my drink to let her know I appreciated her getting the drinks for us. Granny took a bonbon and popped it in her mouth, "But I've your Mammy to look forward to. She'll be home this time next week," she said, savouring the sweet.

I sat up, "And Dad as well, he's coming as well, you know," I said, worried Granny omitting him might mean Dad wasn't coming for some reason.

She nodded, "I know that," she said, getting up to open the door that led into the cupboard space under the stairs. I'd often wondered what lay behind this door, and I peered in but was distracted by what hung from the back of the door.

"Granny, whose is that coat?" I asked.

She stroked it gently, "That's your Grandad's." She closed the door and touched the small crucifix around her neck, *"He's gone a good few years now, God rest his soul."*

Chapter 41: Town Granny

Granny lifted the circular ring on her range with a metal device and plunged a log into the burning furnace.

Her silence spoke to me, and I cradled my Cola, not wanting to break the quiet. I watched as she sprinkled tea leaves into an ornate porcelain tea-pot, pouring steaming water into it from the kettle on the range. She placed the pot on the table, dressing it with a knitted cosy.

All the while, the two of us remained perfectly silent and not awkwardly so. I found comfort in observing her ritual.

She returned from the kitchen with a single cup and saucer, placing it down and taking her seat at the head of the table. And still, the silence remained.

Granny stared ahead; sunlight filtering through her brilliantly white net curtains bathed her face in a glow that altered her looks. She looked like a young woman – the image of my mam.

And still the silence.

Granny knew I was staring at her. It was as though she were performing, showcasing a gentle serenity – giving me her best side.

We were both content, me sipping a sweet nectar, Granny waiting for her tea to brew.

This was the nicest time I'd ever spent with my Town Granny.

There was conversation in our silence. Although nothing was spoken, much was said, *"See, I'm not as hard as you think, Gerard, I have a soft side. You just never give me the time to show it."*

She placed her hand on the top of the tea pot and left it there a while. Somehow satisfied, she picked up the pot and poured her tea. Next came a spoonful of sugar and a drop of milk from the jug and condiments that were a forever fixture on her table.

She began to slowly stir her tea while her silence continued to speak to me, *"I feel left out, Gerard, that you're not bothered about me. When yous do visit, yous can't wait to get away."*

She took a sip of her tea, replaced her cup, and resumed her silent stare.

"My own's all left the nest now, I do look forward to the grand childer's visit, but I know it's a hardship for them to be sitting with an auld one like me."

Her voice jolted me from my thoughts, "Will you take another mineral?" she asked.

"No, I'm alright, thanks."

She took out the bonbons and placed one in front of me, "Now, enjoy that," she said. I popped it in my mouth as Granny took another sip of tea. Putting the cup down, she looked at me, "Are you happy enough sitting there?" I nodded my yes. She looked straight ahead, "It's nice to have the bit of company."

I didn't think I was being much company, but Granny did, and that was enough for me.

No sooner had I swallowed the bonbon than she put another one in front of me, "Granny, they're for you," I said, pushing it back to her.

She flicked it back to me and took another one from the bag, "No harm in sharing," she said, popping it into her mouth.

We sat together, the only sound the chomping chew of our chops – until a rap at the door alerted us both.

Granny stood up, ran her fingers through her hair, straightened her pinny and asked, "Who's that at this time?"

As she left for the door, I stood up, as intrigued as Granny as to who her afternoon visitor was.

I strained to listen but heard nothing. Instead, the door opened and in walked Maria.

Her arrival surprised me, "How come you're here?" I asked.

"Same reason you are," she said.

Granny walked in behind her and pulled out a chair for Maria, "Now, will you have a mineral, or will I get you a cup for the tea?"

Maria didn't hesitate, "I'll have tea, please, Granny." Her beverage of choice further told of Maria's new maturity; before, she'd have gone for the pop, now she was a grown-up tea person.

With Granny in the kitchen, Maria whispered, "Why didn't you tell me you were coming? We could have come together," she asked. With no answer, I head-swivelled as Granny came back with a new cup and saucer.

"And what about Dermot, will he be visiting?" she asked, pouring Maria's tea.

Maria and I exchanged a swift glance while Maria acted as spokesperson, "No Granny, he had an accident on Jim's Honda, and he's on crutches."

Granny topped up her cup, "That'll not stop him off galivanting the fields, so it won't," she said, putting down the teapot with a knowing eye-raise.

Her attention focussed on Maria, "I see Milly's cured your stye," she observed.

And before Maria could answer, I jumped in, "Do you think it was Milly who cured her stye?" Granny looked at me oddly, and I immediately regretted the impetuous nature of my question. I sat back sheepishly while Granny glared at me.

"Who else do you think cured it?" she asked.

I shrugged, sheepish, "Don't know, was just asking, that's all."

She turned her focus to Maria, "Did you go to a doctor or the Chemist, daughter?" she asked.

Maria swivelled her head, "No, it just went away on its own."

A stern look flashed across Granny's face, "Indeed, it did not go away on its own. Milly has the cure of the stye, and it's many she's cured; you're lucky I have her on my doorstep," she said.

Maria agreed, "I know Granny, I'm dead grateful, that's why I came up, to say thank you to her," she said.

Granny raised a second eye, "And did you thank her?" she asked.

Maria smiled, "Yes, I did."

Granny gazed at the window again, "So it's Milly you came to visit, not me," she said, her face visibly dropping.

Maria, ever eager to please, implored, "Aww no, I came to see you both, honest." Granny softened, and as she turned her head towards us, Maria produced a bar of chocolate and slid it over to her, "I bought you this."

She picked up the small bar, looking at it studiously; she reminded me of an elder cat trying to decipher the nature of what's been put in front of her. Slowly her mouth widened into a smile, lighting up her face, "Tiffin and Strawberry bonbons, two of my favourite treats; aren't I the spoiled one today," she said. Maria and I swapped swift glances, and I know she was feeling the same as myself – accomplished.

"I'll be putting these in my treat box," said Granny, walking into her kitchen.

Maria winked at me, "We did good, Gerard," she whispered, squeezing my knee.

Granny returned to us in a mood that changed Maria and I's perception of her persona. She was joyful and ebullient.

"Come up to see the room I've done for your Mammy and Daddy."

Upstairs of Town Granny's house was a hallowed space where only the special were given access. So, as I followed Granny and Maria up the narrow staircase, I knew we were honoured.

We arrived at a small square landing with three closed doors. Granny opened the left-hand door and led us into the room. Stepping into the space was a sensory overload for me, and as usual, my words fell without thinking, "What's that smell?"

Maria tapped my shoulder while Granny looked concerned, "Do you find a bad smell?" she asked.

I shook my head while I tried to compute the strange smell, "No, it's a kind of nice smell," I said, unsure whether it was a pleasant smell or not.

Granny looked around the room, and I saw realisation hit her, "Ah, that'll be the mothballs I put in the wardrobe. I know how fussy your Mammy is with her clothes, and I wouldn't want the moths eating them," she said.

I was fascinated, "How do the balls stop moths eating clothes, Granny?" She opened the wardrobe, and as she did, the smell flooded out.

"They don't like the smell," she explained. And when she closed the doors again, I decided I was with the moths. I didn't like the smell of the balls either, but I was mindful to keep the fact to myself.

I became aware of Maria and Granny in conversation, but I wasn't listening because I was drinking in the room. The size struck me; it was larger than I expected, given the smallness of the house. Then the elegance, the décor and placement of the furniture gave the room a grandeur that beguiled me. A large double bed sat in the centre of the back wall, beautifully made and topped with a delicately coloured patchwork blanket. In the corner was an open fire, already set and framed by an intricately ornate surround. On the right-hand wall was a small table on which sat a large bowl and jug, a tier of fluffy flower-adorned towels nestled beside them.

Bright white nets hung from the front window, accompanied by curtains with a modern brown and orange design. And in front of them sat a beautiful mahogany dressing table with a large circular mirror and matching stool. I stared at this furniture and imagined Mam sitting at it, applying her pan-stick and red lipstick.

The whole room had a glamour that appealed to my aesthetic tastes. My eyes explored the room, taking in all the decorative details; until they settled on a thing that didn't sit with the beauty, it jarred – disgusting!

I walked towards it and homed in to be sure it was what I thought it was. And as per usual, my words fell-forth, "Granny, there's a potty under the bed!" Granny and Maria looked from me to the offending piece of porcelain.

I searched Granny's face, hoping she'd realise her error and remove the item that was completely unnecessary in an adult's room. But instead, she smiled, "Isn't it a beautiful piss-pot, do you like it, Gerard?" Her question made me flinch, how could I like a potty, and moreover, how could Granny describe a piss-pot as, "Beautiful?"

I stood dumbstruck, looking at Maria using my eyes to appeal for her help. And to my relief, she gave it, "It's gorgeous, Granny, is it Willow Pattern?" she asked, stooping to look at the potty.

Granny joined her in mutual admiration of a thing that you pee in.

"I think that's what you'd call it; I saved up the price of it for your Mammy and Daddy coming home. I'm delighted with it, so I am," she said. I wondered if it was a joke, but when they both stood straight, I knew it wasn't and decided to say nothing more on the matter until I was alone with Maria.

Granny turned to me, "Well, Gerard, do you think your Mammy will like the room?" she asked.

I nodded, "It's dead nice, Mam's gonna love it," I said, resisting the urge to ask her to remove the mobile toilet.

She patted my shoulder, "I'm delighted you like it; you've a woman's taste, so you have. I think your Mammy will like it as well."

Granny made for the door, leaving me reeling; what did she mean by, *"I have a woman's taste?"*

Chapter 42: Potty Tastes

"Come on, Gerard, stop dawdling," shouted Maria, as I trailed behind her sucking on a bonbon while ruminating on what Granny had said about me.

I ran to my sister, eager for answers, "Maria, do men and women taste things different?" I asked.

She took my hand and led me down the narrow walkway of Jubilee Terrace, "What do you mean?"

I swallowed my sweet, "Like when a woman eats a strawberry bonbon, it tastes of strawberry, but when a man eats a strawberry bonbon, it tastes of banana," I said.

Maria looked ahead, "No, Gerard, we all taste things the same," she said dismissively.

I felt a gentle rattle of my shackle, "Then why did Granny say I have a woman's taste?"

Maria stopped and paused a moment before answering, "That means you like the same things that women do, you know how you like pretty colours and things, that's your taste; so that's what Granny meant."

I stood with her, not liking her explanation one bit. "But that's bad, shouldn't I have a boy's taste?" And before she could answer, I threw another question at her, "Can my taste be fixed?" I asked, hopeful.

Maria squatted to my eye level, put her hands on my shoulders and gently shook me. "There's nothing broken, Gerard, we all have different tastes. Some girls like boy's things and some boys like girls' things; we all have different tastes," she explained.

Her words were a small comfort; still, I shrugged and resolved to try and change my tastes to those more befitting a boy.

Maria gently shook me again, "Do you understand?"

I smiled, "Yes," I said, not wanting to talk any more of tastes until I'd worked on changing mine.

When we set off again, another question dropped from me, "Why's Granny put a potty in the bedroom?"

Maria chuckled, "In case Mam and Dad wake up in the night and need a pee, they won't have to go downstairs."

I couldn't hide my disgust, "Eurgh – what if they want to do a pooh?"

She laughed, "Mam and Dad aren't going to pooh in a potty, Gerard."

But I couldn't let it go. "I think Mam'll take it out of the room, she'll think it's horrible like I do, and anyway, Mam and Dad'll get up and go downstairs to use the toilet, I know they will," I said, with an emphasis that closed any more talk of potties, pee and pooh.

......

"What made you decide to visit Town Granny?" asked Maria as we strolled down Cavan's main street.

Her question made me visualise Betty Hickey, "I bought some cinnamon sweets for Granny, then thought it was mean not getting any for Town Granny, so I called to give her my bonbons."

She squeezed my hand, "That was nice of you, and you could tell she was dead chuffed to see us."
I chipped in, "She was different today. I think she's nicer when she's not making us eat her dinners."

Maria tugged on my hand, "She doesn't make us eat her dinners. You just don't like eating them."

I didn't respond, as Maria kept talking, "But you're right, she was different, I saw another side of her today." She pondered a moment, "I think she's lonely; I feel bad for not taking more time to visit and get to know her better."

I agreed, "I know, she got Cavan Cola's in for the three of us, and it was just me that got one, so she's got two spares now."

Maria stopped, "Aww, did she really get them in for us?"

"Yeah, she told me, and she said we never call to see her."

Maria continued on, "Now I feel awful and sad." She stopped abruptly, "Gerard, I hope Mam's not gonna be mad with us?"

"Why, what've we done?"

"Hardly visited Town Granny, our Mam's Mam."

"Mam knows I don't like her dinners."

"I know she does, but I'm the oldest, and I should've made more effort to go and see her."

I knew my sister was struggling with guilt, so I took her hand, "It don't matter, you bought her a Tiffin Bar, and she really liked it." And, wanting to change the subject, I asked, "Why isn't Milly a doctor?"

Maria brightened up and took my hand, "Because she isn't."

That wasn't enough for me, so I dug deeper, "But if she can cure your stye, she can probably cure everything with those saint medals on her pinny." I said, searching Maria's face for a conclusive answer.

I didn't get one, "To be honest, Gerard, I think that stye went away on its own. I don't think Milly had owt to do with it." She stopped and tugged my hand hard, "But don't you ever say that to Milly or Town Granny."

"I won't."

She tugged again for extra emphasis, "Promise me? I know what you're like for blurting things out."

Feeling rightly chastised, I shrugged, "Promise."

We carried on hand-in-hand up Cavan's Main Street at a comfortable pace until the Surgical Hospital loomed large ahead. I tightened my grip on Maria's hand, "Come on, let's run."

At a safe space away from the Surgical, I slowed, and Maria caught her breath, "Crikey Gerard, you're strong and fast for a kid."

Her words made me feel good, "Am I?" I asked, wanting further affirmation of these strengths.

"You are. What made you run like that?"

I stood and watched the place I feared, "I don't like the Surgical, it scares me, and I don't like the smell."

Maria looked back, "I know what you mean, but I'm not so scared of it that I have to run like the clappers past it,' she said, chuckling.

Even though I was a kid, at that moment, I knew that running away from fears would always be preferable to confronting them.

Chapter 43: Running

Maria and I arrived at the familiar crossroads called Drumalee. This was the point from which the town ebbed away, and lush green fields and forests flowed. Maria gave me a shy, sheepish look.

"What's up?" I asked.

She twiddled her hair the way she did when she was slightly nervous, "Do you mind if I go down here, on my own?" She asked, pointing to my left. I was becoming accustomed to Maria's change; the sting I'd experienced about her no longer wanting my company had diminished to a dull ache. Also, I felt sorry for her needing to ask my permission to pursue her newfound grown-up pursuits.

"I don't mind, it's up to you," I said. But I was curious, "Where are you going?" She tussled her hair over her face, and through a shy smile, she tapped her nose, implying a secret.

But now I knew her secret and needed to articulate it aloud to prevent my mind from making up dark diversions, "You're going to see the boy with Bruce Lee hair, I know you are!" I said, with a knowing emphasis. Maria giggled, her face flushed, glowing with glee. She placed her finger on her mouth and blew through it, "Shhhhhh," she sounded. I knew I was to say nothing of my sister's secret rendezvous. Maria's confiding in me gave me a newfound connection with her. I was the secret keeper of my sister's new self.

Maria bent down and kissed my cheek, "Love you," she said. I didn't have time to return a salutation as she turned and took off down the lane; her run interspersed with jumps and skips that made her hair leap and twirl as if dancing a salsa in the sunshine.

Only when she disappeared from view did I turn and look at the road ahead. A desire to try and match my sister's joyous sprint rushed through me – and I took off, wishing my hair would salsa like Maria's – but of course, it didn't.

......

Running exhilarated me, and like a dog unleashed, I sprinted at speed until a sight, sound, or smell forced me to stop and investigate. As I peaked the hill that led down to the House in The Hollow, movement ahead halted me. My head jutted forward; eyes squinted to decipher what I saw – a digger.

From the woods beyond Granny's house, I saw the mechanical jaws of a gargantuan digger open up like a hungry dinosaur ready to devour its prey. The sight of this man-made machine amidst the natural beauty of the woodlands I loved was completely incongruous, and I resumed my sprint to uncover more.

But a rumbling sound from behind stopped me. I spun round to see a fleet of mechanical beasts ascending the hill. Standing back into the bush and bramble, I watched diggers, dumper trucks, and tractors pass me by, a marauding herd that actually shook the ground beneath my feet.

It seemed like an age before the Mammoth Mechanical Cade passed me by. When it did, I emerged from the bramble and watched the various beasts turn and disappear into the woodland.

My heart sank when I considered their intentions, and my first thought was for my friend Johnnie, so I took off again, saying to myself as I ran, "They've come to bulldoze your house Johnnie, don't let them."

A swift glance at Granny's house as I sprinted by told me it was safe; the beasts had passed it by, the house oblivious to the marching machines.

But I was stopped for the third time by a smell. I lifted my nose to the air, the usual forest fragrances: the wet earthiness, sweet bouquet of wildflowers, the subtle woodiness, were all gone – overpowered by the pungent odours of petrol and other fuels used to feed a mechanical army.

Then, I knew they weren't going to bulldoze Johnnie's. His house wouldn't need this army to obliterate it.

Most of the Mechanical Cade was parked in a hastily carved roadside clearing. With engines switched off, the machines gently heaved and hummed as they cooled from their march. Their masters, dressed in tough workwear and hard hats, jumped from driver's seats, entering the woodland, propelled by a work men's purpose.

Leaning against a tree, I sighed a sad lament, "This tree won't be here next summer."

Resting against the tree, I realised I had so much to learn about this world – but I found learning difficult because forgetting was easier. I'd forgotten all about the school.

......

There'd been much talk about the new school being built directly across the road from the House in The Hollow.

I'd been so distracted, the construction had already begun and passed me by. The woodland was largely still intact, a fact which had contributed to my erasure of the school's impending build from my mind.

But now, I looked at the snake of machinery by the roadside, a stark reminder that the landscape I loved would soon be gone forever.

This was our last summer together. My sadness deepened with the realisation that when I returned a year older, my beloved woodlands, wherein I felt safe and cosseted from the world, wouldn't be altered or changed. No, they'd be gone – the trees I talked to, up-rooted and rolled away – the slow undulate of the land that soothed my mind, flattened – the flora and fauna that intrigued me, dug up and dumped – my boyhood joys, the tears, and fears, bulldozed into oblivion. And as I looked from tree to condemned tree, my melancholy was worsened by my youth. "I'll probably forget about you when I'm a grown-up," I said, addressing the place as though it were a person.

My land of freedom would be replaced by a place of restraint – *a school.*

Chapter 44: School

I hated school. And what I loved most about my summers in Ireland was its freedom from the institution's authority. But now, its scholastic spectre sullied my final days as the Mechanical Cade prepared to tear into the freedom of the forest environment to create one, I found infinitely oppressive.

Extracting myself from the tree, I turned away, not bringing myself to look at its gnarled old bark for fear I might cry.

But I also knew it had to happen; my experience with Maria had taught me that places, like people, change. Walking away, a thought formulated in my mind, and I said it aloud, "I'm scared of things changing."

......

Back inside The House in The Hollow, everything remained reassuringly the same. Lofty sprawled on his chaise longue deep in conversation with his imaginary foe. My entrance interrupted his dialogue, and he sat up, "Ah Gerard, tis you, come here to me," he said. He rifled in his pocket and produced a shiny fifty pence piece which he handed to me, "There you go, treat yourself."

I pocketed the treasure, "Thanks, Uncle Micky."

He pulled his pipe and tobacco from his pocket and began the ritualistic loading up of his smoking device, "I heard you saw the ghost up above in the farmyard, tell us, were you freckened of him?" he asked.

I shook my head, "No, he wasn't scary; he was just like a normal man. I hope I see him again before I go back to Manchester, so I can ask him some questions."

Mickey pressed the tobacco into the bowl of his pipe, compacting it hard with his thumb, "Ah now, not at all, he'll not be showing his self again."

I shot back, "Dad told me he seen him loads-a-times when he was my age –why do you think I won't see him again?" I asked, intrigued.

He held the pipe elegantly by the shank, "His job's done, you saw him, and you can tell your Daddy when he's home." He lit up his pipe, smiled at me and said, "Good man, Gerard." He inhaled deeply. When he exhaled, a thick plume of smoke engulfed his face, and through the haze, I heard him say, "His spirit can go and rest now."

"Would you look who it is? You're home ahead-a-the rest of them." I spun round to see Granny ascending the steps of her scullery laden with plates.
"Come and have your tea in peace," she said, laying the dishes on the table.

I scanned the table: a plate of sliced ham, quartered tomatoes, soda bread, an oblong pat of butter, and my absolute favourite, a block of Galtee Cheese. This was my favourite way to eat; it gave me control. I could pick and choose what I put on my plate, rather than be faced with the visual overload of a piled-up plate, which for me, presented a mountain to climb rather than food to be enjoyed.

Granny pulled out a chair for me, but before I sat down, I remembered the cinnamon sweets, pulling them from my pocket, "Her you go, Granny, they're your favourite."

"God bless ya gossun," she said, taking them from me and placing them in the sweet tin she kept in the cabinet, which she called a press. Back at the table, she poured me a cup of tea and returned to her scullery. Granny was always busy; I rarely saw her sit down. She only ever attended to her food and refreshment needs when she was sure everyone else was fed and watered. So, I was surprised when she returned and sat with me, cutting a slice of soda bread for herself and me. She buttered hers and placed two pieces of tomato on it with a liberal sprinkle of salt. I buttered mine and put two slices of Galtee Cheese on it.

Once I'd finished my first cheesy slice, my curiosity returned, "Granny, do you think Milly really cured Maria's stye?" I asked, wanting an alternative Granny perspective to my cure conundrum.

"You wouldn't know," she said, taking a sip of tea.

"I don't know; that's why I'm asking you."

She put down her cup, "Well, it did her no harm, and she didn't need a doctor, so there's your answer," she said, taking a slice of ham, rolling it up and biting into it.

And it was good enough for me. Granny's evaluation was open-minded enough for me to form my own conclusion, and I decided that Milly did indeed have the cure of the stye.

I took a slice of ham and matched Granny's roll and eat, "Did you see all the diggers and trucks that passed by?" I asked.

"I heard them alright, they're getting a quare move on. You'll not know the place next summer."

My heart sank as a part of me hoped I'd get one last summer with my forest, "Do you think the school will be built by then?"

She drained her tea, "Indeed it will, long before next summer by the looks of things." She glanced over at Lofty and on out through the window, "God knows, we'll find some change when it opens its doors."

Granny didn't dwell long. She returned to her scullery while I finished my tea, listening to her nurturing symphony.

"You could be going to that school yet." Lofty's words spun me around. He held his pipe aloft in his left hand while he curled his right into a fist, rested his chin on it and stared out the window.

"What do you mean?" I asked.

His stare remained fixed on the woodland, "I mean what I said, you could be learning in the school that's taking over the trees."

I asserted myself, "I won't. I'll be going to Sacred Heart School in Manchester."

"Is right, so," he said, putting his pipe into his mouth and letting it linger there a while before inhaling.

The door flew open as Lofty exhaled and through the smoke emerged Dermot, hopping to the table on one foot, no sign of his crutches. Granny, always aware of a new entrant to the home, immediately followed up the steps from the scullery.

"Dermot, sit yourself down there now," she said, placing a plate of sliced boiled eggs on the table."

Granny sliced a piece of soda bread and buttered it for him, "Thanks, Gran," he said, devouring half of it. And with his mouth still full, he continued, "I've been helping em build the school. It's gonna be miles better than Sacred Heart." He swallowed the bread, glugged some tea and said, "Gran, will you tell Dad to let us come over for good so I can go to the new school here."

Granny straightened up and smiled, "Indeed I won't. You can tell him that yourself, for it sounds like you'd be happy to go to it."

Dermot's enthusiasm bewildered me, "We don't live here; we live in Manchester," I said.

"I know where we live, our-kid, but we can always move over here," he said, chomping on his second mouthful of bread.

"We are going back to Manchester with Mam and Dad, aren't we?" I asked, curious.

Dermot looked at me with a surprised expression, "Blimey our-kid, what's up with you? You look like someone's smacked you in the gob!"

I shook my head, "Nowt's up with me; but we're going back to Manchester, aren't we?" I asked again, the urgency in my voice evident.

Dermot hacked through the soda bread with the butter knife, "Course we are, calm down our-kid, what you panicking about now?" he asked, struggling to slice the bread.

His assertion that we were returning to Manchester did calm me down, and I affected a carefree attitude, "I'm panicking about nowt, just asking, that's all," I said, heading for the door.

Outside I took in a lung-full of relieving air. Because in truth, I was momentarily panicked – *by Sea-Monkeys.*

Chapter 45: Green V Grey

The thought of receiving my Sea Monkeys had sustained me throughout the darker days of my summer of change. My mind wandered back to Maria writing to Mam, asking her if I could send away to America for them when I returned to Manchester.

This idea seeded by Lofty and bolstered by Dermot that we might stay in Ireland led me to a selfish inspired panic that I wouldn't be able to get them should I stay in Cavan.

Moreover, despite the turmoil I'd experienced over my summer, I'd come to see Ireland as my safe haven, a place of colour and character far removed from the cold grey concrete of our Council Estate. I could lose myself amongst the solitude of Cavan's hills and vales and shut the doors of the darkly oppressive corridors of my Victorian Primary School.

I so yearned to keep both places separate. A school being built across the road from the House in The Hollow meant the grey was already encroaching on the green, and I wanted it to stop at that. I could still enjoy my Cavan summers, as although a school would stand where my woods once were, at least it would be closed.

What caused me creeping anxiety was the thought that the grey would collide with the green sometime in the future, and I might have to return to Cavan to attend school. That would suck all the colour from my Cavan experience – of that, I was sure.

......

The slam of car doors pulled me from my thoughts, "How-a-ya,

Gerard," said my uncles Michael and Peter in perfectly synched harmony. They were returning from work, their white coats speckled with chicken's blood, their wellingtons adorned with feathers.

"Hiya – Dermot's helping build the school," I said, hoping they'd give me further insight into any impending Cavan school-days. But no, they ruffled my hair and entered the house for sustenance and emotional nourishment.

The door closing compelled me up the steps, over the road, through the gate and into the woods. I followed the sound of flowing water down to the lagoon and sat on the mossy stump that had become my favourite chair.

I reflected on my summer and searched for answers in the solitude – but I struggled to find anything. I knew Maria experienced a significant event here, a life shift for her, a gear change unfathomable to me. I lifted my head to catch a ray of light filtering through the trees and pondered on what secret she had disclosed to Mam on the postcard enclosed in an envelope and sealed tight. Would it ever be revealed to me?

I hoped it would.

My hands reached into the spongey moss at my feet, and I pulled up clumps and watched the various bugs disperse and run for cover. Feeling guilty, I replaced the moss in a futile attempt to rebuild the homes I'd just destroyed. I stared at the ground and hoped the bugs would meet up with their families and relocate to another home.

And when I looked back up, he was there – watching me.

"Hello, Crow," I said, pleased to see him.

He was perched on a branch on the tree opposite me, the place where we first met.

"You know what, I met the tall-man." Crow remained utterly still, not even a blink of his beady eye. "You won't see him anymore; he's at rest in heaven."

And with that, he took off, flying over my head. It was almost like he'd been waiting for me to tell him before he departed. I turned and watched him flutter into the woodland, "Goodbye, Crow, it was nice knowing you," I said with a wave that held regret.

I wondered if I'd ever see him again. As summer was coming to its end, so was our relationship. But I would always cherish our friendship. I smiled at the recollection of me talking to him, spilling all my hopes and fears to a big black bird in the woods. My smile waned as I felt the mournful twinge of goodbye sting the pit of my stomach. Standing on my tip-toes, I craned my neck and peered through the forest, hoping for a final glance of him.

But no, Crow had flown his way, and soon I would sail my way – back to the grey concrete of Manchester City.

A teary hiccup caused me a sudden spasm, and I walked away from the waterfall to curtail my tears.

A thought gave me comfort, and I articulated it aloud to soothe my sadness, *'At least all the goodbyes coming up won't be as final as Crow's because I'll see everyone in Cavan again – next summer.'*

Chapter 46: Manchester

The summer sun faded as the year grew old. Maria, Dermot and I were back in our Manchester council house. We had swiftly re-transitioned back from country to inner-city kids.

I was happy to be back, especially as I had such an exciting real-life horror tale with which to regale my friends. I'd decided to call my tale 'The Crow from The Clear Lagoon', and I was so excited to tell it to an audience.

But what really made the return to Manchester special was Maria.

I had her back.

As winter's cloak descended, she invited me into the light of her little room. "Right, Gerard, I'm gonna try and copy this one," she said, placing the copy of Jackie Magazine onto her makeup adorned dressing table. I watched transfixed as she expertly applied colours to her eyelids, altered her skin tone with a small beige brick that emerged upwards from a blue plastic container, then finally stained her lips a glossy pink with what looked like a cotton bud plucked from a cylindrical barrel.

She turned from the mirror, holding her hands beneath her face, presenting it to me, "Well, what do you think?" I looked at her awestruck. She'd transformed herself into the beaming beauty that smiled from the cover of her magazine. "Well, come on, tell me," she said, staring at my open mouth.

Eventually, I found the words, "You look dead beautiful, just like a model on the magazines," I said.

She lunged in and hugged me, "Orr, thanks."

Letting go of me, she jumped up, "What do you think, Bruce?" she asked, presenting herself in front of a shirtless Bruce Lee who hung from her wall brandishing his nunchaku.

When he didn't answer, I jumped in front of her, "You look beautiful, will you marry me?" I said, doing my best to sound like Bruce Lee even though I'd never heard him speak.

Maria chuckled and pushed me on the bed. "Don't be daft you, Bruce Lee won't ever marry me, he's got the pick of the world's most beautiful women, I'd never get a look in," she said, sitting back at her dressing table and playing with her hair.

Watching Maria experiment with different hair looks, I couldn't help bring myself back to our summer past, "Will you marry the Boy with Bruce Lee hair?" Her hands stalled at her head, halting the up-do she was creating. She let the hair tumble about her face, and her eyes filled with tears. I immediately regretted asking the question.

"I don't think he'd want to marry me, either – he never did take me to the pictures to see The Godfather."

Knowing I'd crossed some kind of line that had pushed Maria back towards her stye state, I jumped in with a happy diversion, "Shall we put The Sound of Music on?" I suggested, lunging to her LP collection and holding up our favourite.

My tactic worked; she beamed, "Put I am sixteen going on

seventeen on," she said. It was my least favourite, so feeling a little disappointed, I complied, as I'd do anything to ensure Maria remained free from any further evils.

Maria returned to her hair experiments and gently mouthed, "*You wait, little girl, on an empty stage for fate to turn the light on. Your life, little girl, is an empty page that men will want to write on…*"

Chapter 47: Full-Stop

As my seven ebbed away and I flowed towards eight, Christmas beckoned. But this impending festive season brought with it a niggling sense of dread that diluted my excitement. For the first time in my Manchester life, an immediate Irish relative would be travelling from Cavan to spend Christmas with us – Town Granny.

......

It wasn't that I disliked Town Granny. I'd tentatively bonded with her during that afternoon in Cavan. I was merely mindful her strict authority would bring a different flavour to our freer family Christmas. Mam was already fretting a week before her mother's arrival.

"Now you'll not be going to the pub when Mammy's here, do you hear me, Sean?" she said, shackling Dad's weekly Saturday night treat.

"I won't if it keeps the peace," he replied, giving me an eye-roll.

I knew Mam and Dad would act differently with Town Granny at our Christmas Table. They'd be aware of her wants and put her needs above their own, which would result in a more reserved Christmas for us all.

Still, I didn't fret too much, as I knew this was an important visit for Mam. So, I was ready to adjust myself accordingly.

......

Our house gleamed on the day of Town Granny's arrival. Mam,

always fastidious with housework, had gone into overdrive, and the place had an antiseptic cleanliness.

Dad went to pick Granny up – from the Airport.

The Airport! There would be no arduous overnight journey for Town Granny; Mam made sure of that.

It would be just Mam and me to initially greet Town Granny, as Maria and Dermot had sleepovers at friend's houses. I sat freshly preened in my best bib and tucker: waiting.

When we heard the key in the door, Mam and I stood nervously, like subjects about to meet their Queen. Dad opened the door, and in she stepped, wearing a blue woollen coat with matching hat pinned to her newly coiffured hair, her right arm threaded through the strap of a matching handbag.

She stood, observing her surroundings with an imperious eye, before focussing on Mam and me.

"The Aeroplane's a great invention altogether," she said, walking forward.

Mam nudged me, and I launched into my greeting, "Welcome to Manchester Granny."

She nodded, "Thank you, son."

Mam gestured her forward, "Give me your coat Mammy, and I'll get you a cup of tea and some breakfast."

Granny perched on the white leatherette couch, silently surveying our space. I felt her sense of displacement as she sat in the gaudy modernity of our fashionable seventies surroundings that were at odds with the dated décor of which she was familiar. Her own home was sparse and utilitarian, where ours was impractically over-embellished. I sat opposite her, observing her sensory overload while vicariously experiencing her sense of wonder.

Then Dad came to me, "This came for you this morning," he said, handing me a tightly packaged parcel. When I saw the American Post Mark, my hair prickled, my heart soared, and my hands began to tremble – my Sea-Monkeys had arrived.

My acute excitement needed an outlet, and it spilt out in exultant over-greeting for Granny. "Orr, it's lovely to have you here Granny, we're gonna have a great Christmas together, and I can show you all around town and everything, you'll love it."

Town Granny mistook my shaking excitement at receiving my Sea-Monkeys for delight in seeing her – my new pets were already serving me well.

......

When my aunt, uncle and Mam's friends arrived to greet Granny, I slipped upstairs to my bedroom and carefully opened the package.

It contained a kit containing various sachets and the all-important Instruction Manual. I couldn't wait to get going, and hearing the animated chatter downstairs, I knew I had the necessary adult distraction to bring the Sea-Monkeys into my world.

So, I shut the door and began to devour the Instruction Manual.

After two full reads, I felt I was reasonably conversant with my undertakings, and I tiptoed to the bathroom with the designated bowl to fill my Sea-Monkey's home with the all-important element – water.

Back in my room, I duly completed stage one: *Mix sachet with water and leave for 24 hours.* My severe lack of patience rendered me slightly riled with what, for me, seemed like an interminable wait. But on reading for a third time, I realised I wasn't quite as conversant with the instructions as I thought.

For there was a part to stage three that flummoxed me: *When your Sea-Monkeys hatch, they will be the size of the 'period' at the end of this sentence.*

I scoured the end of that sentence over and over, eventually concluding that the manual had mistakenly omitted the illustration of the 'period.'

My frustration grew along with my anger for the manual makers. I ruffled my hair and vented aloud, "Stupid people, how am I supposed to know what my Sea-Monkeys will look like when they hatch when I don't know what a 'period' looks like!"

How could they leave such an important picture out?" I asked myself. I grabbed the Manual and repeatedly flicked through its illustrated pages to be sure I'd not missed the image of the 'period.'

But no, I was sure they'd made an omission, a grave error, and I slumped on my bed with a whirring mind.

Then I had an epiphany – *I'd ask Mam. She had all of life's answers.*

I almost fell down the stairs; such was my haste to get to Mam.

Racing into the living room, I saw quite the gathering had amassed to greet Town Granny.

I stood in the centre of the room and chanted over the chatter – "MAM. MAM. MAM!"

Silence descended, and all eyes fell on me, but I didn't care.

"What is it, son?" asked Mam.

The questions flowed from me with an urgent need for answers, "What does a period look like? How big are they?"

All around me, I became aware of Granny's guests flinching, their heads lowering. When I looked at Granny, I saw her mouth open as though she were trying to catch non-existent flies – her right eye furiously twitching as though it were silently berating me.

Mam broke the silence, "Who told you that word, Son?"

I felt a wave of dread wash over me. "It says in the instruction manual that when my Sea-Monkey's hatch, they'll be the same size of a period, but they forgot to put in the picture of the period." Mam's mouth opened, but no words came out.

I felt myself drowning in dread, and in a flailing attempt to save myself and my Sea-Monkeys, I spluttered, "Never mind, it don't matter no more!"

Soaking in shame, I floundered back to my bedroom.

Chapter 48: Revelation

Muffled voices woke me, Mam and Dad's. They'd given up their bed for Town Granny and were sleeping on make-shifts in the living room.

I couldn't make out what they were saying in my befuddled state, but I heard a simmer in their whispering; they were trying to keep the lid on a row.

I stretched and turned over, and on seeing my Sea-Monkey bowl gone from my bedside drawer, I shot up, wide awake. Scratching my head, I thought I must have left it in the bathroom.

The door was locked. I rapped on it, "Who's that?" asked Town Granny, annoyance in her voice.

"It's me, Granny; open the door; I need a wee"

She shot back, "Would you ever go to the toilet downstairs and leave me to get washed."

On hearing her anger, I made to go back to my room, but Maria's door opened; she put her finger to her lips, "Shhh, come in."

Maria sat on her unmade bed and gestured for me to sit on her little bedside stool. She whispered, "Why didn't you wait for me to do your Sea-Monkeys with you?"

"Why? Have I done something bad?" I whispered back.

313

Maria fidgeted and ran her fingers through her hair, "No, course you haven't, you couldn't be bad if you tried."

She turned and began to brush her hair. We both remained silent, and, in this stillness, Maria's room began a metamorphosis in my mind.

I saw lush green foliage all around me, and the sound of rushing tap water from the adjacent bathroom transported me back to The Clear Lagoon in Ireland. Maria and I were back in the summertime space where I'd felt her change.

When Maria put the brush down, I whispered, "Please tell me, Maria, what've I done wrong?"

Her lip quivered, and I was unsure whether it was with sorrow or smile. Eventually, a sad smile broke, and she swivelled her head, "Nothing," she said, hugging me.

With my head resting in her hug, my eyes scanned her dressing table, and there I saw it – The Sea-Monkey Instruction Manual. A rush of relief coursed through me, "Have you got my Sea-Monkeys?"

But Maria didn't answer. Instead, she held me in her hug. I struggled like a kitten wanting free, "Why did you take them off my bedside drawer?"

She released me, "I'm sorry Gerard, Mam flushed them down the toilet while you were asleep." Her words hit me with a slap that felt physical, and I actually flinched before a profound shock at Mam's actions made me feel sick.

Maria instinctively engulfed me in her embrace. "I promise when I get my Saturday job, I'll send off for another pack, and we'll hatch them together here in my room," she said, squeezing me tight. But her hug was scant compensation for the crushing disappointment I felt for the loss of my Sea-Monkeys.

......

The sense of being back in The Clear Lagoon stayed with me. Back then, in that summer of secrets, I knew Maria was withholding something from me. And now, in this winter of woe, I had the same sense.

I stayed silent in Maria's arms, the continually flowing tap water giving me cold comfort.

And when the tap stopped, I wanted answers. I pushed myself from her, "What've I done wrong? What's Mam punishing me for?" I asked with a newfound assertion.

Maria stood and picked up the Sea-Monkey Manual. She flicked through the pages, stopping at one, "Sit here," she said, tapping the bed. Her fingers ran over the page as I settled next to her. Her index finger stopped, "It's this word 'period'; I think it means something else in America." She sighed, "I wish you'd have waited for me to do this with you."

"What does that word mean in America?" I asked.

"I think it means a full-stop, so it says when your Sea-Monkeys hatch, they'll be the same size as the 'full-stop' at the end of this sentence," she explained.

She made some kind of sense, sort of, "But why didn't Mam tell me that when I asked her?"

Maria let out a stifled chuckle, "Because she probably didn't know." She paused before continuing, "That word 'period' means something else here, and you know what Town Granny's like. She's dead prim and proper."

My intrigue piqued, "What does period mean here then? Is it not proper to say it out loud?"

Maria's reaction puzzled me: she laughed, swivelled her head, inhaled, exhaled, took my hand, and said, "Right, it's all about girls growing up." She stopped, took a deep breath and continued, "When a girl starts growing up, changes start happening in her body, and we call this happening a 'period.' She paused and pushed her hands through her hair, "It's kind of embarrassing for girls and grown-ups, so we don't really talk about it in the open because it's private. That's why everyone went quiet when you said it out loud."

Her words rendered me quiet as revelation washed over me. I was back in The Clear Lagoon, struggling to understand the change, the shift in my sister. Now I knew.

I understood the sealed postcard to Mam and why she wouldn't want to discuss this private matter with her kid brother.

Maria nudged me with her elbow, "Do you understand what I'm saying?"

I tilted my head, "I think so, yes."

She nudged me again, "Please don't be mad with Mam. She was only trying to keep the peace with her Mam, she didn't want anything spoiling Christmas."

I nodded my understanding, "But if a 'period' looks like a tiny little full-stop, why is Town Granny bothered by that?" I asked, bemused.

Maria spluttered and laughed a great big heaving guffaw. When she recovered, she dive-hugged me, "You're so bleeding sweet you are." When she released me, her mirth had morphed into a kind of melancholy, and she sighed, "It's sad we have to grow up," she ruffled my hair, "being a kid's so much easier."

We heard the bathroom door open, and Maria jumped up, "Granny's out of the bathroom, it's my turn," she said, fleeing the room.

......

The Clear Lagoon morphed back into Maria's room, and reality began to bite me. I reflected on her words, "…being a kid's so much easier."

It wasn't easy for me. I longed to be an adult. For they knew life's truths and were thus exempt from their mind's making up tormenting scenarios from the shreds of whispered words and furtive actions.

Had I known the truth of this happening called a period, my mind wouldn't have created the absurdity of my sister's possession, and my summer might have been more carefree.

That summer, my sister had come of age.

And now, in this winter, as I stood on the cusp of eight years old, *my coming of age began.*

Chapter 49 – Manchester: 1976

My Council Estate baked under a relentless sun as the heatwave refused to abate. Paddock Field was parched as hosepipe bans meant us kids had no respite from the heat; our cheap paddling pools remained deflated.

After another scorching day, I returned home as the fading sun left its stinging burn on my exposed skin. I opened the door and walked into the emptiness.

……

The passing of time meant I was now most often the sole resident of our Paddock Field Council House – especially at the weekends.

Saturday nights were an infinite stretch of solitude as Mam worked, Dad reaped the rewards of his working week in the pub, and the age gap between my siblings and I meant they were out enjoying all the thrills of early adulthood.

I was still very much a child, and although I was often home alone, I never felt the ache of loneliness. My own company was something I'd grown accustomed to. Besides, I had the telly to myself, which was a great privilege for an eleven-year-old.

There was something else I'd grown accustomed to – Maria was now a fully-grown woman, and this I accepted with gusto.

I now understood where Maria was in her life; what enhanced mine was how she would include me whenever she could. She no longer dismissed me as an annoying little brother who restricted her womanly pursuits. Instead, she saw me as a friend with whom she enjoyed spending quality time.

And it was these times with Maria that I lived for. The thought of our shopping trips made my dull telly nights alone more endurable.

Maria now worked part-time in the Manchester Department Store, Selfridges, and I'd bristle with excitement on the evenings when she'd come home from work, invite me into her bedroom and regale me with all the glamour of the store.

One mundane Monday evening, I sat bored in front of the telly when I heard the key in the door. This innocuous sound gave me the greatest thrill, as I knew it was Maria returning from her Selfridges shift.

On this evening, she flew through the door and into the living room, her face flushed with excitement, "Orr Gerard, you'll never guess who I served today?"

I jumped from the couch, "Who?" I asked.

She grabbed my hand, "Come upstairs, I'll show you," she said.

I pulled her back, "Show me? Have you brought them back with you?" I asked, looking around for the customer that so invigorated my sister.

Giggling, she pulled me up the stairs, "Don't be daft – come on."

I sat on her bed, twitching with anticipation. Maria placed her bag next to me and took out her purse. I wobbled my feet to try and give me restraint, but it didn't work, "Come on, tell me, who was it?" I asked, impatient.

She gave me a coy smile, "I'll show you." She opened her purse, took out a narrow piece of paper and handed it to me. I looked at the blank till receipt, confused, "What's this?" I asked.

"Turn it over."

I did as she said, and looked at it, then back to Maria, "No way, honestly, you served her?"

Maria beamed and nodded, "Yes, I did."

My finger followed the pen written message – 'To Maria, best wishes, Dana XXX'

That evening we had a glorious time listening to Dana songs while discussing all kinds of everything into the early hours of the morning.

......

This evening, as I tried to salve my burning skin with Mam's Nivea Cream, I knew Maria wouldn't be arriving home with any of her Selfridges Tales of Fabulosity.

Maria was now attending college. Earlier in the day, I'd helped her choose an outfit for a day trip to Blackpool with her newfound college friends. Together, we chose a fitted yellow t-shirt with a sunset motif, worn with tight denim flares that fell stylishly over her multi-coloured platform shoes. She looked super stylish.

Of course, I ached to go with her, but I knew this was her adult world, and she'd want to be free to behave in ways that were not for her kid brother's eyes.

She checked her image in the full-length mirror, and happy with what she saw, she turned to me, "We're a great team, you and me. I love this look," she said, bending to hug me. She applied a slick of lip-gloss, popped it into her small shoulder bag and said, "I'll bring you back loads of rock." She bent and kissed my cheek, "See you tomorrow, Gerard."

I listened to her excitedly descend the stairs before the bang of the front door meant I was alone. I sat on Maria's bed, surrounded by the sound of silence.

......

Another Saturday evening, and the silence was replaced by the sunny cheer of The Generation Game. I knelt in front of the telly, fully immersed in the family-friendly game show.

I watched it without family, but that didn't impede my enjoyment of the show. I sang along unselfconsciously to the theme tune, "Life is the name of the game, and I wanna play the game with you."

Little did I know then, I was about to meet a person who would re-shape my life and re-route my future.

Chapter 50: A Star visit

The sun's sear slowly ebbed as night began its fall. Sitting on the leatherette sofa, my head became heavy, and tiredness caused it to fall forwards. But as I was about to succumb to sleep, a noise jolted me awake. It was a sound inconsistent with this time on a Saturday evening – the key in the door.

Someone was returning home unexpectedly.

I stood up with an intuitive feeling that something incredible was about to happen. I began fixing my hair in accordance with the unfolding of a momentous moment.

When the door banged shut, I heard footsteps crumple the plastic sheeting used to protect our hallway carpet – this was more than one person.

My most plausible thought was Dermot returning with a friend, and I puffed up to meet his mate, readying myself to affect a blokey banter.

They went into the kitchen; I heard the tap being turned on and the water running. I thought to shout out, "Hello, is that you, Dermot?" But some kind of sense made me mute.

I heard a muffled voice, with a strange sound I couldn't place.

My skin prickled, and I moved to the window and opened the latch. This window was often my escape route from my irate brother. Now, it was a potential getaway from a key-holding intruder.

But I stayed put and listened intently – rustling and giggling combined with the strange sound of a voice I didn't understand. The sounds and situation were foreign to me, and I called out wanting clarification, "Hello!"

The sounds stopped, halted by my hello. Then, after what seemed like an eternity, "It's alright, Gerard, it's only me," said Maria. I didn't respond, as I guessed it wasn't only my sister. Her following words, not directed at me, confirmed my suspicion, "Come on and meet him."

I pulled the latch closed and tensed as I heard footfall coming up the plastic sheeting.

My jaw dropped, and I stumbled backwards, struck by a star.

Maria stood smiling so wide her light replaced the summer sun. And a man stood beside her smiling as brightly – *it was Bruce Lee.*

Chapter 51: Bruce Lee

'It's him, it's really him. Bruce Lee is standing in my living room next to my sister,' my inner voice yelled, leaving me standing open-mouthed and mute.

Bruce extended his hand, "Very nice to meet you, Gerard. I hear lots about you." His English was broken; his handshake wasn't. It was strong and firm.

But I still couldn't speak, so I nodded and smiled shyly. He looked exactly like he did on Maria's posters. Slim hipped, taut, athletic; and – the hair: inky black, a sleek and shiny face frame.

This wasn't the boy with Bruce Lee hair – this was the real deal.

Maria seemed shy as well, although not as debilitatingly so as me. She smiled at me sweetly, "Has the cat got your tongue, Gerard?"

I swivelled a 'No,' as Bruce Lee spoke again, "You have cat?" he asked, his eyes searching our living room for any animals.

His question made Maria giggle, and she play-tapped him on the shoulder, "No, we don't have a cat. That's what we say when someone's being quiet," she explained.

Bruce laughed, "I have lots to learn about English." He scanned the room, taking in every nook and cranny of our gaudily decorated living room. Eventually, he homed in on the Chinese lady that took pride of place atop our television. "Ah, she looks like my sister," he said, rushing to admire my favourite ornamental piece in our house. This exotic lady sat cross-legged in her brightly-bejewelled catsuit, her hands clasped in elegant prayer. Her black hair scraped tightly back, emphasising the almond shape of her chocolaty brown eyes; but what spoiled her aesthetic for me was the light bulb screwed into the top of her head, and the synthetic light shade with plastic gems stuck to it – she was a lamp that we never switched on.

But the bulb didn't bother Bruce. On the contrary, he was both awed by her beauty and impressed with her job as a bringer of light. Watching the wonder in Bruce Lee's face as he traced her contours with his finger before he switched her on filled me with pride.

I was proud that we had appealed to Bruce Lee's aesthetic; my family's style choice had impressed a movie star.

Maria was also cheered by Bruce's appreciation of our familial ornamentation. In fact, she seemed to swoon with delight while watching him discover other trinkets, which through his widened eyes were viewed as treasure.

My eyes met Maria's; she smiled wide before her eyes left mine and returned to Bruce. She gazed at him with what looked like adoration. Eventually, she spoke, her words shattering my stricken star, "Gerard, this is Raymond."

My head swivelled from him to her, "What – wait – who?"

He turned around and said, "No, my name is Waiman, but other students say it like English name Rayman, so that what they call me in college," he explained.

I knew he wasn't really the movie star. My suspended disbelief snapped as he offered me his hand again. I took it, and this time I managed to say a shy, "Hello."

Raymond looked at Maria, then back to me, "You come to Blackpool?" he asked.

Confused, I answered, "It's nearly night. Are you going back to Blackpool?"

Maria smiled, "No, we've just got back, we had such a laugh," she said, nudging Raymond,

"Yes, it is very fun." He addressed me again, "You come to visit me with Maria, and we take you on all the fun rides," he said.

My ease with him grew, and I asked, "Ah, do you live in Blackpool?"

Maria looked a little wistful as she answered for him, "Raymond's going to work in a restaurant there, for the summer."

The Seaside Town, Blackpool, was a thrilling place, and the thought of going there with Maria and Raymond filled me with such excitement that I couldn't curb my enthusiasm.

"Can we, please Maria, can we visit Raymond and go on the Log-Flume and all the other rides?" I asked.

Maria looked at Raymond and smiled, "Yes, we can," she said.

He nodded, "Okay, I go to work now in Fish and Chip Shop," he said, taking Maria's hand and leading her back out the door and up our plastic laden hall.

He was gone as swiftly as he'd arrived, and I stood in awe at this twist to my Saturday night.

I waited, wondering would Maria return. Listening, I heard muffled words and stifled giggles punctuated by moments of silence. I wanted to go to my bedroom but felt trapped, lest I intrude upon some kind of courting ritual.

So, I sat on the couch and continued to wait.
Wait for what?
I didn't know.
I did know that I had an innate sense that I shouldn't be sat on the couch at this time, that I was some kind of hindrance despite having nowhere else to go.

The bang of the front door raised me to my feet, "Maria, have you gone?" I called out. There was quiet before the plastic hallway crumpled.

Maria stopped in the doorway. She looked at me with a side-wise head tilt and a kind of sorry, sheepish look on her face that I didn't understand.

"What?" I spoke.

She smiled shyly, "What do you think?"

"Of what?"

She lifted her head, "Of Raymond," she said as if her question should be obvious.

"Oh right, he's dead nice. I thought he was Bruce Lee for a minute."

She sat on the far end of the couch and turned to me, "I think he's even nicer looking than Bruce Lee."

I'd become mindful of not commenting on male looks, so I smiled without comment.

She nudged me with her elbow, "Well, what did you think of him?" she repeated.

"He's dead friendly."

She seemed disappointed in my answer, "Is that all? Don't you think he's dead nice?"

I nodded, "Yes, I told you he is."

I paused a moment, then asked, "Is he your boyfriend?"

She sighed, "I don't know."

"Why don't you know?" I asked, sure she should know this simple fact of life now that she was a college student.

She shrugged her shoulders, "I know he likes me, but he likes Hillary McCroy as well, and she's prettier than me."

"You're really pretty – is it a competition – do you have to win him as a boyfriend?" I asked, intrigued to know what Hillary McCroy looked like.

I could see her pondering my question before she answered. "In a way, I suppose it is a bit like a competition; college definitely is. We're all competing with each other for marks and that," she turned to me, "I wish we didn't have to compete for romance." Maria stood and stared at her reflection in the mirror, assessing herself. When she turned away from her reflection and looked at me, I saw the disappointment on her face.

I jumped up, "Stop it, Maria, you're dead pretty, honest you are," I implored.

She smiled and took my hand, "Come to my room, there's a record I want to play for you."

......

Maria's room, my favourite place in the world. As soon as I entered her sanctuary, I was soothed by the musky smell of Avon's Sweet Honesty, Maria's signature perfume. I sat on my corner of her bed as she took a Woolworths carrier bag from her top drawer.

Opening the bag, she revealed a record, a single. This was unusual as Maria rarely bought singles, preferring long-playing records.

My excitement mounted, "Is it Save your kisses for me?" I asked, hoping it was the Eurovision winner we adored.

She lifted the lid on her record player and removed the black vinyl disk from its cardboard sleeve, which she deliberately hid from my view.

The disk dropped from the metal pole, and as the needle bar found its groove, I leaned in and listened.

Bongo drums gave way to a stirring string intro that made me sit up. The opening lyric sang out, *"Though we gotta say goodbye, for the summer...."*

I recognised the song, and it made me immediately reflect. As the song continued, I was taken back to the darkness of Summer 1972... *"Baby, I promise you this, I'll send you all my love every day in a letter, sealed with a kiss. Yes, it's gonna be a cold, lonely summer, but I'll fill the emptiness; I'll send you all my dreams every day in a letter, sealed with a kiss. I don't want to say goodbye for the summer, knowing the love we'll miss, so let us make a pledge to meet in September, and seal it with a kiss."*

A cold chill shivered through me as the mournful tune rekindled thoughts of demonic possession and self-inflicted pain. When the song ended, Maria's voice pulled me from the darkness, "It's such a gorgeous song, isn't it?"

I head-swivelled, "It reminds me of Ireland, that summer when you had that horrible stye," I said.

"Does it?"

"Yes, it does."

But still, she beamed, "It reminds me of Raymond, that's why I bought it."

"Why does it remind you of him?" I asked, intrigued.

"Well, you know he's going away to work in Blackpool for the summer."

"Yes, to work in a restaurant."

She looked around at her Bruce Lee posters, then focussed back on me, "He said he's going to write to me..."

…I jumped in, "Every day in a letter, sealed with a kiss."

She giggled, "He didn't say that bit, but the fact he said it is dead romantic."

I sat upright, "Did he tell Hillary McRoy he's going to write to her?" I asked. Immediately I regretted my question as the wistfulness fell from her face and her whole body tightened.

She rested her chin on her fist, "I didn't think of that." She rose from the bed and walked towards her record player, stooping to remove the record. As she placed the disk back in its sleeve, I noticed she looked mournful. She opened her drawer and picked out a bundle of t-shirts. "I run away with myself I do, get ideas above my station," she said, putting the record in her drawer, placing the t-shirts on top and shutting it away.

She did this almost ritually. Her sadness touched me – *Maria had buried her hope.*

Chapter 52: Hairs and Veils.

I pulled open my top drawer and dug deep, pulling out my favourite shirt for what I hoped would be a sunny spring day.

About to put on the shirt, my reflection in the mirror above my bedside drawer stalled me. I threw the shirt on my bed and leaned in for a closer look. I cringed at the whiteness of my skin and my almost skeletal frame, but it was something else that caused me concern. I drew in even closer, and to be sure, I placed my hand on my chest and swiped left and right.

But the offending fuzz remained. This wasn't some bed fluff; this was real hair – growing from my chest. I craned in even further to see three black shoots sprouting from the centre of my torso. I wondered if they were just an anomaly, an aberration that would correct itself over the coming days?

I associated chest hair with men, old men – although now twelve, I was still a kid.

A sharp rap on the door jolted me, and I grabbed the shirt to cover my chest lest someone enter and see my three hairs, "Hello," I said.

"Hurry up, Gerard, we've got to leave soon," said Maria, hastily descending the stairs.

I put on my shirt and quickly buttoned it up; with the hairs out of sight, they were out of mind – for the moment.

Maria was in the kitchen with a glass of Vimto. When I entered, she looked at me bemused, "Gerard, are you being serious?"

"About what?" I asked, confused.

She nodded at me, "That."

"What?" I asked, looking down at myself.

She put her hand to her throat, "Your shirt, you've got the top button fastened."

My hand shot to my collar, "I know, I like it like this," I said, feeling myself flush.

Maria laughed and approached me, "Don't be daft, it's the style to have buttons open and your collar out wide," she said, her hands reaching out to my neck.

"NO!" I shouted, jumping back.

Maria jolted at my reaction, "What's up with you today?" she asked.

I grappled at my top button, "Nowt, I'll unbutton it meself, that's all," I said, opening only one button to ensure the three hairs remained unseen.

……

On the bus, Maria and I were quiet, deep in thought. While mine were all about my evening plans to shave off the three hairs using Dad's razor, I had a good idea what Maria's were focussed on.

I glanced at her as she stared out the window with a wistful look; I knew she was thinking about Hillary McCroy – we were on our way to her wedding.

......

Of course, we hadn't been invited because Maria and Hillary were no longer friends. They'd had a big bust-up over boyfriends, and now Hillary was marrying hers.

I didn't understand why Maria wanted to put herself through what to me would feel like agony, but when I asked her, she answered matter of factly, "I just want to see what her dress is like."

......

We stood outside the church as the final guests arrived and entered. Maria gazed at the blue sky, "Things always go right for Hillary, no chance of rain on her wedding day," she said, her words weighted with sadness.

I took her hand, and she squeezed it; the thing she did to let me know she was alright. I felt her tense, "She's coming," she said. "Where is she?" I asked, seeing no sign of any wedding confection. Maria nodded down the road at an approaching car, festooned with white ribbon.

It stopped opposite us, and the smartly dressed driver opened the back passenger door.

My heart began to quicken as a man in tails, holding a top hat, emerged. He bent and offered his hand inside the car to help out his daughter. My gasp at the sight of her was involuntary. Her veil billowed upwards in the soft breeze, then out came Hillary, dressed in a spectacular opulence of silk and lace.

The skirt was bell-like, and as she followed her father's lead, she seemed to glide like a swan on a lake. Hillary raised her hand to catch her veil, and as she did, she turned – and caught Maria's eye.

She stood tall to give us a full-frontal view of her Bridal-Beauty. Then to my surprise, she spoke, "Maria, come to the evening do," she pointed at me, "and bring your Gerard with you." Maria nodded and smiled back, "Thanks."

We watched as she and her father entered the church. Maria let go of my hand and swiftly turned, walking away at pace as if to rid herself of the sight of Hillary – I wiped her sweat off of my hands and followed.

......

On the bus home, Maria broke our silence, "She took your breath away, didn't she?" My reaction had been obvious. I couldn't lie, "Yes," I said, immediately feeling a guilty pang for having betrayed my sister, somehow.

Her stare remained fixed out the window, "I knew she'd wear cream." I didn't answer because I didn't know what she meant. Then in a whisper, she said to herself, yet was meant for my ears also, "When I get married, I'll be wearing white."

When she remained silent, I nudged her, "Are you getting married?" I asked. She smiled and resumed her silent stare out the window. I grabbed her arm, "Maria, answer me."

I tugged her arm, "Maria?" She turned to me with a cheeky grin and leaned in, "Promise me you won't say anything," she said, grabbing my arm and pulling me into her.

I pulled back and looked at her, my mouth open. Maria looked all around the bus, then back to me, "Not a word to Mam, Dad, or Dermot, cross your heart and hope to die," she said.

I struggled to find words as my head spun. Maria tugged my arm again, "Gerard, promise me!"

Eventually, I found the words, "You can't get married without telling Mam and Dad."

She giggled, "I'm gonna tell them at the weekend."

I shook my head, "Don't you mean, ask them?"

She shook her head, "I'm eighteen," she paused before continuing, "and anyway, they love Raymond as much as I do." She nudged me, "You love him too, aren't you happy for me?"

I nodded, "You'll have a proper wedding and all that, won't you?"

"Of course, you can help me pick the dress."

I nodded again and asked, "When?" Maria leaned back, "When what?" she asked.

"When are you getting married?"

Uncertainty clouded her face, "We're not sure yet. He only asked me last week."

I was happy with the gap in our conversation. I needed time to compute the momentous revelation – *my sister Maria was marrying her Bruce Lee.*

Chapter 53: The Telling

Mam and Dad adored Raymond. He'd bonded with our family and successfully assimilated into the local community and wider city of Manchester in such a short time.

His strong work ethic ensured he was in demand for work within the restaurants and businesses of the city's China Town. Mam and Dad were fond of him personally and impressed with his professionalism; his ambition was fierce. "That young fella will be a millionaire by the time he's thirty," said Dad to Maria, as he readied himself for the pub on Saturday night.

I glanced at Maria, and when she caught my eye, I mouthed, "Tell him, now," thinking his positive appraisal of Raymond would be a good time for Maria to tell Dad she was going to marry him.

But Maria shut me up with an urgent head swivel and a silent but angry, "NO!" Feeling chastised, I left the room and went to my bedroom.

I sat on my bed and listened to footfall coming up the stairs. A pause at my door, then a knock, "Can I come in?" asked Dad. My stomach tumbled, had Maria told him?

"Yes," I answered, apprehensive.

Dad didn't come in; he popped his head around the door, "Are you alright?" he asked.

Immediately I knew she hadn't told him, "Yeah, why?"

"You left the room in a huff there, so you did."

"I didn't. I'm alright."

He looked me up and down, "Are you sure now? Is everything alright at school?"

I gave him a reassuring smile, "Yeah, honest." Satisfied, he returned a smile, "Then go down and keep Maria company; she gets lonesome when Raymond does be working at the weekends," he said.

"Alright, I will."

I felt angry with myself for putting Maria in a potentially embarrassing situation. When I heard Dad leave, I left my room and went tentatively downstairs. Sheepishly, I peeped into the living room. When Maria caught my eye, I said, "Sorry." She stood up, the look on her face forgiving, "Come into the kitchen. I'll make us some cocoa."

I luxuriated in the warm drink, made extra comforting by the addition of cream; it was a literal hug in a mug. Maria sipped her cocoa, "I've decided to tell them tomorrow. You know they're always in a good mood on Sundays because it's their day off."

I nodded my understanding, "Is Raymond gonna be with you?" I asked.

"No, he's working – again," she took another sip, "I'd prefer to tell them myself anyway, in case Mam gets mad, I wouldn't want Raymond witnessing that." Maria drained her mug; in her face, I saw a concern coupled with doubt in her eyes, "They'll be alright with it, won't they?"

she asked. My stomach tightened with angst at my grown-up sister asking her kid brother for an assurance I wasn't entirely sure of myself.

I affected a confident air, "Course they will, they'll be dead chuffed," I said.

She kissed my cheek, "You're right. I'm worrying over nothing."

But in truth, I had a niggling worry about Mam's reaction to Maria's pronouncement of marriage to Raymond. I'd become aware of a tension between Mam and Maria, something I'd never seen in the past. Perhaps it had always been there, but my being so young meant I hadn't noticed. My growing maturity had made me more aware of the dynamics of adult relationships, and I was acutely aware of the shift in Mam and Maria's. At times I wondered if they even liked each other, let alone loved the way a mother and daughter should. With this question front of mind, I wondered if it was time to ask, 'Do you love Mam?'

But I pulled back on opening a potential can of worms, preferring instead to push it to the back of my mind.

She took my cup and began to wash it in the sink. "I'll tell them in the morning before Dad puts his Irish records on," she said, her confidence returned, while mine continued to wane – a potential adverse reaction from Mam to Maria's news niggled at me.

……

"Red and yellow and pink and green,
Purple and orange and blue.
I can sing a rainbow,
sing a rainbow,
sing a rainbow too.

Listen with your eyes,
listen with your ears,
and sing everything you see.
I can sing a rainbow,
sing a rainbow,
sing along with me."

Val Doonican's velvety vocal roused me from the soundest sleep. I threw my arms upwards, stretched and yawned aloud, feeling remarkably refreshed.

Then realisation hit me, and I sat upright; it was Sunday morning – had Maria told Mam and Dad? Seeing Dermot's bed unslept in, I knew he'd stayed over at a friend's house. This meant Maria had Mam and Dad to herself, so I surmised she'd already told them.

I hoped Dad's playing Doonican was a celebratory song choice. But I couldn't be sure. So, I crept out of bed and gently tapped on Maria's door, "Are you there?"

No answer. I opened the door and peeked in; her bed was freshly made – she'd been up for a while. Surely, she's told them. Yet I was reluctant to go downstairs lest I walk in at an inopportune time and spoil Maria's pronouncement.

I slinked back to my room, sat on my bed with the door open and took Val Doonican's advice to listen with my eyes and listen with my ears.

Peering over the bannister and into our long hallway, I saw the kitchen door ajar – this meant the three of them were in the living room. My heart quickened – she was probably telling them right now.

My ears pricked up, and I strained to listen. "There was Johnny McEldoo and McGee and me, and a couple of two or three went on a spree one day. We had a bob or two which we knew how to blew, the beer and whiskey flew, and we all felt gay...."

All I heard were the dulcet tones of Val Doonican filling the house. Feeling confident Maria had told them, I decided to go downstairs and enter the living room with an unknowing, nonchalant attitude.

But with barely a foot on the stair, Val's cheerful song abruptly stopped, replaced by Mam's cheerless pronouncement, "No. No. No!"

I froze.

Dad's voice, "Calm down, Kathleen."

I ran back to my room and slumped on the bed in time for Mam's response, a singular, emphatic – "No!" her voice flaming with anger.

There was banging, clattering, and finally, the race of footfall up the stairs chilled me to the bone. Maria burst into my room; her body language mute, her face ashen.

Our widened eyes locked, and with Maria speechless, I spoke, "I didn't think she'd take it that bad."

Maria shook her head and remained mute while I gibbered. "She'll be alright, she'll come around to it, you know what she's like, Dad'll convince her – she really likes Raymond – she loves spring-rolls – special fried rice – that crispy duck thing with roll-up pancakes that he does when we go to the restaurant where he works – and she even drinks the Chinese tea, even though she hates it...." Maria raised her hand to halt my babble.

Eventually, she found words. "She's happy for me; they both are." Seeing my confusion, she focussed on me intently, "Gerard, thank God, I told them before they got that news."

I jumped up, "What news?"

Maria took my hand and guided me back to the bed. Sitting next to me, she stared ahead and softly said – *"Town Granny's dead."*

Chapter 54: Death

I couldn't understand Mam's angry reaction to her mother's passing. She'd received the death notice via a phone call from a relative in Cavan, and her ire towards the messenger seemed wholly misplaced.

My own response was shock, followed by sadness for a Granny who I was only just getting to know. There'd been a growing bond between us after my Sea Monkey debacle. When Maria had explained the miscommunication, she giggled like a little girl. She said, "God Love you, Gerard, I'll give you the money to send off for another pack of them, so I will." I actually looked forward to visiting her and getting to know her more on my next Cavan Summer.

But sadly, that wouldn't come to pass now she was gone. Moreover, I had no outlet to express my sadness. Mam shed no tears; instead, when her anger diminished, she transformed into an organising automaton: packing, phone calls to inform siblings, family, and friends, telling work of her leave of absence, booking flights – and then Mam was gone, waved off in a taxi to bury her mother in Cavan.

With the taxi out of sight, Dad, Dermot, Maria, and I breathed a collective sigh of relief that Mam's tension had left the house with her. Knowing I could now ask questions, I didn't hold back, "Dad, how'd she die?" He was clearly shaken.

I saw a slight tremble in his hand as he wiped his face, "She dropped dead in the Convent Chapel. I'd say it was a heart attack, Son."

Dad walked to his beloved record playing system and plucked out

Jim Reeves. Sitting down, he lost himself in Jim's melancholy voice, "I fall to pieces each time I see you again. I fall to pieces; how can I just be your friend?"

Dermot always fled from Dad's songs, and he was gone before Jim sang his first word. Maria gently tapped my arm and gestured to follow her.

On the upstairs landing, I tugged Maria's arm, "Is Dad alright?"

Maria was sure, "Yeah; he's feeling sad, he reacts to things differently than Mam." She turned her ear to the final verse of Jim's song and smiled, "He told me that's his and Mam's song. When Mam left Cavan to be a nurse over here, Dad followed her." She took my hand and guided me to her room, "They were friends first, just like Raymond and me."

Back in my bedroom, I asked, "Maria, are you sad Town Granny's dead?"

My question irked her, "Course I am, why do you even have to ask me that?" she said, hitting me with her elbow.

Lowering my head, I had to think why I asked her, "None of us has cried, not even Mam," I said.

Maria thought a moment, "I suppose it's because we're all a bit shocked," she paused and pondered, "and because we're not that close to Town Granny."

This was my first death experience in my family, and I was confused by our collective reaction to it. Maria added to her evaluation of our response, "Who knows, Gerard, our tears might come later on when we get over the shock."

A thought struck me, "She might come back as a ghost; her house is haunted, you know, even you said it was."

Maria chuckled, "I thought you'd grown out of all that ghost stuff."

Her words reminded me of my summer of tumult, "Remember when I was looking for that ghost in Cavan, the tall-man?" I asked.

She let out a little sigh, "I do."

I made sure our eyes met, "I didn't really meet a ghost, did I?"

Her smile was soft, "No, I don't think you did; Uncle Tommy was messing and being kind with you."

"What do you mean?"

"He knew how much it meant to you; he was playing along with the story so you wouldn't be disappointed and had something to tell Dad."

"Yeah, I realise that now – I really believed all that stuff then; I still kinda do." I paused, then decided to confess something still hidden in that distant summer, "I thought you were possessed by the Devil back then."

Maria's eyes widened, and her head swivelled like a thing possessed, "You what?"

"You heard what I said."

"I did – what made you think that?"

"Because you changed, become dead distant from me; then you got a stye, and I thought that was proof you were possessed – I was gonna shoot you in the eye to get rid of that stye."

Maria shook my shoulder, "Gerard, I hope you're messing. Please tell me you weren't really going to do that?" she asked, aghast.

My eyes narrowed, and I began a slow head swivel. Only when Maria's face began to contort with horror did I burst out laughing, "With a water pistol filled with Holy Water."

Maria exhaled with relief and tapped my shoulder, "You daft sod, you had me there." She nudged me, "Why didn't you do it?"

I pondered, then recalled, "The pistol went off in my pocket and soaked me in holy water; you all thought I'd pissed myself."

We both burst out laughing and instinctively covered our mouths to stifle our mirth.

I removed my hand first, "Maria, we shouldn't be laughing."

She composed herself, "I know," she took my hand, "come into my room, I've got things to show you," she said, swiftly exiting the boy's room.

I loved being in Maria's floral festooned sanctuary, albeit somewhat changed. Bruce Lee no longer adorned her walls now she had her own real-life version to look at. Instead, her walls bloomed in delicate pink and yellow flowers, with pale green foliage, wallpaper that transformed the room into a summer woodland – it was my happy space.

Sitting on her bed, my heart fluttered with anticipation at the things she had to show me. Maria lifted the lid on her bedside foot-stool, pulled out a pile of magazines and sat next to me. "I'm getting married, Gerard – we need to start looking at wedding dresses," she said, opening the first of the stock-piled Bridal Magazines on her lap.

Town Granny was dead, but life goes on; and in that moment of loss, all Maria and I could think of was – *The Wedding.*

Chapter 55: 1977 Salford, Manchester, England

My ears pulsed to the beat of my heart. I unclenched my hands and wiped the sweat on my suit trousers, instantly feeling fresh beads prickle my palms.

I was about to watch Maria marry her sweetheart, Raymond – and I was nervous.

Mam and I sat in the front pew of St Joseph's. She looked behind her, then turned to whisper in my ear, "This chapel hasn't seen the likes of it, it's like the United Nations."

Looking back, I was struck by the multi-cultural guests. Chinese, Muslim, African, English, and Irish were sitting together in the childhood church where my story began.

My aunts, Susan, Eileen, and their daughters Carmel and Brenda, had travelled from Cavan to represent our wider Irish family.

In the days leading up to the wedding, I'd acted as tour guide for my Irish relatives. I enjoyed showing them around Manchester, albeit bittersweet – because while I showed them the sights, I said silent goodbyes to the city.

These were my last weeks as a city boy. I'd had a good six months to get used to the idea of my life's change and sitting in the church waiting for Maria to arrive, I was resigned to it.

Mam and Dad called me into the kitchen. There was a solemnity about them indicating big news to come. Mam spoke, "When I was over burying Mammy, I got the news that she's left me the house."

I nodded, "That's good, isn't it?" I asked.

When Dad took over, I noted his nervous shuffle. "Now that Maria's getting married, we thought we'd leave the house to her and Raymond, and we'll go home to live in Town Granny's house."

Unsure of what he was implying, I asked, "I'm living with Maria and Raymond, then?"

They exchanged a concerned glance before Mam cut to the chase, "No, Dermot has his job here, he'll be living with them, you'll be coming home with us."

Mam nudged me, "Doesn't our Dermot look fierce well."

Looking over at Raymond's best-man, Dermot, I saw he was precisely that now – a man. When our eyes met, he winked and gave me a thumbs up, which I returned while answering Mam, "Yeah, he looks dead smart and handsome." I envied him his life's path; it wasn't punctuated by the change I was facing.

"I'm dead jealous of you, our kid, going to live in Cavan. It'll be like a never-ending holiday," said Dermot, the evening Mam and Dad had given me the news of our move. I knew he suspected I was apprehensive, and this was his way of buoying me up. I gave him a thumbs up and said nothing of how I felt. How I wanted us to remain a family, how I'd miss him crashing into bed in the early hours of the morning, how I'd miss our fights over the telly, our Sunday evening battle to pick the remnants of the roast chicken. I couldn't articulate how much I was going to miss – him.

Mam leaned in and whispered in my ear, "I wonder will she wear the hat or the veil?" she asked.

I shrugged, "Don't know, but we'll find out soon," I answered, affecting a nonchalant unknowing air.

"I've decided, Gerard." Maria leaned forward for her big reveal, "I'm going to wear the hat." She leant back to feast on my reaction.

My heart surged. The hat was my choice, "It's miles nicer than the veil, honest it is," I said, taking a celebratory slug of lemonade. We were in the café of Debenhams Department Store in Manchester. We'd been to the bridal department where Maria had bought the final pieces for the wedding day – two pale blue, floral headbands for her flower girls. She beamed, "It's far trendier than the veil; Chris said the veil's more for an older bride," she said, taking a bite of her cheese and onion sandwich. Chris was Maria's best friend and bridesmaid; she was stunningly stylish and beautiful. I was thrilled such a doyenne had agreed with my fashion choice for the big day.

Maria brimmed with pre-bridal energy, "And after the wedding, I can take the silk and lace off it and wear it as a sun hat on honeymoon." Her mention of honeymoon made me deflate, for it was after their week in Wales that Mam and I would return to Cavan. Dad would leave the Monday after the wedding to start his new job. Maria noticed my mood change, "Eh, you, don't be getting down in the dumps on me," she said, play-slapping my hand.

I perked up, "I'm not, honest." She looked at me with her knowing face, "Please don't fret about moving to Cavan; don't forget you can come and stay with us every summer." I forced a smile, "I'm not, I'm kinda looking forward to it," I lied.

The truth was, I wanted to cry. The lie prevented me from doing so; I didn't want to dampen Maria's pre-wedding parade.

Mam looked behind her, then at her watch, "She's late, that girl can never be on time, God knows." she said, irritation in her voice. I glanced at my digital watch that Raymond had bought me – Maria was running fifteen minutes late.

"Have you told Derek and Jeanette you're moving to Ireland?" asked Maria.

They were my best friends on the council estate, "Yes," I said.

"What did they say?"

"Nothing." And they had said nothing because I hadn't told them nor intended to; they were two goodbyes I could avoid. Whenever my friends began their excited banter about starting our first year of Secondary School in Sacred Heart, I went quiet because I wouldn't be turning up for the eagerly anticipated first day, nor any English school day thereafter.

There was a shuffling accompanied by low-level murmurings amongst the guests in St Joseph's. I glanced at my watch again: 2. 23. Maria was on track for being a half-hour late. Mam looked at her watch, her irritation rising. I wiped my sweaty palms on my trousers and looked behind me – every guest was doing the same, their eyes peeled on the door awaiting the bride's arrival.

"You'll make new friends, and you've got all our cousins to help you settle in." Maria continued to sell Cavan life to me, regaling me with all the positives. But I didn't speak of the negatives that weighed

me down. And the biggest one was, she wouldn't be around. Maria was the only person with whom I could fully relax and be myself. When my doubts and fears made me flail, she gave me direction, she assured me of my fit – with an ocean between us, I'd be without her steer.

But of course, I said none of this. Instead, I smiled in agreement, looked at my watch and said, "Chris is late. I thought she was coming for cake with us?"

Maria shook her head, "Forgot to tell you, I saw her last night, she changed her mind, cancelled."

I wiped my brow and glanced at my watch: 2. 36. Maria was heading for an hour late. She'd joked about being fashionably late, but not this late – something was wrong.

"Gerard, what's wrong?" asked Maria, wrapping me in her arms. She'd arrived home early from work and heard my sobbing. I'd been with Derek, Jeanette, and some other estate kids who'd all been discussing teachers and all things Sacred Heart. Not being able to join in with their excited banter, I'd made my excuses and fled to my bedroom. My tears were borne of frustration with my inability to tell my truth. But in Maria's arms, I let flow a tsunami of sadness. I didn't need to tell her why I cried, my tears spoke to her, and she answered them with comforting words.

"Listen, Gerard, if you don't settle in, you can always come back here to live with us. Mam and Dad will understand, don't feel like you're being forced to do this." She paused and rubbed my back, "All you have to do is give it a go, give it a chance."

My tears began to subside, and she put her hands on my shoulders and levelled her face with mine, "Do you hear what I'm saying?"

I wiped my eyes, "I'll be alright when I get there, I'm just being daft."

Sitting on my bed, she put her arm around me, "You're not being daft, I'm feeling sad about you leaving." She pulled me closer, "To be honest, I'm scared as well."

I pulled away from her, "What you scared of?" I asked, concerned, protective.

My reaction made her pull me closer, "It's a new life for me as well, being a wife, worried I might not be a good one, worried about how Dermot and Raymond will get on, worried about work and money. She lowered her head and continued, "Mam says I'm too young, wants me to wait until I'm 23." I had no idea Maria harboured these feelings, and as she continued to speak, I couldn't find words of comfort – so I hugged her.

A loud clattering from the back of St Josephs startled me. With the door slightly ajar, I saw a family friend, Michael, gesturing animatedly. He slipped through the door and made his way urgently up the aisle – *he looked harassed.*

Chapter 56: No show.

Michael raced up to Raymond and whispered something in his ear. I studied Raymond's face, trying to read his reaction; he glanced towards the back of the church, his expression blank.

Mam's head swivelled back and forth, "What's going on?" she asked, her voice raised. Michael approached our pew and knelt in front of us, "A disaster – the car didn't show up; I threw a bit of ribbon round mine and drove them here myself."

Mam couldn't hide her annoyance, "And it paid for in full," she exclaimed.

Michael steered Mam's focus back to the star of the show, "Maria's fierce upset about it, but she's here now," he said, taking his place in the pew behind us.

I slumped back in my pew, and as the first peels of 'Here comes the bride' rang out, I'm sure I heard a collective sigh from the congregation.

Maria looked an ethereal vision. Her dress fluttered like a cloud on a gentle breeze in a clear blue sky, while the hat circled her face in light, an illuminating halo. It was clear to me she was trying to fight her tears, a battle she lost when Raymond mouthed, "Wow."

Dad took her hand in his and guided it over to her betrothed. When Raymond took Maria's hand, Dad wiped his tears and took his place next to Mam in our pew.

Mam's emotions were at odds with Dad's. As he tried to compose himself, she plotted, "I'll get that car fella tomorrow, he'll not be ripping us off, I'm telling you." Dad nodded in placid agreement, then lowered his head and gently cried.

I was caught between the conflicting emotions of my parents. While Mam seethed, Dad sobbed. My tummy knotted as I tried to appease both.

......

The parental tension distracted me from the wedding-ceremony until a gentle song eased me back into it, *"Love, soft as an easy chair. Love, fresh as the morning air. One love that is shared by two, I have found with you..."*

Applause rang through the chapel as the bride and groom returned from the registrar with their witnesses. Barbra Streisand's Evergreen voice was also a balm to Mam and Dad, who linked arms and beamed as they accompanied their daughter up the aisle and out into her new life as a wife.

......

Outside, an explosion of confetti was accompanied by a cacophony of cheering and the flipping of Zippos as people lit celebratory cigarettes.

Needing to escape the cheery chaos, I pushed through and into the playground of my old primary school, St Joseph's. From a distance, I watched the scene in front of me through a televisual slow-motion lens. My beautiful sister glowed triumphantly in her gorgeous gown as people thronged around her, taking photographs and throwing congratulations. Maria smiled and shook every hand offered to her, while Christine, her beautiful bridesmaid, stood dutifully aside to let her best friend bask in the glory.

My sister was now Raymond's wife, but in this moment, Maria was my Miss World.

She'd already told me the day would be a whirlwind and had apologised in advance if she didn't get to give me much of her time, and I was alright with that. This was her big day, and her little brother wasn't going to get in her way.

It was a sad day for me, but a week before the wedding, Maria had made a promise to me, which made it easier to bear. *"Listen, Gerard, when I get back from honeymoon and you and Mam are leaving, I'm not saying goodbye, because I promise you it's not that, it's, 'see you later.' Do you understand?"*

"See you later is all it is," I concurred.

We had nothing else to say, so we said it with a silent hug instead.
…..
An approaching boy made me switch off Miss World and turn the real world back on, "Hello Gerard, I'm Sang," he said, offering me his hand. He was the son of the couple Raymond worked for.

"Hello, did you like the wedding?" I asked, not really knowing what else to say.

"It was nice, now we take pictures and then have a party," he said.

I waved over towards the guests, "We do; let's go back or else we won't be in any of the photos."

Sang followed me, and although I didn't know him, I felt an affinity, which was affirmed when he said, "I leave Hong Kong to live in England, and you leave England to live in Ireland. Raymond tell me that."

I stopped and asked him, "Do you like it here?"

He didn't hesitate, "Sometime good, sometime bad." I said nothing in return because his words resonated.

I suspected my move would be an ever-changing sea of sometime good and sometime bad.

And I was ready – *to board that boat.*

Epilogue: Liverpool, September 1977

Back on the B+I line's Boat, The Munster; I was taller, older, a little wiser, but above all – alone.

Mam had pre-booked a cabin. She was exhausted after organising the transplanting of our lives from one country to another. So, no sooner had we boarded the boat than she announced, "Gerard, I'm going to bed; you mind yourself and don't be staying up late, do you hear me?"

Mam didn't wait for my reply; instead, she rushed to slumber – I didn't begrudge her the rest.

The bustle of people around me had reduced to only a few flustered late arrivals, hurriedly placing cases in the luggage room. Most passengers were settled into Pullman lounges or in the bars and cafes. But the excited peels of children running the corridors intensified my minds meander.

Reminiscences lay heavy on my heart, making me ache with melancholy. Without my siblings, this journey wasn't an adventure such as in the past. The Cavan summers I had known were over – this was a voyage into the unknown, on my own.

Wanting to escape the melancholy, I ventured into the gift shop – and walked right back into it. Vivid images of our journey five years earlier returned to me. My mind played flickering footage of Dermot messing up the merchandise in his haste to find the item he so coveted. Instinctively, I asked the shop assistant, "Do you have those pens with the boat that sails when you turn it upside down?" She didn't hesitate,

"Sorry, love, they've been discontinued."

Discontinued. No longer available, like my brother and sister, along with my Manchester life.

"Visit old Johnnie, see if he's still got the one you gave him during your summer of tumult and change – at least then you'll know it continues," I told myself, by way of comfort.

Leaving the shop, I decided to go on deck, hoping the wind might blow away the mourning lodged in my mind's eye.

But outside, the smell of diesel hit my olfactory nerve, heightening my mournful memory. I heard my sister's voice calling on the wind, *"Dermot, get back inside this boat, now!"* her anxious sound tempered with concern and caring for the welfare of our wilful brother who'd fled on deck, the place we three children were told not to venture.

With the boat's shuddering departure, I stupidly sat on a raised deck area and felt the slippery slick of oil permeate my trousers. Standing up, I looked at my smeared backside and waited for my sister to wipe me down; but how could she when she wasn't with me. Reality hit: even though she would always be my sister, she was now, first and foremost, Raymond's wife.

Wiping the back of my trousers with my hand, a man halted me, "Here you go, lad, it's a clean one," he said, handing me a hankie.

I took it, "Thanks," I said shyly.

"You watch yourself out here, could do yourself an injury," he said, with a departing wave. As he walked away, he reminded me of someone from the past – Penman.

The man I'd thought was a monster on the Munster, who I fretted may have harmed my brother on our first journey together without adult supervision.

Wiping myself down, I said to myself, "That was nice of him. I like Hankie-man."

The wind whipped up as I approached the boat's bow and the claxon boomed, and in between the contrasting sounds, I heard my brother's voice, *"I have to go bomb-searching on deck. Someone's got to do it, our kid."*

This memory made me smile; Dermot was now a working young man who spent his weekends with his mates, searching for *bombshells* of the female variety.

"Our kid," that's what I still was, a kid. My siblings were young adults, and in effect, the years between us made me an only child. I'd lost them to adulthood. And now, on the boat that played an integral part in our childhood life's adventure, I grieved for my loss – I missed my brother and sister so much I physically hurt. But it was a pain I buried deep, for I didn't want my hurt to be seen, lest it stain Mam and Dad's return home.

......

A compulsion pulled me towards the Pullman lounge. I tried to fight it, but the force was too strong, and I soon found myself standing back in our seating/sleeping space. The Lounge was busy, and I craned my neck to search. When I saw them, the seats Maria, Dermot, and I sat in when we were three kids, I grief-gulped. They were amongst the only remaining empty seats, and the sight of them caused tears to sting my eyes – I swiftly turned away. Back in the corridor, my hand reached out to grab Maria's, but of course – she wasn't there.

Determined not to shed any more tears, I wiped my eyes and put my hand in my pocket to prevent it from flailing for the past.

......

I walked the corridors of the boat, steeling myself for a new life and secondary school in Ireland. My great uncle Lofty's voice returned, *"You could be going to that school, yet."* His proclamation had come to pass. What I feared most was actually happening – school stipulations would sully the freedoms of my Cavan World.

Questions mired my mind, but the one that continually looped was: would I find a place to fit in this new life?

I was cruising into the unknown. But what I knew for sure, I was sailing without an anchor – my sister, Maria.

......

Restless energy compelled me to keep walking, picking up my pace, searching for something amongst the narrow walkways that might give answers to my mind's quandary.

That summer of tumult in Cavan was front of mind – my fraught search for a ghost I didn't find and my misinterpreting Maria's coming-of-age for malevolent-possession. And while still only twelve years old, on a boat back to the present Cavan, I was being chased by my memories from its past. I sprinted for the deck door, needing an escape from the marauding, melancholic phantoms.

Back outside, the fresh sea air eased me a little while flickering lights caught my eye and beckoned me, *"Come over here, I've got something to show you,"* said a now-familiar inner voice. I'd grown to welcome this voice; where once I feared it, now I instinctively trusted the insights it gave me. I walked towards the light, eager to see if I'd find answers in it.

At the stern of the ship, I held tight to the rails and watched Liverpool's lights become ever more distant. When their flicker gave way to the merest twinkle, I raised my hand and faced my fear – I waved, *"Goodbye."*

The boat picked up speed and sailed out into the Irish Sea, finally extinguishing Liverpool's lights and all sight of England.

But in the darkness, something kindled, and I stepped back further when I saw a spark of recognition. My seven-year-old self returned to me while my mind's eye recalled flashes of my frantic summer-time search for that ghost.

The flashes ignited, and, in their flare, I finally found him – the tall-man. I raised my hand and whispered without fear, *"Hello."*

With my salutation, the spirit emerged from the darkness and presented itself with great clarity and feeling. I not only keenly felt but clearly recognised the apparition in front of me. I looked behind, and on seeing I was the only terrestrial on deck, I turned to speak with the celestial, "I know who you are," I said quietly. When its aura reached out to me, I stepped back; not to avoid its touch, but to take in all aspects of the multifaceted revenant before me.

"I'm not sure other people would recognise you; if I told Dad who you were, he'd probably tell me I was a bit daft."

A gentle waft waved through me, and despite the sea chill, I felt its warmth. I turned with the warming breeze, "Don't go, stay for a while," I whispered.

With darkness behind me, the myriad lights of the Munster twirled and swirled, creating all manner of patterns as the ship pulsed to the rhythm of life. And to this steady beat, my inner voice spoke to confirm my finding,

"You're right Gerard, the ghost is the Spectre of:
the passing of time,
change,
coming-of-age
growing up,
growing apart,
leaving,
loss,
grief,
bereavement,
death.
I interrupted the inner voice, nodded and whispered to myself, "Now I know why you were so hard to find, because you're all those things hiding in one word: GOODBYE. I walked with newfound knowing towards the door of the boat's interior.

At the door, I looked through the glass panel into the light and softly said, "All ghosts are goodbye – because even though they might not know it, goodbye haunts everyone."

......

As my words were blown out to sea by the September breeze, I opened the door and stepped back into the bustle of the boat.

My melancholy lifted, replaced by an inner calm that gave me comfort. My hand traced a chain of shamrocks painted on the corridor's wall, and I followed their undulating flow.

The shamrock motif returned me to my seven-year-old self, Dad pinning the national plant to my lapel as we readied ourselves for Manchester's St Patrick's Day Parade.

"He banished the snakes son, but he could do nothing about the ghosts. They still ramble and roam at home."

Dad's telling me of ghosts so young made me unafraid of all things ghoulie.

Now I knew what they really were; I embraced them fully.

I'd grown, had confronted goodbye and was ready for life's change.

My heart settled, and I sailed home on the crest of a hopeful wave.